Kaplan Publishing are constantly finding new ways to make a difference to your studies and our exciting online resources really do offer something different to students looking for exam success.

This book comes with free MyKaplan online resources so that you can study anytime, anywhere. **This free online resource is not sold separately and is included in the price of the book.**

Having purchased this book, you have access to the following online study materials:

D0192224

CONTENT	AAT	
	Text	Kit
Electronic version of the book	✓	✓
Progress tests with instant answers	✓	
Mock assessments online	✓	✓
Material updates	✓	✓

How to access your online resources

Kaplan Financial students will already have a MyKaplan account and these extra resources will be available to you online. You do not need to register again, as this process was completed when you enrolled. If you are having problems accessing online materials, please ask your course administrator.

If you are not studying with Kaplan and did not purchase your book via a Kaplan website, to unlock your extra online resources please go to www.mykaplan.co.uk/addabook (even if you have set up an account and registered books previously). You will then need to enter the ISBN number (on the title page and back cover) and the unique pass key number contained in the scratch panel below to gain access. You will also be required to enter additional information during this process to set up or confirm your account details.

If you purchased through Kaplan Flexible Learning or via the Kaplan Publishing website you will automatically receive an e-mail invitation to MyKaplan. Please register your details using this email to gain access to your content. If you do not receive the e-mail or book content, please contact Kaplan Publishing.

Your Code and Information

This code can only be used once for the registration of one book online. This registration and your online content will expire when the final sittings for the examinations covered by this book have taken place. Please allow one hour from the time you submit your book details for us to process your request.

Please scratch the film to access your MyKaplan code.

Please be aware that this code is case-sensitive and you will need to include the dashes within the passcode, but not when entering the ISBN. For further technical support, please visit www.MyKaplan.co.uk

FOUNDATION CERTIFICATE IN ACCOUNTING

FOUNDATION DIPLOMA IN ACCOUNTING

SYNOPTIC ASSESSMENT

STUDY TEXT

Qualifications and Credit Framework

AQ2016 Level 2 Foundation Certificate in Accounting

This Study Text supports study for the following AAT qualifications:

AAT Foundation Certificate in Accounting – Level 2

AAT Foundation Diploma in Accounting and Business – Level 2

AAT Foundation Certificate in Bookkeeping – Level 2

AAT Foundation Award in Accounting Software – Level 2

AAT Level 2 Award in Accounting Skills to Run Your Business

AAT Foundation Certificate in Accounting at SCQF Level 5

British Library Cataloguing-in-Publication Data

A catalogue record for this book is available from the British Library.

Published by
Kaplan Publishing UK
Unit 2, The Business Centre
Molly Millars Lane
Wokingham
Berkshire
RG41 2QZ

ISBN 978-1-78415-990-0

CONTENTS

STUDY TEXT

WORK EFFECTIVELY IN FINANCE STUDY TEXT

SYNOPTIC ASSESSMENT CONTENT

KAPLAN PUBLISHING

INTRODUCTION

HOW TO USE THESE MATERIALS

These Kaplan Publishing learning materials have been carefully designed to make your learning experience as easy as possible and to give you the best chance of success in your AAT assessments.

They contain a number of features to help you in the study process.

The sections on the Unit Guide, the Assessment and Study Skills should be read before you commence your studies.

They are designed to familiarise you with the nature and content of the assessment and to give you tips on how best to approach your studies.

STUDY TEXT

This study text has been specially prepared for the revised AAT qualification introduced in September 2016.

It is written in a practical and interactive style:

- key terms and concepts are clearly defined

- all topics are illustrated with practical examples with clearly worked solutions based on sample tasks provided by the AAT in the new examining style

- frequent activities throughout the chapters ensure that what you have learnt is regularly reinforced

- 'pitfalls' and 'examination tips' help you avoid commonly made mistakes and help you focus on what is required to perform well in your examination.

ICONS

The study chapters include the following icons throughout.

They are designed to assist you in your studies by identifying key definitions and the points at which you can test yourself on the knowledge gained.

 Definition

These sections explain important areas of Knowledge which must be understood and reproduced in an assessment.

 Example

The illustrative examples can be used to help develop an understanding of topics before attempting the test your understanding exercises.

 Test your understanding

These are exercises which give the opportunity to assess your understanding of all the assessment areas.

Quality and accuracy are of the utmost importance to us so if you spot an error in any of our products, please send an email to mykaplanreporting@kaplan.com with full details, or follow the link to the feedback form in MyKaplan.

Our Quality Co-ordinator will work with our technical team to verify the error and take action to ensure it is corrected in future editions.

KAPLAN PUBLISHING

SYNOPTIC ASSESSMENT GUIDE

Introduction

AAT AQ16 introduces a Synoptic Assessment, which students must complete if they are to achieve the appropriate qualification. In the case of the Foundation Certificate in Accounting, students must pass all of the mandatory assessments and the Synoptic Assessment to achieve the qualification.

As a Synoptic Assessment is attempted following completion of individual units, it draws upon knowledge and understanding from those units. It may be appropriate for students to retain their study materials for individual units until they have successfully completed the Synoptic Assessment for that qualification.

All units within the Foundation Certificate in Accounting are mandatory. Four units are assessed individually in end of unit assessments, but this qualification also includes a synoptic assessment, sat towards the end of the qualification, which draws on and assesses knowledge and understanding from across the qualification.

- Bookkeeping Transactions – end of unit assessment
- Bookkeeping Controls – end of unit assessment
- Elements of Costing – end of unit assessment
- Work Effectively in Finance – assessed within the synoptic assessment only

Note that Using Accounting Software is a unit assessment only and is not assessed as part of the synoptic assessment.

Scope of content

To perform this synoptic assessment effectively you will need to know and understand the following:

The synoptic assessment will ask you to apply knowledge and skills gained across the qualification in an integrated way, within a workplace context. Scenarios will change over time to ensure the validity of the assessment.

Assessment objective 1	Demonstrate an understanding of the finance function and the roles and procedures carried out by members of an accounting team
Related learning outcomes	**Work Effectively in Finance** LO1 Understand the finance function within an organisation LO2 Use personal skills development in finance LO3 Produce work effectively LO4 Understand Corporate Social Responsibility (CSR), ethics and sustainability within organisations
Assessment objective 2	Process transactions complete calculations and make journal entries
Related learning outcomes	**Bookkeeping transactions** LO2 Process customer transactions LO3 Process supplier transactions LO4 Process receipts and payments LO5 Process transactions through the ledgers to the trial balance

Assessment objective 3	Compare, produce and reconcile journals and accounts
Related learning outcomes	**Bookkeeping Controls** LO3 Use control accounts LO4 Use the journal LO5 Reconcile a bank statement with the cash book **Elements of Costing** LO2 Use cost recording techniques LO3 Provide information on actual and budgeted costs and income
Assessment objective 4	Communicate financial information effectively
Related learning outcome	**Work Effectively in Finance** LO3 Produce work effectively

Summary

Underlying unit	LOs required
Work Effectively in Finance	LO1, LO2, LO3, LO4
Bookkeeping Transactions	LO2, LO3, LO4, LO5
Bookkeeping Controls	LO3, LO4, LO5
Elements of Costing	LO2, LO3

THE ASSESSMENT

Test specification for this synoptic assessment

Assessment type

Computer based
synoptic assessment

Marking type

Partially computer/
partially human marked

Duration of exam

2 hours

The following weighting is based upon the AAT Qualification Specification
documentation which may be subject to variation.

Assessment objective	Weighting
A01 Demonstrate an understanding of the finance function and the roles and procedures carried out by members of an accounting team	24%
A02 Process transactions, complete calculations and make journal entries	24%
A03 Compare, produce and reconcile journals and accounts	34%
A04 Communicate information effectively	18%
Total	**100%**

The specimen synoptic assessment comprises seven tasks and covers all
four assessment objectives.

STUDY SKILLS

Preparing to study

Devise a study plan

Determine which times of the week you will study.

Split these times into sessions of at least one hour for study of new material. Any shorter periods could be used for revision or practice.

Put the times you plan to study onto a study plan for the weeks from now until the assessment and set yourself targets for each period of study – in your sessions make sure you cover the whole course, activities and the associated questions in the workbook at the back of the manual.

If you are studying more than one unit at a time, try to vary your subjects as this can help to keep you interested and see subjects as part of wider knowledge.

When working through your course, compare your progress with your plan and, if necessary, re-plan your work (perhaps including extra sessions) or, if you are ahead, do some extra revision / practice questions.

Effective studying

Active reading

You are not expected to learn the text by rote, rather, you must understand what you are reading and be able to use it to pass the assessment and develop good practice.

A good technique is to use SQ3Rs – Survey, Question, Read, Recall, Review:

1   Survey the chapter

Look at the headings and read the introduction, knowledge, skills and content, so as to get an overview of what the chapter deals with.

2   Question

Whilst undertaking the survey ask yourself the questions you hope the chapter will answer for you.

3   Read

Read through the chapter thoroughly working through the activities and, at the end, making sure that you can meet the learning objectives highlighted on the first page.

4   Recall

At the end of each section and at the end of the chapter, try to recall the main ideas of the section/chapter without referring to the text. This is best done after short break of a couple of minutes after the reading stage.

5   Review

Check that your recall notes are correct.

You may also find it helpful to re-read the chapter to try and see the topic(s) it deals with as a whole.

Note taking

Taking notes is a useful way of learning, but do not simply copy out the text.

The notes must:

- be in your own words
- be concise
- cover the key points
- well organised
- be modified as you study further chapters in this text or in related ones.

Trying to summarise a chapter without referring to the text can be a useful way of determining which areas you know and which you don't.

Three ways of taking notes

1   Summarise the key points of a chapter

2   Make linear notes

A list of headings, subdivided with sub-headings listing the key points.

If you use linear notes, you can use different colours to highlight key points and keep topic areas together.

Use plenty of space to make your notes easy to use.

 KAPLAN PUBLISHING

3   Try a diagrammatic form

The most common of which is a mind map.

To make a mind map, put the main heading in the centre of the paper and put a circle around it.

Draw lines radiating from this to the main sub-headings which again have circles around them.

Continue the process from the sub-headings to sub-sub-headings.

Highlighting and underlining

You may find it useful to underline or highlight key points in your study text – but do be selective.

You may also wish to make notes in the margins.

Revision phase

Kaplan has produced material specifically designed for your final examination preparation for this synoptic assessment.

These include pocket revision notes and a bank of revision questions specifically in the style of the new syllabus.

Further guidance on how to approach the final stage of your studies is given in these materials.

Further reading

In addition to this text, you should also read the 'Accounting Technician' magazine every month to keep abreast of any guidance from the examiners.

WORK EFFECTIVELY IN FINANCE – UNIT GUIDE

Work Effectively in Finance is assessed as part of the synoptic assessment only and not as a standalone unit.

Purpose of the unit

This unit will help students to develop the professional skills and behaviours needed in the workplace. Learners will be able to work independently or as part of a team. While this unit is set in the context of the finance function, these skills are transferable to many other working environments.

Students will understand the work of the finance function and why that work is important to an organisation. They will understand that finance employees require more than numerical skills: they also need interpersonal and written communication skills. Students will learn the importance of being an effective employee and what this means, and how to work as part of a finance team. Students will be able to identify activities that develop current skills and knowledge, and those that will help them achieve future career aspirations. Students will understand how to ensure data security and the importance of maintaining confidentiality of information. Students will understand why corporate social responsibility is important and what actions individuals can take to ensure that they behave ethically and support sustainability.

Studying this unit helps to prepare students for Advanced level Ethics for Accountants. The communication and numeracy skills included within this unit will be beneficial to those studying all AAT qualifications. The written communication skills element of this unit will prepare students for work and further study by developing their reading and writing skills. The basic numerical functions covered in this unit are important in all financial computations and, as such, students who successfully complete this unit should have an increased confidence in dealing with financial computations.

Work Effectively in Finance is a mandatory unit in this qualification.

Learning outcomes

On completion of this unit the learner will be able to:

- Understand the finance function within an organisation.

- Use personal skills development in finance.

- Produce work effectively.

- Understand corporate social responsibility (CSR), ethics and sustainability within organisations.

Knowledge

To perform this unit effectively you will need to know and understand the following:

Chapter

1   Understand the finance function within an organisation

1.1   Identify the role of the finance function   1

Students need to know:

- the role of the finance function: responsibility for production of statutory financial statements, providing a service (information, support advice and guidance) to both internal and external stakeholders.

1.2   Demonstrate an understanding of how finance staff   1 and 5
contribute to an organisation's success

Students need to know:

- the importance of establishing good business relationships

- the principles of effective communication: content is written clearly, complete, accurate, timely, concise and meets the needs of the recipient, and an appropriate medium is used in a suitable environment

- actions of finance staff that support efficient working practices, solvency and long-term financial stability, legal and regulatory compliance

- the importance to an organisation's survival of remaining solvent and managing funds effectively

- the different types of policies and procedures affecting finance staff: finance function-specific and organisation wide.

1.3 Indicate the role of information in the work of the finance function   1

Students need to know:

- types of information received by the finance function: budgetary, inventory control and costing information, information from suppliers and customers, purchase orders, remittance advice, statements, supplier invoices, credit notes

- types of information produced by the finance function: information to help management decision making, budgetary information, cash information, taxation information, information for suppliers and customers, sales invoices, credit notes, statements

- the importance of providing useful information

- characteristics of useful information: complete, accurate, timely and fit for purpose.

1.4 Identify the importance of data security   5

Students need to know:

- why it is important to ensure the security of data and information

- the implications for the organisation if data and information is not secure

- how data and information is retained securely: using passwords, archiving, backups and restricting access.

Chapter

2 Use personal skills development in finance

2.1 Identify the interpersonal skills required by finance staff   **4**

Students need to know:

- a range of interpersonal skills: respecting others, developing trust, being responsible, being reliable, communicating effectively, negotiation, problem solving, decision making

- how to use active listening skills

- how to use appropriate business language

- the importance of appropriate language, personal appearance and body language in different business situations to project a professional image

- how interpersonal skills help build good business relationships.

2.2 Identify the features of an effective finance team   **4**

Students need to know:

- the characteristics of an effective team: good communication channels, shared values, a mix of complementary skills, clear leadership, common purpose and clearly defined roles and responsibilities

- the skills, competencies and behaviours required of individuals within a high-performing team: trust, shared goals and values, clear roles and responsibilities, effective communication, numeracy skills, clear leadership, every member feels valued, a mix of complementary skills and diversity

- the actions a team member can take to support the success of the team: work independently but aware of the work of others, help others in the team wherever possible, take responsibility for completing work within targets and to standard, communicate effectively, contribute ideas, understand role within the team, understand individual and team objectives, have commitment to achieving team and individual objectives.

		Chapter

2.3 Identify development needs   6

Students need to know:

- the importance of continuing professional development (CPD) to finance staff.

Students need to be able to:

- review own performance and use feedback from others

- identify development objectives and activities to address objectives.

3   **Produce work effectively**

3.1 Produce accurate work in appropriate formats   2

Students need to know:

- standard business communications: business letters, emails, formal business reports, spreadsheets

- how standard business communications are usually structured and presented: business letters, emails, business reports, spreadsheets.

Students need to be able to:

- choose the appropriate format to present business information

- produce accurate information, which is technically correct and free from spelling and grammatical errors

- use numerical functions for business calculations in any combination: addition, subtraction, multiplication, division, percentages, proportions, ratios, averages and fractions.

KAPLAN PUBLISHING

		Chapter

3.2 Communicate information effectively   2

Students need to be able to:

- communicate using acceptable business language

- produce written communication that is clear, structured and follows a logical progression

- prepare logical and clearly structured notes to plan for verbal communications.

3.3 Plan workload to meet the needs of the organisation   3

Students need to know:

- the importance of communicating with others during the completion of tasks or when deadlines are in danger of not being met

- the importance of meeting agreed deadlines and adhering to working practices

- the impact on others of not completing specified tasks.

Students need to be able to:

- work independently, and manage workload using time-management techniques and planning aids

- plan, prioritise, monitor and review workload within deadlines.

4 **Understand corporate social responsibility (CSR), ethics and sustainability within organisations**

4.1 Demonstrate an understanding of corporate social responsibility (CSR)   7

Students need to know:

- what CSR is

- organisational actions that support CSR

- good practice in organisations with a strong CSR commitment.

Chapter

4.2 Identify how finance staff can support ethical business 7
practices

Students need to be able to:

- maintain confidentiality of information

- behave professionally in finance: acting with honesty and fairness, ensuring that professional knowledge is up to date.

4.3 Establish the features and benefits of sustainable 7
business practices

Students need to know:

- areas of sustainability: economic, social, environmental

- organisational actions that support sustainability

- the impact of sustainability activities on the organisation: costs, benefits

- the impact of sustainability activities outside the organisation: on stakeholders, on the environment, on society.

Delivering this unit

This unit has the following links across the AAT Foundation Certificate in Accounting.

Unit name	Content links	Suggested order of delivery
Bookkeeping Transactions	Numerical skills, communication of information and professional behaviour may be linked with Bookkeeping Transactions.	Bookkeeping Transactions might be delivered before, at the same time as or after Work Effectively in Finance. It is recommended that the synoptic assessment is only attempted after the contributing units are completed, although this is not compulsory.

Unit name	Content links	Suggested order of delivery
Bookkeeping Controls	Numerical skills, communication of information and professional behaviour may be linked with Bookkeeping Controls.	Bookkeeping Controls might be delivered before, at the same time as or after Work Effectively in Finance. It is recommended that the synoptic assessment is only attempted after the contributing units are completed, although this is not compulsory.
Elements of Costing	Numerical skills may be linked with Elements of Costing.	Elements of Costing might be delivered before, at the same time as or after Work Effectively in Finance. It is recommended that the synoptic assessment is only attempted after the contributing units are completed, although this is not compulsory.

The role of the finance function

1

Introduction

This introductory chapter covers role of an accountant and the policies and procedures that they may come across in the finance function.

ASSESSMENT CRITERIA	CONTENTS
1.1 Identify the role of the finance function	1 Where accountants work and what they do
1.2 Demonstrate an understanding of how finance staff contribute to an organisation's success.	2 Key aspects of accounting and solvency
1.3 Indicate the role of information in the work of the finance function	3 Policies and procedures within the finance function
	4 Information received from stakeholders

1 Where accountants work and what they do

1.1 Where do accountants work?

An accountant may work in industry, in an accounts or payroll department or in a practice firm.

1.2 What do they do?

Most accountants work as part of a team and often have to liaise with staff in other departments so they need to be good at working with others and have good communication skills.

These are examples of duties that an accountant or someone working in an accounting environment may undertake:

(a) Prepare statutory financial statements including a statement of profit or loss and a statement of financial position

(b) Reconcile reports, identify and correct discrepancies

(c) Maintain and improve accounting procedures and processes

(d) Analyse reports

(e) Banking of cash and cheques

(f) Preparing sales invoices and credit notes

(g) Maintaining the sales and purchase ledgers.

The above are just some of the duties someone working in accounts may be involved in but it differs depending on each business.

2 Key aspects of accounting and solvency

Financial accounting information and **management accounting** information will both use the same basic data but they will be presented differently and fulfil different roles.

2.1 Financial accounting

The **financial accounts** record transactions between the business and its customers, suppliers, employees and owners. The managers of the business must account for the way in which funds entrusted to them have been used and, therefore, records of assets and liabilities are needed as well as a statement of any increase in the total wealth of the business.

Financial accounts are presented in the form of a **Statement of Profit or Loss,** detailing all income and expenses, and a **Statement of Financial Position**, which shows details of all assets and liabilities.

 Definition

Financial accounting is:

- the classification and recording of monetary transactions; and

- the presentation and interpretation of the results of those transactions in order to assess performance over a period (usually 12 months) and the financial position at a given date

- the recording of day to day transactions and the analysis of capital and revenue expenditure and income

- maintaining both the sales and purchase ledgers and keeping close control on the receivable and payable balances. This will mean that payables balances can be settled when they fall due and other expenses can also be paid on time.

These controls have a direct effect upon the cash flow of the business and thus its financial strength and **solvency** (its ability to pay its way).

2.2 Management accounting

Management accounting is a wider concept involving **professional knowledge and skill** in the preparation and presentation of information to all levels of management in an organisation. The source of such information is the financial and cost accounts. The information is intended to assist management in decision making and in the planning and control of activities in both the short and long term.

> ### 🔍 Definition
>
> An integral part of management concerned with identifying, presenting and interpreting information which is used for formulating strategy, planning and control, decision making and optimising the use of resources. Management accounting includes:
>
> - the allocation and control of resources
>
> - preparing cash flow forecasts. This accounts for day to day revenue expenditure and income and also future payments of capital expenditure, dividends to shareholders and legal requirements e.g. taxation
>
> - analysis of the accounts to improve performance going forward. For this reason management accounts are usually prepared more often than financial accounts e.g. monthly.

2.3 Financial accounts and management information

It may be helpful to look at a simple statement of profit or loss to see the role of management accounting:

XYZ Company		
Statement of profit or loss for the period X		
	£	£
Turnover		200,000
Cost of sales:		
Materials consumed	80,000	
Wages	40,000	
Production expenses	15,000	
		(135,000)
Gross profit		65,000
Marketing expenses	15,000	
General administrative expenses	10,000	
Financing costs	4,000	
		(29,000)
Net profit		36,000

This statement may be adequate to provide outsiders with an overview of the trading results of the whole business, but managers would need much more detail to answer questions such as:

- What are the major products and are they profitable?

- By how much has inventory of raw materials increased?

- How does the labour cost per unit compare with the cost incurred in the previous period?

- Is the expenditure incurred by the personnel department higher than expected?

The management accounting system reports will provide the answers to these (and many other) questions on a regular basis. In addition, the management accounts will contain detailed information concerning raw materials inventory, work in progress and finished goods, which will provide a basis for the valuation necessary to prepare periodic and final accounts.

2.4 Summary of the differences between management and financial accounting

The main differences between financial accounts and management accounts can be summarised in the following table.

Financial accounts	Management accounts
Limited companies are required by law to prepare them.	Records are not mandatory.
Accordingly, the cost of record-keeping is a necessity.	Accordingly, the cost of record-keeping needs to be justified.
Objectives and uses are not defined by management.	Objectives and uses can be decided by management.
Mainly a historical record.	Regularly concerned with future results as well as historical data.
Information must be compiled prudently and in accordance with legal and accounting requirements.	Information should be compiled as management requires – the key criterion being relevance.
Prepared for external reporting.	Prepared for internal use only.

2.5 Solvency

 Definition

Solvency refers to the financial soundness of a business that allows it to discharge its monetary obligations (such as paying payables on time) as they fall due. To this end they must ensure that they have cash available to meet these obligations.

Management accounting is concerned with the allocation and control of resources. The Management Accountant forecasts the cash flow based on information from the financial accounting function. This would account not only for day to day revenue expenditure and income but future payments for capital expenditure, dividends and taxation, including VAT.

This has an effect on the overall **solvency** of the business.

2.6 Ways to ensure and improve financial solvency

- Regular reconciliation of bank balances e.g. to highlight bank charges, interest (both paid and received), direct debits going out and BACS receipts from customers.

- Awareness of bank balances e.g. you know if you are likely to go overdrawn and can therefore plan for any charges, or find other ways to avoid an overdraft.

- Awareness of how much is owed to the company e.g. Sales Ledger Control Account.

- Credit control measures e.g. chasing bad debts.

- Awareness of amounts owing e.g. long term obligations (loans or mortgages) and when they are due for repayment.

- Awareness of payments to suppliers e.g. current liabilities and when due.

- Completing weekly payments to suppliers e.g. taking advantage of credit terms and ensuring that the company is making full use of free credit available.

- Awareness of forward planning e.g. cash flow statements – ask suppliers to extend credit terms if you know you cannot pay in time.

3 Policies and procedures within the finance function

3.1 Policies and procedures within the finance function

Members of staff working in the finance function will need to comply with both internal and legal policies and procedures. These policies and procedures will be looked at in more detail in Chapter 5.

Below are some examples of policies and procedures which accounting and payroll staff may need to comply with:

Legal	Internal policies
• VAT return submission and payment date	• Overtime payment procedures
• Corporation tax	• Purchase ledger payment procedures
• Health and safety regulations	
• Data protection act	• Expenses policy
• The submission of statutory financial statements	• Authorised signatories

4 Information received from stakeholders

4.1 Stakeholders

 Definition

Stakeholders are parties that have an interest in an organisation or project, they can be internal or external to the organisation. Stakeholders in a typical organisation include; its investors, employees, customers, suppliers, the government and the community.

The finance function within an organisation has a responsibility to supply information to both internal stakeholders (other departments) and external stakeholders.

4.2 Types of information

The finance function will receive different types of information from stakeholders. This includes:

Bank statements – received from an external stakeholder (the bank or building society) showing a breakdown of receipts and payments made from the bank.

Invoices and credit notes – received from external stakeholders (suppliers) for goods purchased on credit and for goods returned.

Statement of account – received from external stakeholders (suppliers) showing a breakdown of the transactions during the period.

Internal business documentation – received from internal stakeholders (other departments), for example, they will receive a monthly analysis from payroll of amounts paid to employees.

As well as receiving information, the finance function will also provide information. This includes; information to help managers make decisions, budgetary information, taxation figures and cash flow information.

4.3 Useful information

It is important that the finance function provide useful information as this information is often used by stakeholders to make decisions. The characteristics of useful information are:

Completeness –enough information to allow decisions to be made but not so much to confuse the issue.

Timeliness – information must reach the stakeholder in time to fulfil their decision needs.

Accurate –information is correct and reliable.

Fit for purpose – it should meet the needs of the person requesting the information.

5 Summary

This introductory chapter outlined the differences between management and financial accounting and how their roles ensure and improve solvency within an organisation.

Stakeholders and the importance of useful information were reviewed. Legal and internal policies and procedures were also introduced.

Comparison and communication of information

2

Introduction

In this chapter we will be dealing with comparisons of current actual costs with information from different sources. We must consider where the information for comparison comes from and how to make meaningful comparisons. It will also consider the most common methods of reporting.

ASSESSMENT CRITERIA

3.1   Produce accurate work in appropriate formats

3.2   Communicate information effectively

CONTENTS

1   Comparisons required

2   Previous periods, corresponding periods and forecasts

3   Methods of reporting

4   A note

5   A letter

6   Electronic mail

7   Memorandum

8   Reports

9   Word-processed documents

1   Comparisons required

For information to be meaningful there must be a purpose to its production. Much information is produced in order to be able to compare results and costs with other relevant comparators – such as different periods, competitors and a company's own budgets/targets.

Different periods and budget comparisons are discussed below:

1.1   Previous periods

In some cases you will be required to compare current costs and income to the same costs and income from previous periods in order to determine any significant differences, i.e. have costs changed, and if so, does an equivalent change in income suggest that this was to be expected?

The costs and income for the previous period will have been summarised in various management reports, and you need to know where and how to find this information. You should therefore ensure that you understand your company's procedures for filing these reports, or know how to access them on your computer system (i.e. how documents are named and whether passwords are required to access them).

1.2   Corresponding periods

In some businesses the income and costs tend to vary with particular seasons, and therefore a comparison of one period to the next may not be particularly meaningful. For example in a retail business the period just before Christmas may be unusually busy; therefore a comparison of income between December and January may not provide any useful information. In such cases it is likely to be more useful to compare one period to the corresponding period of the previous year. In the case of the retailer the figures for December could more usefully be compared to those of the previous December.

Another way in which meaningful comparisons can be made with a corresponding period, is by comparing the year to date costs or income to the same cumulative period in the previous year.

1.3   Budgets

You may also be required to compare current costs and income to the budgets that were created for this period. Budgets refer to the plans that are produced by companies showing the figures that they feel they should be able to achieve for income, costs etc. for a given period. Comparisons are particularly important here to ensure that such plans are realistic.

2 Previous periods, corresponding periods and forecasts

2.1 Comparison of information

There are many ways in which you might be asked to compare current costs and income to previous and corresponding control periods. In this section some typical examples will be considered.

It is always important to ensure that you understand precisely what is required of you, as this comparison is likely to be a time consuming process and you do not want to waste time extracting information that is unnecessary. Therefore if you have any doubts about precisely what information is required always check with the appropriate person.

Example 1

Your organisation operates its sales function in three divisions, A, B and C, and records sales separately for each division. You have been asked to compare this month's sales (June) to those of the previous month. You have obtained the May information from the management accounting filing system and it is as follows:

	£
Division A	113,000
Division B	258,000
Division C	142,000

You have also obtained the sales ledger accounts for June which are as follows:

Sales account – Division A

	£		£
		Sales June	129,000

Sales account – Division B

	£		£
Sales returns June	15,000	Sales June	250,000

Sales account – Division C

	£		£
		Sales June	120,000

You are required to compare the sales for June to those for the month of May in a suitable manner.

Probably the simplest method of comparing this information would be in the form of a table showing the sales for each division and in total for each month. Care should be taken with Division B's sales and the returns must be deducted from the sales figure therefore a net sales balance should be found on that account as follows:

Sales account – Division B

	£		£
Sales returns June	15,000	Sales June	250,000
Balance c/d	235,000		
	250,000		250,000

Now a simple table can be prepared.

Divisional sales for May and June

	May	*June*	*Increase/ (decrease)*
	£	£	£
Division A	113,000	129,000	16,000
Division B	258,000	235,000	(23,000)
Division C	142,000	120,000	(22,000)
Total	513,000	484,000	(29,000)

It might also be useful to include a further column to show the percentage increase or decrease in sales. The percentage change would be calculated as a percentage of the May sales as follows:

Division A $\dfrac{16,000}{113,000} \times 100 = 14.2\%$

Division B $\dfrac{(23,000)}{258,000} \times 100 = (8.9\%)$

Division C $\dfrac{(22,000)}{142,000} \times 100 = (15.5\%)$

Total $\dfrac{(29,000)}{513,000} \times 100 = (5.7\%)$

The table would then appear as follows:

Divisional sales for May and June

	May	June	Increase/ (decrease)	Increase/ (decrease)
	£	£	£	%
Division A	113,000	129,000	16,000	14.2
Division B	258,000	235,000	(23,000)	(8.9)
Division C	142,000	120,000	(22,000)	(15.5)
Total	513,000	484,000	(29,000)	(5.7)

 Test your understanding 1

You have been asked to compare the month 2 labour cost from last year to the month 2 labour cost for this year.

From the filed management accounts for last year you discover that the month 2 labour cost was broken down as follows:

	£
Production labour cost	336,000
Selling department labour cost	248,000
Administration department labour cost	100,000

The wages expense account for month 2 of this year is as follows:

Wages expenses account			
	£		£
Gross wages cost	990,000	Work-in-Progress account	510,000
		Selling costs account	350,000
		Administration costs account	130,000

You are required to compare the labour costs for month 2 of the current period with the corresponding period last year.

2.2 Comparison to corresponding period

Rather than comparing figures from one month to the next or one quarter to the next it might be more useful to management to compare the figures for a particular period this year to the same period the previous year and determine any increases or decreases.

Example 2

In an earlier example we were given the total costs for the year to date as at 30 September for a variety of cost codes as follows:

Code	Year to date at 30 September 20X5
	£
021113	32,477
021114	146,229
021115	25,110
022113	66,001
022114	7,698
022115	13,332

The current year is 20X5 and you now find in the management accounting records the figures for the same cost codes in the year to date to 30 September 20X4. Comparison can then be made:

Code	Year to date at 30 September 20X4	Year to date at 30 September 20X5	Increase/ (decrease)
	£	£	£
021113	30,551	32,477	1,926
021114	151,345	146,229	(5,116)
021115	26,790	25,110	(1,680)
022113	73,465	66,001	(7,464)
022114	6,124	7,698	1,574
022115	11,531	13,332	1,801
	———	———	———
	299,806	290,847	(8,959)
	———	———	———

2.3 Comparison to budgeted figures

Comparison might also be required between forecast or budgeted figures for a particular period and the actual results of that period. Upon comparing actual costs to budgeted costs, there may be a difference or discrepancy between them – this is known as **a variance**. If the actual cost is greater than the budgeted cost, this is an **adverse** variance. If the actual cost is less than budgeted cost this is a **favourable** variance.

 Example 3

The budgeted costs for week 17 for material and labour production costs were found in the filing system and were as follows:

	£
Material X	117,000
Material Y	270,000
Labour	226,000

The actual costs of the period are as follows:

Stores ledger card

MATERIAL DESCRIPTION Material X									
Code			M100						
	Receipts			**Issues**			**Balance**		
Date	Quantity	Unit price £	Total £	Quantity	Unit price £	Total £	Quantity	Unit price £	Total £
Bal b/f							10,000	15.00	150,000
Week 17				8,000	15.00	120,000	2,000	15.00	30,000

MATERIAL DESCRIPTION Material Y									
Code			M101						
	Receipts			**Issues**			**Balance**		
Date	Quantity	Unit price £	Total £	Quantity	Unit price £	Total £	Quantity	Unit price £	Total £
Bal b/f							130,000	2.50	325,000
Week 17				100,000	2.50	250,000	30,000	2.50	75,000

Wages Expense account

	£		£
Gross wages cost	470,000	Production costs	230,000
		Selling costs account	110,000
		Administration costs	130,000

You have been asked to prepare a comparison of the budgeted cost of materials and labour for production in week 17 to the actual cost for the week.

Solution

Costs – week 17	Budget £	Actual £	Variance £	
Material X	117,000	120,000	3,000	adverse
Material Y	270,000	250,000	20,000	favourable
Labour	226,000	230,000	4,000	adverse

Note how variances can be either favourable or adverse depending upon whether the actual cost is smaller or larger than the budgeted cost.

 Test your understanding 2

The budgeted costs for expected production of 100,000 units last week are given below:

	£
Labour	45,000
Materials	60,000
Production expenses	17,000

The actual costs were:

	£
Labour	42,000
Materials	62,000
Production expenses	16,000

You are required to compare budgeted costs to actual costs.

2.4 Sales and variances

Sales figures can be compared as well as costs. This helps businesses to determine if they are achieving expected growth, or if there is something stopping them from growing that needs to be investigated. However some care should be taken with determining whether the sales variances are favourable or adverse. If actual sales are higher than budgeted sales then this is a favourable variance. Whereas if actual sales are lower than the budgeted sales then this is an adverse variance. This is, of course, the opposite to the effect we see with costs (i.e. we would like to see higher sales than expected; as this is a **good** thing it will give rise to a **favourable** variance).

Example 4

Given below are the budgeted and actual **sales** for three products for the month of July and their variances. Make sure that you are happy with why the variance is favourable or adverse.

Product	Budgeted sales £	Actual £	Variance £
X	450,000	430,000	20,000 adverse
Y	500,000	530,000	30,000 favourable
Z	410,000	400,000	10,000 adverse

 Example 5

XYZ Ltd has the following budget and actual results for August 20X6

	Budget August 20X6 £	Actual August 20X6 £
Sales	434,000	489,000
Costs		
Materials	178,000	193,000
Labour	50,000	56,000
Direct expenses	24,000	33,000
Indirect expenses	37,000	28,000
Total costs	289,000	310,000
Net profit	145,000	179,000

Compare budgeted and actual revenue, costs and profit, calculate the variances and state whether the variances are favourable or adverse.

Solution

	Budget August 20X6 £	Actual August 20X6 £	Variance £	
Sales	434,000	489,000	55,000	Fav
Costs				
Materials	178,000	193,000	15,000	Adv
Labour	50,000	56,000	6,000	Adv
Direct expenses	24,000	33,000	9,000	Adv
Indirect expenses	37,000	28,000	9,000	Fav
Total costs	289,000	310,000	21,000	Adv
Net profit	145,000	179,000	34,000	Fav

2.5 Investigation of variances

Variances are of interest to management as they form part of the management process of control, and managers will often need to investigate the cause of any variances. However, in many organisations not all variances will be investigated, only those that are considered to be significant. Therefore you might be asked to prepare calculations showing each variance as a percentage of the budgeted figure indicating which are most significant and may need investigating.

Note: Businesses will investigate both favourable and adverse variances. By investigating favourable variances they may be able to identify trends that they are able to exploit further in order to make additional savings.

 Example 6

Given below are the actual costs and budgeted costs for a manufacturing process for the month of March:

Cost	Budget £	Actual £
Material X	100,000	105,600
Material Y	80,000	77,300
Labour	140,000	138,700
Expenses	60,000	67,400

We can now calculate the variances for each expense together with the percentage that each variance is of the original budgeted figure.

Cost	Budget £	Actual £	Variance £	Percentage
Material X	100,000	105,600	5,600 adverse	5.6% adverse
Material Y	80,000	77,300	2,700 favourable	3.4% favourable
Labour	140,000	138,700	1,300 favourable	0.9% favourable
Expenses	60,000	67,400	7,400 adverse	12.3% adverse

If the business has a policy of only investigating variances that are more than 10% of the budgeted figure then in this case only the expenses variance needs to be highlighted for investigation to management.

Example 7

	Budget August 20X6	Actual August 20X6
Consider again the information for XYZ Ltd from Example 10	£	£
Sales	434,000	489,000
Costs		
Materials	178,000	193,000
Labour	50,000	56,000
Direct expenses	24,000	33,000
Indirect expenses	37,000	28,000
Total costs	289,000	310,000
Net profit	145,000	179,000

Compare the budget and actual revenue and individual costs and calculate the percentage difference for each as a percentage of the budget figure. Calculate the variance to two decimal places.

XYZ Ltd has a policy of investigating any variances that are more than 10% of budget. Which variances would they investigate?

Solution

	Budget August 20X6 £	Actual August 20X6 £	Variance £	Percentage difference %
Sales	434,000	489,000	55,000	12.67
Costs				
Materials	178,000	193,000	15,000	8.43
Labour	50,000	56,000	6,000	12.00
Direct expenses	24,000	33,000	9,000	37.50
Indirect expenses	37,000	28,000	9,000	24.32
Total costs	289,000	310,000		
Net profit	145,000	179,000		

XYZ Ltd would investigate all the variances except materials.

3 Methods of reporting

When a request is made for such a comparison of information it will normally be requested in a particular format. This can range from an informal note through to a formal report. In this chapter we will consider each of the different methods of reporting.

3.1 House style

Although the basic requirements of each method of reporting will be covered in this chapter it is important to realise that each organisation will have its own style and methods. These will normally be contained in the organisation's policy manual and house styles should always be followed.

3.2 Confidentiality

It is extremely important that the information that has been requested is sent to the appropriate person and only that person and any others that you are specifically asked to send it to. Often the information is confidential and therefore should be treated with the highest degree of respect and care.

4 A note

Probably the most simple and informal method of reporting information to another person in the organisation is by way of a note.

4.1 Format

There is no set format for a note although obviously it must be addressed to the appropriate person, be dated and be headed up correctly so that the recipient knows what it is about. You should also include your name so that the recipient knows who it is from.

In most cases the information that you are reporting on will be important management information and therefore it is unlikely that a note would usually be the most appropriate format. Only use a note if specifically asked to by the person requesting the information.

5 A letter

A slightly more formal method of communicating information is in the form of a letter. Although it would be quite unusual to communicate to another person in the same organisation in this way, a letter may be appropriate if the person to whom you are sending the information works in a separate location, such as Head Office.

5.1 Format

A letter should always have a letter heading showing the organisation's name, address, telephone number etc. Most organisations will have pre-printed letterheads for you to use (an example of 'House Style').

5.2 Rules of letter writing

There are a number of **rules** that should be used when writing a formal or business letter:

- Try to write as simply and as clearly as possible and do not make the letter longer than necessary.

- Remember not to use informal language like abbreviations – I'M, CAN'T, HAVEN'T – these should, of course, be written as: I am, cannot, have not…

- Your address – The return address should be written in the top right-hand corner of the letter.

- Date – Different people put the date on different sides of the page. You can write this on the right, parallel with the last line of the address to which you are sending the letter, or on the left 2 lines below the address you are writing to. Write the month as a word (in full).

- Salutation or greeting: Dear Sir or Madam, – If the name of the person to whom the communication is being sent is not known, use this. It is always advisable to try to find out a name. When using Dear Sir/Madam the closing will be Yours faithfully.

- Dear Mr Jenkins, – If the name is known, use the title (Mr, Mrs, Miss or Ms, Dr, etc.) and the surname only. When writing to a woman and it is not known if she uses Mrs or Miss, Ms would be acceptable, (this is used for married and single women). In this case the closing will be Yours sincerely.

- Signature – the letter should be signed, and the name of the sender printed beneath the signature. If it is unclear if the sender is male or female, then the sender's title should be shown in brackets after the name. If appropriate the job title could also be shown below the name.

6 Electronic mail

Most organisations are now fully computerised and most individuals within an organisation can communicate with each other via electronic mail or e-mail.

6.1 Format

An e-mail must be addressed to the person to whom it is being sent using their e-mail address. It should also be given a title so that the recipient can see at a glance who it is from and what it is about.

In terms of format of the content of the e-mail there are no rules other than any organisational procedures that should be followed.

Care should be taken to ensure that the e-mail is properly addressed to the intended recipient. Most users tend to send many e-mails to many people and it is easy to pick the wrong recipient from a list. It is also essential to take care to preserve confidentiality – customer and supplier e-mail addresses should be kept confidential, unless they are already in the public domain. Therefore if you are sending any sort of blanket e-mail it is important to use the BCC (or blind copy) function. By using this you are ensuring that none of the recipients can see who else the communication has been sent to.

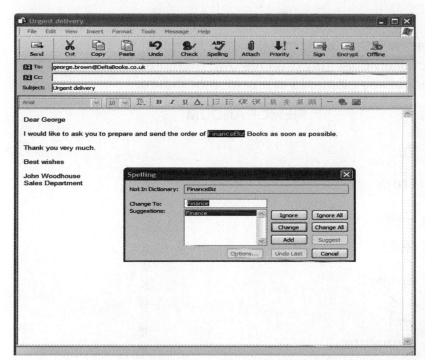

Always spell check your e-mails before sending them!

Common spelling errors to check for include: to/too; their/there; lose/loose.

Also check them for sense and tone. It is easy for the tone in e-mails to be misunderstood by the recipient.

7 Memorandum

🔍 Definition

A memorandum (or memo) is a written communication between two persons within an organisation. The plural of memorandum is memoranda.

A memorandum serves a similar purpose to a letter. However the main difference is that letters are usually sent to persons outside the organisation, whereas memoranda or memos are for communication within the organisation itself. Memos can range from brief handwritten notes, to typed sets of instructions to a junior, to a more formal report to a superior. In general a memo can be used for any purpose where written communication is necessary within the organisation, provided this is according to the rules of the organisation.

7.1 Format

Many organisations will have pre-printed memo forms. In smaller organisations each individual may draft his own memoranda. However there are a number of key elements in any memorandum.

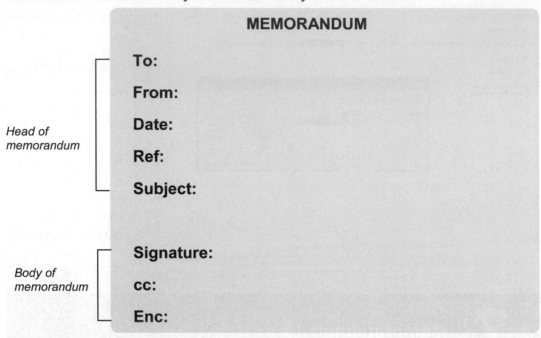

All memoranda will show who it is they are being sent to and who it is from. The date and a suitable reference, for filing purposes, are also essential. The memorandum then must be given a heading to summarise its essential message.

The content of the body of the memorandum will be discussed in the following paragraph. Whether or not a memo is signed will depend upon the organisation's policy. Some organisations insist on a signature on a memorandum, others do not.

It is highly likely that a number of copies of the memo will be sent to people in the organisation other than the main person that it is addressed to and these people copied in should be listed. Finally if there are any enclosures i.e. additional pieces of information that are being sent out with the memorandum, then these should be noted under this final heading of Enc.

7.2 Content of a memorandum

The details of the content and style of a memo will depend upon who is sending the memo, to whom they are sending it, the degree of formality required and the actual subject matter of the memo.

Some memos will simply be handwritten notes from one colleague to another.

If a memo is to be sent to a superior in the organisation, either showing information requested or making recommendations, then both the tone and the content might perhaps be slightly more formal.

Again if a manager is writing to junior personnel in his department his style may be of a more formal nature than if he were writing to another manager within the organisation.

Whatever the precise style and content of the memo some general rules apply:

- There should be a heading to give an indication of the subject matter.

- There should be an introductory paragraph setting the scene.

- The main paragraphs of the memo should follow in a logical order, so that the recipient clearly understands the arguments being put forward.

- There should be a summary of the main points.

8 Reports

Accountants are used to dealing with figures, but they must also learn to express themselves clearly in words. Accountants are (or should be) well prepared for the degree of precision and organisation required in report writing, but may need practice to improve their written style.

8.1 Format

The following guidelines for report writing should be observed.

(a) **Reporting objectives**

Every report has several objectives. Generally these will be to:

- define the problem

- consider the alternatives

- make a reasoned recommendation for a specific alternative.

(b) **Recipient**

The writer should consider the position of the recipient and design the report accordingly. Some recipients will require detailed calculations; others will have little time to study a lengthy report and should therefore be given one of minimum length consistent with providing the required information.

(c) **Heading**

Each report should be headed to show who it is from (or rather, who it has been prepared by) and to, the subject and the date.

(d) **Content**

A simple report will begin with a short introduction explaining the reason for its production. There may also be an 'Executive Summary', which, if present, would appear before the introduction. This is a brief summary of the content of the report which can help readers to decide if it is of use to them (and therefore if they should read the whole report). This will be followed by the body of the report detailing the main issues and discussions. Finally a conclusion will be reached and recommendations made.

(e) **Possible reports sections**

- Contents
- Executive summary
- Introduction
- Main body with main discussion points
- Conclusions and recommendations
- Appendices (referred to within the report and containing detailed figures and sources of information).

(f) **Paragraph point system – each paragraph should make a point; each point should have a paragraph**

This simple rule should always be observed. Important points may be underlined.

(g) **Jargon and technical terms**

The use of jargon should be avoided at all times. If it is necessary to use technical terms, these should be fully explained, as should any techniques with which the recipient may be unfamiliar e.g. decision trees, linear programming, marginal costing, etc.

(h) **Conclusion and recommendations**

A report should always reach a conclusion. This should be clearly stated at the **end of the report**, not in the middle. The report should make it clear why you have arrived at the stated conclusion – it is not enough simply to state all the alternatives and then to recommend one of them without supporting reasons.

KAPLAN PUBLISHING

(i) Figures

All detailed figures and calculations should be relegated to appendices, only the main results appearing in the body of the report. Remember that comparative figures will often be useful. The report should be made as visually stimulating as possible, for instance, by the use of graphs or charts instead of, or to supplement, figures.

9 Word-processed documents

All of the aforementioned documents would usually be produced using word processing software. Memos and short reports should follow your company style (house style). An example report and memo follow.

REPORT

To: Managing Director

From: Candidate

Date: Dec 20X5

Subject: Net Present Value technique

The Net Present Value technique relies on discounting relevant cashflows at an appropriate rate of return. It would be helpful to know:

1   Whether there are any additional cashflows beyond year five.

2   Whether the introduction of a new product will affect sales of the existing products E, C and R.

On the basis of the information provided, the project has a positive Net Present Value of £28,600 and we should therefore proceed.

INTERNAL MEMO

To: Bobby Forster, Accounts Assistant

From: General Manager

Date: 28 October 20X4

Subject: Budgeted production costs for 20X5

As you know we have begun our budgetary planning exercise for 20X5.

I understand that you have been working on the analysis of budgeted production costs.

Could you please pull together all the information you have gathered and carry out the allocation and apportionment exercise for production overhead costs for 20X5.

Then we will have the necessary information that we need to calculate the pre-determined overhead absorption rates for 20X5.

Thanks.

 Test your understanding 3

Define the terms:

- **budget**
- **variance**

Test your understanding 4

Hockeyskill Ltd manufactures hockey sticks and divides its sales function into four main areas:

(1)   Scotland and the North

(2)   Midlands

(3)   South East

(4)   South West.

Its cumulative sales for five months in 20X3 and actual sales for June were:

		Jan–May £	June £
Area	1	31,000	7,100
	2	33,500	8,200
	3	49,000	9,750
	4	41,000	8,210
		£154,500	£33,260

The budget for the six months was:

		£
Area	1	37,500
	2	40,500
	3	57,500
	4	46,500
		£182,000

Prepare a statement for management to show the budget and actual sales for each sales area for the six months ended 30 June showing clearly the variance for each area and in total.

Test your understanding 5

Northcliffe Feeds produces animal feed. It has three main products: A1 Plus, B Plus and Feed Plus. Its planned sales for the quarter ended 30 June 20X3 (budgeted) was:

	Sales tonnes	Selling price per tonne
		£
A1 Plus	12,000	100
B Plus	11,000	120
Feed Plus	9,500	125

Actual sales for the quarter ended 30 June 20X3:

	Sales tonnes	Sales value
		£
A1 Plus	12,600	1,272,600
B Plus	11,000	1,331,000
Feed Plus	9,000	1,116,000

Tasks

- **Present a statement to management to show, for each product and in total, the budgeted sales value and the actual sales value and the variance for each.**

- **Calculate for each product the average actual selling price per tonne.**

- **Calculate the percentage increase or decrease on the budgeted selling price per tonne per product for the period.**

- **Present a statement showing for each product and in total the budget and actual tonnage for the period.**

Test your understanding 6

The costs of production of a business for the months of April 20X1 and April 20X0 are given below:

	April 20X1	April 20X0
	£	£
Materials	253,400	244,300
Labour	318,200	302,600
Expenses	68,700	72,400

Draw up a table showing the difference between the costs of the current month and of the corresponding month in £s, and as a percentage of the April 20X0 costs.

 Test your understanding 7

Given below are the budgeted and actual costs for the two production cost centres of a business for May 20X1.

	Budget	Actual
	£	£
Cost centre 1		
Materials	48,700	46,230
Labour	37,600	39,940
Expenses	5,200	3,700
Cost centre 2		
Materials	56,200	62,580
Labour	22,500	20,400
Expenses	4,800	5,600

You are required to draw up a table showing the amount of the variances for the month. You are also to indicate which variances should be reported to management if it is the business's policy to report only variances that are more than 15% of the budgeted figure.

10 Summary

This chapter focused on the comparison of information and the way in which it can be communicated. When actual costs are compared to the budget the differences are referred to as variances. These differences, whether adverse or favourable, need to be reported to those persons responsible in a meaningful manner so that action can be taken.

The various ways in which information can be communicated was also considered.

Test your understanding answers

Test your understanding 1

Labour cost – month 2

	Prior year £	Current year £	Increase/ (decrease) £
Production	336,000	510,000	174,000
Sales	248,000	350,000	102,000
Administration	100,000	130,000	30,000
Total	684,000	990,000	306,000

Test your understanding 2

	Budgeted £	Actual £	Variance £
Labour	45,000	42,000	3,000 favourable
Material	60,000	62,000	2,000 adverse
Production Expenses	17,000	16,000	1,000 favourable

Test your understanding 3

- A budget is a forecast of figures for costs and income for a future period.

- A variance is the difference between the budget allowance for a level of Test your understanding and the actual cost incurred.

Test your understanding 4

Hockeyskill Ltd

Sales report by region

Budget to actual for period ended 30 June 20X3

Region	Budget	Actual	Variance F/(A)
	£	£	£
Scotland & North	37,500	38,100	600 F
Midlands	40,500	41,700	1,200 F
South East	57,500	58,750	1,250 F
South West	46,500	49,210	2,710 F
	182,000	187,760	5,760 F

Test your understanding 5

Northcliffe Feeds Ltd

Sales report by product

Budget to actual period ended 30 June 20X3

Product	Budget value	Actual value	Variance F/(A)
	£	£	£
A1 Plus	1,200,000	1,272,600	72,600 F
B Plus	1,320,000	1,331,000	11,000 F
Feed Plus	1,187,500	1,116,000	71,500 A
	3,707,500	3,719,600	12,100 F

Selling price per tonne

	Budget	Actual	% increase (decrease)
	£-p	£-p	%
A1 Plus	100.00	101.00	1.00
B Plus	120.00	121.00	0.83
Feed Plus	125.00	124.00	(0.80)

Budget and actual sales in tonnes for period ended 30 June 20X3

Product	Budget tonnes	Actual tonnes
A1 Plus	12,000	12,600
B Plus	11,000	11,000
Feed Plus	9,500	9,000
	32,500	32,600

Test your understanding 6

	April 20X1 £	April 20X0 £	Difference £	Difference %
Materials	253,400	244,300	9,100	3.7
Labour	318,200	302,600	15,600	5.2
Expenses	68,700	72,400	(3,700)	(5.1)

Test your understanding 7

	Budget £	Actual £	Variance £	Variance %
Cost centre 1				
Materials	48,700	46,230	2,470 fav	5.1
Labour	37,600	39,940	2,340 adv	(6.2)
Expenses	5,200	3,700	1,500 fav	28.8
Cost centre 2				
Materials	56,200	62,580	6,380 adv	(11.4)
Labour	22,500	20,400	2,100 fav	9.3
Expenses	4,800	5,600	800 adv	(16.7)

The two variances which are to be reported to management are the two expense variances.

Planning and organising work

Introduction

Planning at the organisational level is the process of deciding what should be done, who should do it and when and how it should be done. At the individual level it involves scheduling routine tasks so that they will be completed in time (to deadline), whilst fitting into the working day any urgent tasks that may interrupt the usual working routine.

Work planning means establishing priorities and allocating and scheduling tasks using planning aids such as lists, action plans, timetables, diaries and charts.

ASSESSMENT CRITERIA	CONTENTS
3.3 Plan workload to meet the needs of the organisation	1 Organisation charts
	2 Organisational objectives
	3 Work planning
	4 Planning methods
	5 Time management
	6 Difficulties in meeting deadlines

1 Organisation charts

1.1 Structural relationships

There are different ways of looking at this topic. We can start with the structural types of roles and relationships that show how power, authority and influence are built into the organisation. Working relationships can also be considered in terms of their contractual, ethical and legal effect. Overlaid on the structural factors, there are interpersonal relationships, which include team working, interdepartmental relations and networking.

The **formal** structure, communications and procedures of the organisation are based on authority, responsibility and functional relationships. You need to know what areas you have authority over and how far that authority extends – including who you report to and who reports to you.

The basic relationship in an organisation is that between superior and subordinate. The superior has authority, i.e. the right or power to make decisions or give instructions or orders to their subordinate/s.

There are also the peer relationships – people you work with and who share similar goals to you. Your plans and schedules need to dovetail with those of other individuals and teams with whom your work is linked.

In most organisations this role and the responsibilities involved in the role will be determined by the job description. Every employee should have a detailed job description. Only then can one fully appreciate one's own role and responsibilities.

As well as being aware of your role and responsibilities, in some organisations there is a process of management by objectives (MBO), in which your supervisor or manager will agree specific, measurable goals with you on a regular basis. He or she will also agree on working methods and schedules, as well as agree the resources needed and available to complete the job. You are then responsible for attaining these goals within a certain time. After this time has elapsed you should meet up with your superior again to discuss results and establish new objectives. This process is generally known as 'performance appraisal'.

1.2 Authority and responsibility

Organisation structure is the division of work among members of the organisation and the co-ordination of their activities so they are directed towards the goals and objectives of the organisation.

It means grouping people into departments or sections, defining tasks and responsibilities, work roles and relationships, channels of communication and allocating authority and responsibility.

Definition

Authority can be defined as the right that an individual has to direct certain actions of others i.e. it is the right to use power.

Responsibility is the duty of an official to carry out his or her assigned task or to ensure it is completed.

Delegation is the act by which a person transfers part of their authority to a subordinate person.

This creates a hierarchy or chain of command where authority flows downwards from the top management to each level of the organisation. This chain is illustrated below with the arrows down showing the delegation:

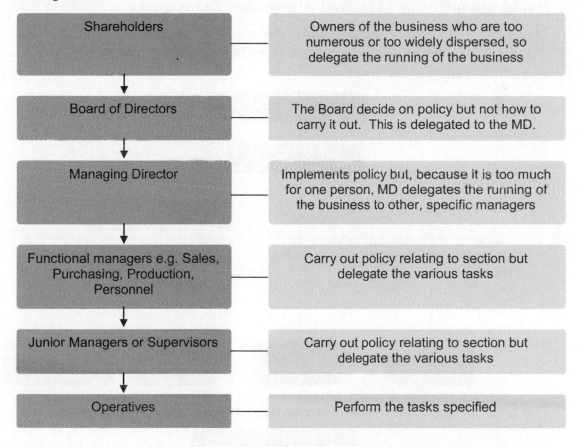

Shareholders	Owners of the business who are too numerous or too widely dispersed, so delegate the running of the business
Board of Directors	The Board decide on policy but not how to carry it out. This is delegated to the MD.
Managing Director	Implements policy but, because it is too much for one person, MD delegates the running of the business to other, specific managers
Functional managers e.g. Sales, Purchasing, Production, Personnel	Carry out policy relating to section but delegate the various tasks
Junior Managers or Supervisors	Carry out policy relating to section but delegate the various tasks
Operatives	Perform the tasks specified

The chain of delegation gives employees the means to resolve or refer any problems or queries regarding work activities to the appropriate person.

1.3   Organisational and departmental structure

An organisation must be set up in a formal manner to give it some authority or structure. This means that those within the organisation must be organised so that they know what to do and who to ask for advice.

- An organisation chart describes in diagrammatic form the structure of the organisation. It illustrates who communicates with whom, how the control system works, who is in control, who has authority and above all, who is responsible. It shows:

    - direction of responsibility (the chart indicates the direct relationship between a group and its immediate supervisor and subordinates)

    - relationships between various sections within a department.

It can outline areas of responsibility for each department and line manager and be extended down to individual employees if necessary.

There are a number of ways to show the grouping of people in the organisation. The functional structure (see below) shows responsibility allocated to specialised functions:

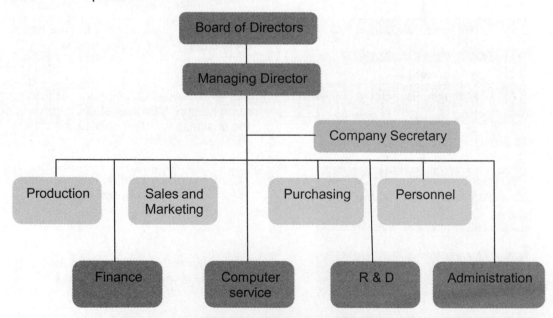

The organisation chart of the Finance department might be shown as:

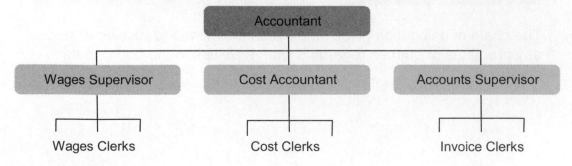

1.4 Teams and teamwork

The basic work unit of organisations has traditionally been the functional department, such as Accounting or Sales. In more recent times, organisations have adopted smaller, more flexible and responsible units – set up as matrix structures, which tend to favour team working. This allows work to be shared among a number of individuals so that it is completed more efficiently and effectively than by individuals working alone. Teams are particularly effective for increasing communication, generating new ideas and evaluating ideas from different viewpoints.

A team may be set up as a separate unit on a more or less permanent basis, with responsibilities for a certain product or stage of a process. Alternatively, it may be on a temporary basis for the attainment of a particular task or project and after it is completed, the team is disbanded or members are re-assigned to a new task.

Multi-skilled teams bring together individuals who can perform any of the group's tasks. These can be shared out in a flexible way according to availability and inclination.

Multi-disciplinary teams bring together individuals with different specialisms so that their skills, knowledge and experience can be pooled or exchanged.

2 Organisational objectives

2.1 Introduction

An organisation will establish goals, objectives and strategies and then determine the policies and procedures necessary to achieve these stated aims. Its effectiveness is generally determined by how well the objectives are being achieved.

Once the objectives are set management will structure the tasks that need to be performed, and decide which department and which individuals will complete which task and when.

2.2 Work methods and practices

The work methods and practices are influenced by:

- the job that needs to be done – its purpose, manner, order and deadline

- the law – making sure the job is done in a safe and secure manner in accordance with all relevant regulations and codes of practice

- the culture of the organisation – the 'way we do things round here' based on the organisational values.

The work methods chosen should consider all of the above to ensure jobs are completed in the right order and in the best way possible, in accordance with legal requirements and the organisation's procedures. There should be no duplication of tasks, or risk that some tasks will not be completed, and efforts should be directed towards a common goal.

2.3 Legal, regulatory and organisational requirements

Laws or agreements of confidentiality will cover some information from within your organisation. For example, you may be required by contract not to disclose financial information. Many of the activities and procedures in the finance section of an organisation will be aimed at producing returns and forms to conform to the legal and regulatory requirements associated with payroll, VAT and tax returns.

Additional legal and regulatory requirements that you must consider are those under the **Data Protection Act** and the **Companies Act**.

2.4 Deadlines

Companies have important deadlines and the most important are those where penalties arise if returns and payments are not made in time. Examples include:

- If a Company Tax Return is filed late, the company or organisation will be charged a flat-rate penalty of £100. HMRC will charge a further £10 penalty per day for every day the return exceeds 3 months late.

- Failing to register for VAT at the correct time will result in penalties and the company paying over any unpaid VAT since the date that they should have registered.

- Failing to submit returns on time.

- Incorrect returns – errors discovered by the HMRC may carry % penalties based on the unpaid tax as a result of the return being incorrect.

- Record-keeping –all business transactions must be recorded and documents kept, including bank statements, bills, receipts and cheque stubs to back them up.

3 Work planning

3.1 Planning and organising

All levels of management are involved in planning. At the top level decisions are made on what to do, and as you come down the hierarchy the plan is fleshed out to incorporate how it is to be done and when it is to be done.

Organising is the next stage after planning. It means working out the actual jobs that must be completed in order to fulfil the plans agreed upon, grouping activities into a pattern or structure, giving specific jobs to people in the organisation and setting deadlines for their completion.

At the individual level work planning involves scheduling and timetabling routine tasks so that they will be completed at the right time, and handling high priority tasks and deadlines which interrupt the usual timetable of work.

The basic steps and objectives in work planning include the following:

The establishment and effective treatment of priorities (considering tasks in order of importance for the objective concerned).

↓

Scheduling or timetabling tasks and allocating them to different individuals within appropriate timescales, (e.g. continuous routine work and arrangements for priority work with short-term deadlines), to achieve work deadlines and attain goals.

↓

Co-ordinating individual tasks within the duties of single employees or within the activities of groups of individuals.

↓

Establishing checks and controls to ensure that priority deadlines are being met and work is not 'falling behind', and that routine tasks are achieving their objectives.

↓

Agreeing the mechanism and means to re-schedule ordinary work to facilitate and accommodate new, additional or emergency work by drawing up 'contingency plans' for unscheduled events. Because nothing goes exactly according to plan, one feature of good planning is to make arrangements for what should be done if there were a major upset, e.g. if the company's computer were to break down, or if the major supplier of key raw materials were to go bust. The major problems for which contingency plans might be made are events that, although unlikely, stand a slim chance of actually happening.

The tasks you complete at work will fall into four categories:

1   **Daily**, e.g. routine tasks such as recording sales invoices in the sales day book or recording cash received.

2   **Weekly**, e.g. preparing journal entries to post totals from books of prime entry to the nominal ledger.

3   **Monthly**, e.g. bank reconciliation or sales ledger reconciliation.

4   **One-off**, e.g. information for a report.

Most employees in an organisation will spend the majority of their time working on the routine tasks that are part of their job and responsibilities. However at times unexpected and non-routine tasks may arise. These must also be dealt with without affecting the routine responsibilities. The performance criterion states that you should:

*   Identify and prioritise tasks according to organisational procedures and regulatory requirements.

*   Recognise changes in priorities and adapt resources allocations and work plans accordingly.

*   Check that work methods and activities conform to legal and regulatory requirements and organisational procedures.

3.2   Agreeing timescales

The planning of work involves the allocation of time to the requirements of work to be done. This must be applied to the organisation as a whole, to individual departments and sections, and to single employees. Planning must be geared to periods of time, and the degree of flexibility built into planning will vary according to the length of time being planned for. The principles of planning will revolve around:

(a)   determining the length of time covered by the plans

(b)   planning by departments and groups of individuals

(c)   planning by individuals.

There are three time ranges, which are normally involved in planning work:

(a)   long-term

(b)   medium-term

(c)   short-term.

These three terms are really only expressions of convenience. Time is relative. For example, a length of five years might be considered long-term within an organisation producing footwear but short-term in, say, the aviation industry. It may well be that three years is short-term to an organisation but to a department within that organisation it may be medium-term whilst to an individual employee it may be long-term. It is important that, whatever the relevant time span may be to a group or individual, work is allocated accordingly.

3.3   Identifying priorities

Much office work is of a routine nature although there are exceptions. Priorities must be established with regard to the cyclical nature of routine work and unexpected demands.

The cyclical nature of routine work often means that certain tasks have to be completed by a certain time. In such cases other work may have to be left in order to ensure that the task with the approaching deadline date is given priority. Such tasks might include:

- the preparation of payroll sheets for a weekly computer run

- the despatch of monthly statements to account customers

- the checking of stock levels at predetermined intervals and appropriate action such as re-ordering.

Unexpected demands are often made at departmental, sectional or individual level. If management requires urgent or additional work to be carried out then, obviously, some other tasks will have to be postponed.

Given that routine tasks may be anticipated and that unexpected demands cannot, this area of priority identification can be divided into routine tasks, which can be accommodated within normal sensible planning, and 'emergency-type' tasks that must be performed at short notice.

Routine work usually includes a number of tasks that, as a matter of course, fall into a natural order in which they should be performed. This 'natural order of events' approach can usually be incorporated into the normal routine of the office and/or the individual to such an extent that often it is not apparent that there has ever been a problem with the identification of priority tasks.

Where tasks/events of an 'emergency' nature arise the main problem facing an individual will be that of deciding which of the routine tasks should be postponed. However, the postponement of one routine task will automatically delay successive tasks.

3.4 Guidelines for determining priorities

In determining priorities, the following should be noted:

- Wherever it is possible for a priority to be anticipated, such as in the case of the 'natural order of events' described above, then associated difficulties will usually be overcome by sensible, logical planning.

- If an 'emergency type' task occurs, then normal routine work will automatically take second place. It is here that decisions must be taken to decide which routine tasks should be postponed. Also, plans should be formulated and implemented to ensure that the routine work being postponed is carried out as soon as possible, resulting in minimum disruption to the normal routine.

Often these situations may arise where one priority comes into conflict with another. Here the task deemed more important by a responsible individual should take preference.

Unfortunately, individuals within one department or section often become blind to the needs of other departments or sections. A task that is classed as low priority within one department or section may be of the utmost priority to another. Thus in arriving at any decision the individual making that decision must ensure that the effect on each department is considered when making a decision.

A responsible individual should determine priorities. Often, especially in the matter of routine cycles, the individual responsible for that work will be qualified to determine any priority. However, the greater the effect and the wider the span of influence of priority determination, the more responsible the individual should be.

When an unexpected task is given to you then you must have the flexibility to be able to reschedule your routine work in order to complete this task.

3.5 Setting priorities

Activities need to be sequenced and scheduled. There may be conflict between the two planning tasks since the best sequence of activities to put the plan into place might not be consistent with the schedule of when particular activities need to be completed. The sequence of activities may be determined by the following:

- An activity must precede another when it is a pre-requisite for later activities. Assembly of a car cannot precede the manufacture or purchase of its components.

- The sequence of activities may be dictated by the ease with which they can be completed.

- An activity may be considered more important than others, e.g. in the building industry priority will be given to outdoor work when the weather is favourable to minimise the risk of delays later.

The organisation's operations require proper scheduling of resources to run efficiently and avoid periods of over and under utilisation. Some activities must occur at precisely the right time, e.g. specific day and time slot for advertising a new product. The scheduling of tasks can also affect customer service in terms of delivery.

3.6 Prioritisation of routine tasks

Routine tasks may be tasks that are performed a number of times each day, tasks performed once or twice each day, tasks necessary each week or at the end of each month perhaps.

Examples of routine tasks might include the following:

- sending out of invoices to customers each day

- opening the post at the beginning of the day and again after the second post has arrived

- filing all copy invoices at the end of the week

- preparing a list of outstanding customer balances at the end of each month.

Priorities are tasks listed in order of importance. Each day employees will need to prioritise the tasks that they are required to complete during that day.

The first job of the day might be to open the post, as the post may contain urgent items to be dealt with by yourself or other members of the department, or items that are needed in order to perform a later task. This will therefore be a high priority job and should not be left until the middle of the morning.

If your job includes responsibility for sending out invoices to customers then it will be a fairly high priority that these invoices are sent out on the same day as the sale or customer order. The task of filing copies of the invoices is less urgent. It may be possible to leave this until later in the day, or even later in the week.

Another skill you can use to analyse jobs is sequencing. When you put things in sequence, you arrange steps in the order that you do them. When you work out the sequence to carry out the tasks, you are judging two things:

- How urgent is the task?
- How important is the task?

These are not the same thing. Urgent tasks need to be completed within a particular time limit. Important jobs may affect a lot of people or cost a lot of money. They may also have major implications if they are not done, or if they are done badly. If you are going abroad on holiday, it is important that you have a passport. If your holiday isn't for six months, it isn't urgent. It becomes urgent if you leave it too late.

3.7 Prioritisation of unexpected tasks

Unexpected or non-routine tasks will normally occur for one of two reasons:

1   The unexpected tasks may be due to additional activity in the organisation, such as a new product launch or takeover of another company.

2   Unexpected tasks can also occur due to some 'emergency' within the organisation such as a fellow member of staff being off work sick or an error being found which must be dealt with immediately.

They should be fairly easy to identify, as they will normally involve instruction from a more senior member of staff. For example if a member of your department is off sick, and is unlikely to return for the rest of the week, it is likely that the manager or supervisor will re-schedule that person's tasks to be dealt with by the other members of the department.

However some unexpected tasks might not be so clearly signalled. For example suppose that you answer the telephone for a colleague during his lunch break.

If the call is from a customer with an urgent request for information, then this customer query may be an unexpected task that you will need to deal with.

If an unexpected task is identified then this must also be prioritised and fitted in with the routine tasks of the individual's job. Unexpected tasks will not necessarily always be urgent, although many will be. When an unexpected task is identified the individual should ensure that he or she fully understands the following points:

- the precise nature of the task

- the resources or information required to carry out the task

- the time required to obtain those resources or information

- the time that the task is expected to take (remember that as an unexpected task it is unlikely that the individual will have performed this task before)

- the time allowed for this task and deadline set for it

- the importance of the task

- the priority it should be allocated in respect of the work being carried out.

Only when aware of all of these points is it possible to correctly prioritise the task and schedule it together with their remaining routine tasks.

For example suppose that you are required to produce a report for a Board meeting on Wednesday 12 March. Today is Monday 3 March. In order to produce the report you will require a number of files from the central filing system which are likely to take two days to be accessed and delivered. The manager of the department who has commissioned this report estimates that there will be approximately one full day's work obtaining the relevant information from the files and another half day in actually preparing the report itself. Owing to backlogs in the typing department your manager suggests that the report is with the typist by next Monday morning, 10 March, at the latest in order that it can be typed, proof read and any adjustments made in time for the Board meeting on Wednesday 12 March.

In this instance the only task that you will need to perform immediately, a high priority today, is to inform central filing of the files that are required for the report. As the files will not reach you until Wednesday then there can be nothing else done for this task until that day. You must then ensure that during Wednesday, Thursday and Friday approximately a day and a half is set aside to prepare and write the report. You must also ensure that when the report is returned from typing at the beginning of the following week the proof reading is again given a high priority.

As a further example suppose that a colleague in your department has called in sick with flu this Monday morning. Your manager thinks that your colleague will not return to work this week, and therefore all of his responsibilities must be dealt with by the other members of the department for the entire week. One of your colleague's responsibilities, which your manager has allocated to you, is to deal with customer complaints. It is the organisation's procedure to ensure that all complaints are dealt with, even if this is simply an acknowledging letter, on the same day as the complaint is received. Therefore, in order to comply with organisational procedures, you will need to give priority to any complaints received in the post each morning and any telephone complaints received during each day. Again you must also ensure that your own priority routine tasks, such as sending out invoices on the day of the order, are completed at the appropriate time.

 Test your understanding 1

List all of your routine daily tasks.

Make a separate list of all non-routine tasks that may arise, and state why they arise. (By their nature non-routine tasks are unexpected and you may need to invent possible non-routine tasks!)

 4   Planning methods

4.1   Introduction

Different organisations, groups and individuals have individual characteristics, tastes, styles, preferences and objectives. These particular objectives may well be attained via different methods and systems of scheduling work.

As a method of planning group work, it is vital that these efforts are co-ordinated – not only with each other but with all actions taken. The method used can be a means of communication and support within the group, ensuring that all members of the group progress towards their goal.

The following planning methods and systems are probably the most common:

(a)   checklists

(b)   bar charts

(c)   bring-forward, bring-up and follow-up systems

(d)   activity scheduling and time scheduling

(e)   action sheets

(f)   other systems, including planning charts and boards, and diaries.

Each of these methods and systems will be discussed individually overleaf.

However, any combination may be in use at any one time within an organisation or by an individual employee. It is vital therefore that these efforts are co-ordinated, not only with each other but with all actions taken.

4.2   Checklists

Checklists are often used on an individual basis and are perhaps the simplest system, being essentially a list of items or activities. The preparation of a typical checklist would involve the following:

(a)   the formulation of a list of activities and tasks to be performed within a given period

(b)   the identification of urgent or priority tasks

(c)   the maintenance of a continuous checklist with the addition of extra activities and tasks as and when required.

This system is obviously limited in its application because of its simplicity. It is suited to fairly mundane or routine tasks, but it is these tasks which are often the very essence of the attainment of objectives.

Typical uses of checklists would include the following:

(a)   purchasing requirements

(b)   points to cover at an interview

(c)   points to cover at a meeting (e.g. an agenda)

(d)   organising a conference or meeting.

Below is a checklist to show when certain returns associated with PAYE are due.

STATUTORY RETURNS SCHEDULE			
Returns	Description	Date Due	Forward To
P60	This is a total of the employee's year-end earnings including Tax and NI.	05.2006	Employee
P9D	Must be completed for all employees earning less than £8,500 (including reimbursed expenses and the taxable values of benefits) and for Directors for whom forms P11D are not required.	07.2006	Employee and HMRC
P14	Summary of deductions such as Tax, NI, SSP, SMP.	05.2006	HMRC
P35	Statement of Tax, NI, SSP and SMP for each employee together with an overall summary of the NI monthly or quarterly payments made by the employer in respect of that tax year.	05.2006	HMRC
P38S	Relates to students who work for an employer during their holidays.	05.2006	HMRC
WTC	Year-end summary of Working Tax Credits paid to employees throughout the year.	05.2006	HMRC
DPTC	Year-end summary of Disabled Person's Tax Credit paid to employees throughout the year.	05.2006	HMRC

4.3 Bar charts

A bar chart has two main purposes:

(a) to show the time necessary for an activity

(b) to display the time relationship between one activity and another.

Bar charts are particularly useful for checking the time schedules for a number of activities that are interdependent. A bar chart for the building of a house extension might be shown over a period of six months and an example is given over the page.

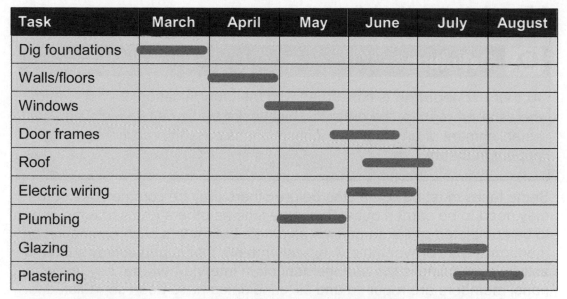

Task	March	April	May	June	July	August
Dig foundations	▬					
Walls/floors		▬				
Windows			▬			
Door frames				▬		
Roof				▬		
Electric wiring				▬		
Plumbing			▬			
Glazing					▬	
Plastering						▬

This illustrates the importance of bar charts in showing:

(a)   overall progress to date, thus assisting in monitoring

(b)   the progress attained at an individual stage of a multi-stage process.

4.4   Bring-forward, bring-up and follow-up systems

These systems are more sophisticated than checklists and bar charts. They are particularly useful for coping with documentation and are utilised in many offices. The systems involve the filing of details of work to be done and the dates on which this work is to be done. A routine is established with a view to allocating necessary tasks to the precise day.

The systems all operate around the following principles:

A note is made of anything to be done in the future, showing details of the appropriate action or format (e.g. make a telephone call or write a letter).

↓

The note is filed away in a concertina folder with separate files for each day.

↓

Each appropriate file is checked at the start of each day and the action required that day noted.

↓

The action is carried out.

4.5 Activity scheduling

 Definition

Activity scheduling is concerned with the determination of priority and the establishment of the order in which tasks are to be tackled. The establishment of an order of priority is not as easy in practice as it may appear in theory.

Some tasks must be completed before others may be commenced, some may need to be carried out at the same time as others and some may need to be completed at the same time as others but factors such as finance or manpower may prevent this. A typical problem that is particularly suited to activity scheduling is the arrangement of an interview where, say, three panel members are required and six candidates have been short-listed for interview. Obviously, mutually convenient dates must be found when all nine parties are available and the room, which is to be used for the interview, must be free for use on these days.

Activity scheduling involves the identification of key factors and their assembly on a checklist. In the example given above, the two key factors are room availability and people availability. It may be used for any task, which involves a number of actions that must necessarily be undertaken in some sequence.

4.6 Time scheduling

 Definition

Time scheduling is an extension of activity scheduling by indicating the required time for each task. It follows the preparation of an activity schedule and involves the determination of time required for each activity.

Given that within an activity schedule some tasks will be performed simultaneously, it should be noted that the time period in which the series of activities will be completed may not equate to the total of the individual activity times.

Effectively a time schedule determines the order in which activities are scheduled on a checklist, the time required for each activity also being shown alongside each item. Tasks that can be done in parallel are noted. The total of the individual activity times, with allowances for simultaneous activities, will produce the time allowed for one complete group of activities.

Time scheduling is thus particularly useful in the process of planning, especially as it enables the initial deadlines to be set.

4.7   Action sheets

This system is a natural progression from activity and time scheduling. Action sheets summarise the time that the stages of the individual task should take, and contain estimates of the start and finish dates of each stage.

The example below depicts an action sheet for a wedding.

Activity number	Detail	Number of weeks in advance	Certification of completion (initials or signature)
1	Book church	26	
2	Book reception hall	26	
3	Send out invitations	12	
4	Receive replies	4	
5	Order food/refreshments	3	
6	Check arrangements	2	
7	The wedding day	–	

Action sheets are widely used and are often utilised in conjunction with bar charts.

4.8   Planning charts and boards

These usually show information in summary form and any required item of information may be seen at a glance. They are often used to show details of future events that affect departments (e.g. to plan staff holidays).

4.9   Diaries

Diaries are an obvious and consequently often overlooked aid to planning. They can range from simple hand-written diaries showing an individual's appointments, meetings etc through to sophisticated computerised diaries, either as part of the organisation's computer network or alternatively in some form of electronic personal organiser. Diaries can also usefully be used not just to show appointments etc, but also to highlight matters that should be followed up or chased up on a particular date. For example, suppose that you have been involved in a number of telephone discussions with a potential customer. The potential customer has indicated that he will have decided whether or not to go ahead with an order by Thursday of this week at the latest. You may wish to make a note in your diary for Wednesday to give the potential customer a telephone call in order to determine whether there is any additional information that you can provide.

Diaries are especially suited to individual employees but only if the employee ensures that all relevant details of any appointments are entered as a matter of course. This matter of full details is important because the failure to note down full and appropriate information regarding a particular appointment could have serious repercussions for the organisation, particularly if an appointment has to be rescheduled or handled by someone else. It is sensible to have a routine for making appointments and indeed to create a 'checklist for appointments'.

Test your understanding 2

Kate has recently joined a busy administration department in a manufacturing organisation. She is slightly shocked that the organisation seems to lack formal procedures. She feels that her job is one of 'fire-fighting'. Once one crisis is over another one arrives. She feels there is never a spare moment in the day from 9am when she arrives to 5.30pm when she goes home. She is constantly responding to so called 'urgent' requests from other people to: "just do this for me Kate please, it won't take a moment", or "this job's top priority – can you rush it through please?" Every job seems to be 'top priority'!

How will this 'Crisis Management' method of working impact on Kate? What are the consequences for her work? What time management techniques could Kate use to help organise and prioritise her workload?

5 Time management

5.1 Timetabling tasks

Work planning ensures that commitments to others are met within agreed timescales and necessitates planning and organising on the part of the organisation and the employee.

Your time needs to be properly managed if you are to work efficiently and effectively. The first way to start to organise your time is to plan your use of time.

Example 1

Here is Joe's diary for the coming week:

May 2006				
Monday	Tuesday	Wednesday	Thursday	Friday
1	2	3	4	5
9am Meeting Mr Green	3pm Group Meeting	2.30pm Visit other site	Mum's Birthday!	

This shows his meetings with other people but not how he will use the rest of his time.

Solution

Here is a more useful version of his diary for the same week:

May 2006

	Monday	Tuesday	Wednesday	Thursday	Friday
9am	Meeting Mr Green	Record Cash	Record Cash	Record Cash	Record Cash
10am	Record Cash	Update cash book	Bank reconciliation	Finish bank reconciliation	Prepare cash flash figure
11am/ 12pm					
1pm	Lunch	Lunch	Lunch	Buy card	Lunch
2pm	Record cash continued	Prepare for meeting		Prepare info for report	Prepare journals
			Site Visit		
3pm	Speak to Pat about new system?	Group meeting			Count petty cash
4pm	Home early				Request cash

Notice how all the major tasks have been timetabled. Joe has estimated the amount of time to complete each task and blocked out that time. This ensures that Joe has sufficient time to complete tasks before the necessary **deadline**.

Test your understanding 3

Do you allow your days to be filled with routine tasks? If so you may be neglecting longer term goals because of this. Draw three columns and in each write down one objective or target you would like to achieve in the next 12 months. Under each objective you need to plan how it will be achieved. Set any interim targets or shorter-term deadlines that you will need to meet and what action or resources you need to succeed. (If you find setting objectives for the next 12 months too long a time-frame then try setting them on a quarterly basis).

5.2 Timing of tasks

Whatever function you perform at work, you will always have tasks to complete, which fall into four categories:

Category		Examples
1	Daily	Recording cash received.
		Recording sales invoices in sales day book.
		Recording purchase invoices in purchase day book.
2	Weekly	Preparing journal entries to post totals from books of prime entry to nominal ledger.
3	Monthly	Sales ledger reconciliation.
		Purchase ledger reconciliation.
		Bank reconciliation.
4	One-off	Information for reports.

Joe also keeps a list of quick tasks to complete at appropriate times. As he completes them, he crosses them off his list.

5.3 Review of work plans

Each evening before he goes home, Joe reviews his work schedule and updates it for:

(a) tasks to carry over

(b) any other changes (e.g. meeting times changed).

Even if you do not have the opportunity to schedule your work, try scheduling your studies and your free time! You should find that you get more out of your time.

6 Difficulties in meeting deadlines

6.1 Introduction

The syllabus area here is that you *'report anticipated difficulties in meeting deadlines to the appropriate person'*. There will always be occasions when, for one reason or another, the deadline or target cannot be met. Often individuals are vague regarding the information they require, which may mean that wrong or incomplete information is provided. It may be that the deadline cannot be met because of problems encountered by the supplier of the information.

Perhaps if a student is required to provide some information, he/she might be unable to gather the information by the deadline either because of lack of sufficient working hours, or due to personal circumstances, such as doctor's/dentist's appointments.

Alternatively the problems with meeting the deadline may be due to a third party. Perhaps the information required has to be acquired from a third party. If this person does not provide the information by the deadline you have set, then you are obviously unable to pass this information on by your deadline.

Identified below are typical examples of problems that may be encountered:

(a)   Files, books, etc may be borrowed and not returned.

(b)   Reference journals may not be kept up to date.

(c)   Access to information may be denied due to security/confidentiality considerations.

(d)   Computer systems may 'crash'.

(e)   International time differences may mean that offices are not open when required.

(f)   Files, books or journals may be incorrectly filed.

(g)   Wrong or insufficient information is provided.

(h)   Delays may occur because information has been archived.

(i)   Unexpected tasks become necessary and take priority.

Whatever the reason for not achieving the target or deadline it is vital that students understand the importance of reporting and explaining this fact.

6.2   Difficulties are promptly reported

It is tempting in any situation to put off dealing with any problems. In a business context if it appears likely that a deadline is not to be met then it is tempting to put off telling the appropriate person about this in the hope that the information can eventually be reported by the required deadline.

This really is the wrong attitude. As far as your manager or colleague, who has requested the information, is concerned it is far better that he or she knows of any possible delays at the earliest opportunity. It is therefore far better to report any possibility of non-achievement of a target at an early stage than to leave such news until the last minute. This gives the manager a chance to revise his or her plans accordingly.

The rule is therefore that if you become aware of the possibility of not being able to meet a deadline for the supply of information then this should be reported immediately. If the circumstances are eventually favourable and the information is reported by the deadline this will be an added bonus. However if the anticipated circumstances exist and the information is not available then at least the manager concerned has had advance notification, giving them the chance to be able to work around the problem.

6.3   Explanation of delays

If you are unable to perform a duty by a specified deadline then, not only must this fact be reported, but it must be reported in an appropriate manner. Not only must politeness be considered but also professional behaviour.

Even if you believe that the deadline that has been set is impossible to meet, there will be nothing to be gained from an aggressive or impolite attitude towards the person requiring the information. There will be instances when deadlines are set that are earlier than is absolutely required, and provided that you give your explanation of not being able to meet that deadline in a reasonable manner then it is possible that the deadline may be able to be extended.

In other circumstances the deadline will be vital. Again any aggressive approach by the student concerned will only heighten the displeasure of the manager at the deadline not being met. The best way to deal with any situation where a target or deadline is not achieved is to explain politely and rationally why this has not been achieved. This may be, as mentioned earlier, due to personal circumstances or due to delays from third parties.

Test your understanding 4

In which example below does the assistant have the authority and ability to delegate to the operatives?

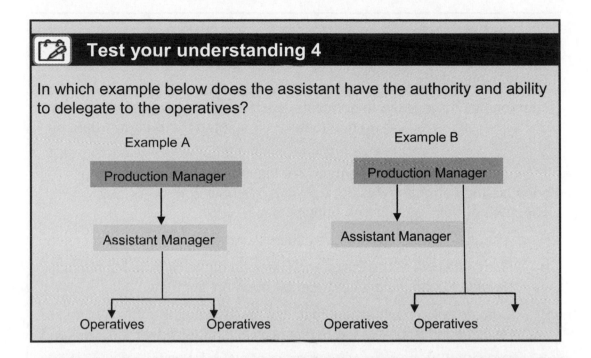

Test your understanding 5

Prepare a checklist of information you would collect and retain relating to a meeting at another organisation's premises.

Test your understanding 6

Today is Friday.

Thomas has three tasks to complete, each of which will take two hours. His supervisor is expecting him to have completed them all by 10am on Monday.

Thomas was unable to perform any of the tasks on Friday morning because the computer was not working. It is now 2pm on Friday. Thomas normally goes home at 5pm.

What should Thomas do in these circumstances?

A   Complete one of the tasks and start one of the others. He should be able to complete all of them by noon on Monday

B   Complete the most urgent task and take home the other two tasks. He is bound to be able to find time to finish them over the weekend

C   Contact his supervisor immediately and explain the problem. He should suggest that he finishes what he considers to be the most urgent task first before starting one of the others

D   Start all of the tasks and do parts of each of them. This way he has at least done something towards each of them before he goes home

 Test your understanding 7

Which one of the following statements about an organisation is NOT true?

(i)   An organisation chart provides a summary of the structure of a business.

(ii)   An organisation chart can indicate functional authority but not line authority within a business.

(iii)   An organisation chart can improve employees' understanding of their role in a business.

(iv)   An organisation chart can improve internal communications within a business.

7 Summary

This chapter should help you to focus on the way you manage your own workload. How you plan, prioritise and organise both routine and non-routine work is of critical importance to how efficient and effective you will be.

Now that you have read the chapter you should be aware of the importance of anticipating problems before they arise and asking for assistance where necessary. Identifying any weaknesses in your own skills, level of experience, or ability to meet deadlines is critical to working effectively as a member of a team.

Test your understanding answers

 ### Test your understanding 1

Possible routine tasks for someone working in, for example, purchase ledger, could include:

- opening and distributing the post

- taking telephone calls from suppliers

- processing supplier invoices

- posting supplier invoices to purchase ledger

- filing all invoices received

- maintaining up to date records of the outstanding creditor position and when payments are due.

Possible non-routine tasks could include:

- provide up to date aged creditor analysis to new investor

- raise sales invoices when colleague off sick.

 ### Test your understanding 2

Kate appears to have to always respond to others demands upon her time and has little control over planning her own time or work. The likely impact of this method of working on Kate is that it will be stressful and unsatisfying. The consequences for her work are that it is likely to deteriorate in quality and important deadlines may be missed as others encroach upon her time.

It is important that Kate learns strict time management techniques such as daily lists and action plans. She needs to prioritise her tasks perhaps in negotiation with those supplying her with the tasks. To do this she needs to communicate very firmly and clearly with those supplying her with work. Next time someone asks her to do something that is supposed to be 'top priority' she must ascertain exactly when the work is required by and firmly negotiate a reasonable deadline. In this way colleagues may learn to respect that she is a busy person who has other demands upon her time than simply responding to their demands.

Test your understanding 3

	Objective/ Target 1	Objective/ Target 2	Objective/ Target 3
Overall goal:			
How?			
Action required?			
Interim targets?			
3 months?			
6 months?			
12 months?			
Resources required?			

Test your understanding 4

In example A, because the flow of authority is shown as passing down from the production manager to the assistant manager and then on to the operatives. In example B the production manager can delegate to the assistant manager and to the operatives, but the assistant manager is not shown as having any authority over the operators.

Test your understanding 5

Ensure that the following information is included:

(a) the full name and title of the person(s) you intend or are required to meet

(b) the full and precise name and address of the relevant organisation

(c) the telephone number of the organisation together with the area code (STD code) and the extension of the person you must see

(d) the time, date and anticipated length of the meeting

(e) the exact location of the meeting (e.g. which room on which floor in which block)

(f) outline details of the matter to be discussed

(g) travel directions and details of entrance points and security procedures.

It is, of course, equally important for those details to be sent to people who may be intending to visit you.

 Test your understanding 6

C – Contact his supervisor immediately and explain the problem. He should suggest that he finishes what he considers to be the most urgent task first before starting one of the others.

 Test your understanding 7

(ii) is not true because an organisation chart does indicate line authority within a business.

Working relationships

Introduction

The efficient running of organisations requires that all the members of the organisation work together towards the achievement of the organisation's objectives. This working together requires the adequate understanding of what others are doing. It requires a high level of coordination and control and, fundamentally, it requires communication which is efficient and effective.

ASSESSMENT CRITERIA	CONTENTS
2.1 Identify the interpersonal skills required by finance staff	1 Co-ordination
	2 Communication
2.2 Identify the features of an effective finance team	3 Methods of communication
	4 Confidential information
	5 Interpersonal skills
	6 Teams
	7 Handling disagreements and conflicts

1 Co-ordination

1.1 Co-ordination and communication

As we have already noted, an appropriate organisation structure will ensure that all sections of the business are pursuing common objectives, and clearly defined job descriptions will improve appreciation of how tasks are inter-related and should prevent overlapping or areas of responsibility being missed. Standard instructions and procedures are a way of reducing the risk of conflicting practices occurring within the company.

However, your role and responsibilities are an integral part of the organisation's structure and cannot be treated in isolation from other people. Your colleagues will have joint objectives and goals, which will necessitate pooling resources, information and efforts.

Any business activity is in part about ensuring the co-ordination of organisational and individual endeavour, and of co-ordinating the work of individuals and teams. Some activities will be dependent on the successful and timely completion of other activities, so you need to be aware of your own requirements as well as the plans and deadlines of others in the organisation.

Poor co-ordination is often at the heart of complaints from customers or colleagues, e.g. two departments giving different information. It can cause workflow problems if work arrives unexpectedly or later than planned from another unit. This can cause conflict between departments with one blaming the other for the problem instead of both working together and co-operating to perform as effectively and efficiently as possible.

In any organisation the communication of information is necessary to achieve co-ordination.

1.2 Social skills

You will see that social skills are important to the organisation, as well as to the individuals employed and this is what we mean by working relations. There will be jobs where co-operation with colleagues is essential. It would, of course, be no good to have a large number of employees who all argue and disagree with each other. Apart from the disruption caused to each other, the organisation would also suffer since the amount of work carried out would probably be very small and perhaps even counter-productive. This would have a negative effect on productivity.

What is meant by social skills? It means the ways in which we discuss work related matters with others, or obtain information from them. You will be aware of the situation when you want to take some annual leave and need to ask your supervisor whether you can have the time off when you require it. The supervisor may tell you right away, ask you to put it in writing or need to ask their manager later. What is important is the way you 'get on' with your supervisor and perhaps the way in which they perceive you. If the approach is right, then you might be told right away there are no problems, even though there may be some particular way in which you should go about it. Your social skills or the way you put the question over is important, not only to you – especially if you want time off – but to the organisation because it is in this way that a certain amount of confidence builds up between you and your supervisor.

It is not unknown to find a clash of personality between individuals in an organisation, and it is up to the senior officer in the organisation to take the appropriate action. Whilst there can be no hard and fast rules on what should be done, the interests of the organisation must take priority, although there may be certain circumstances where the individual's interests should be taken into consideration.

When dealing with other people in your organisation you should be as courteous and polite as when dealing with external customers.

1.3 Contractual and legal relationships

Employment is a legal relationship with your employer. There are underlying duties to your employer under your contract of employment, including:

- **Duty of care** – there is implied into every contract of employment a duty that the employee performs his/her contract with proper care.

- **Duty of co-operation** – even where the employer promulgates a rulebook containing instructions for the execution of the work, the employee is under an obligation not to construe the rules in a way designed to defeat the efficiency of the employer's business. This means working to the spirit of the rules sometimes, rather than to the letter – therefore not being deliberately obtuse.

- **Duty of obedience** – in the absence of express provisions an employee is required to carry out all reasonable and lawful orders of the employer. Some orders clearly do not require obedience e.g. falsify sales records on employer's instructions or drive an un-roadworthy vehicle, which may lead to his prosecution under the Road Traffic Acts.

- **Loyal service** – this duty is to use all reasonable steps to advance his employer's business within the sphere of his employment and not to do anything which might injure the employer's business.

1.4 Equal Opportunities Legislation

'Equal opportunities' is a term describing the belief that there should be an equal chance for all workers to apply to be selected for jobs, to be trained and promoted in employment and have that employment terminated fairly. There are three main reasons for adopting equal opportunities policies:

(i) It is morally wrong to treat parts of the population as inferior or inadequate.

(ii) Organisations do not benefit from excluding any potential source of talent.

(iii) It is the law.

The legislation on equal opportunities is made up of several Acts:

• **The Sex Discrimination Act of 1975** renders it unlawful to make any form of discrimination in employment affairs because of marital status or sex.

• **The Race Relations Act of 1976** ensures that there should be no discrimination on the grounds of colour, nationality, ethnic origin or race.

• **The Equal Pay Act 1970** is concerned with equality of pay and related matters. The Act aims to ensure that where men and women are employed in 'like work' or 'work of equal value' or 'rated as equivalent', they will receive the same basic pay.

• **The Disability Discrimination Act 1995** provides for disabled people not to be discriminated against in a variety of circumstances including employment.

• **The Rehabilitation of Offenders Act 1974** provides that a conviction, other than one involving imprisonment for more than 30 months, may become erased if the offender commits no further serious offences during the rehabilitation period.

Discrimination may operate in all kinds of areas including sex, sexuality and marital status, race and colour, religion, politics, disability and conviction of a criminal offence. Forward-looking organisations will have a positive attitude to equal opportunities and operate non-discriminating procedures in all aspects of personnel management, including recruitment and selection, advertisements, access to training and promotion, disciplinary procedures, redundancy and dismissal.

As an employee you also have responsibilities under the equal opportunities legislation not to discriminate or show prejudice against people on the grounds of sex, race or disability.

 KAPLAN PUBLISHING

1.5   Carrying out instructions

An employee who will not carry out instructions will not be welcomed by most firms. The instructions are given so that the work to be performed can be understood and will fit into the total workload of the department. Failure to carry out instructions may:

(a)   delay a piece of work needed urgently by a customer

(b)   adversely affect the rest of the work performed by others

(c)   endanger lives or health of other employees or customers (e.g.by operating a machine without following instructions or smoking in 'non-smoking' areas).

Employees should expect their employers to give proper instructions at the right time, in the right manner and in the right place. Failure to do so can mean that the employees might lose pay or bonuses because they are unable to complete the work within a prescribed time. It can also lead to poor morale due to workers arguing about what should be done as none of them are fully aware of what exactly is required.

In addition, instructions to protect employees' physical well-being which are not given properly, or not given at all, can result in disability or even death.

1.6   Asking for clarification when necessary

It is possible for instructions to be genuinely misunderstood or for completely wrong instructions to be given. If this happens to you at any time, you should ask for clarification of the instructions. Simply to carry on with the job when the instructions are genuinely not clear, or where they are obviously wrong, can cause all sorts of problems. Your employer or supervisor would therefore expect you to question the instructions in such cases.

Of course it is possible to be obstinate and obstructive by deliberately trying to misinterpret instructions. You must be careful to ensure that your manager or supervisor understands your proper concern at the lack of clear instructions, and does not mistakenly assume that you are being unnecessarily awkward.

If you are ever unclear about instructions that you have been given you should always check them with the appropriate person.

1.7   Asking for assistance

If an individual feels that they are not up to the demands of a particular job, or that a deadline cannot be met, then this is likely to be due to either a lack of time, a lack of skills or a lack of experience. A lack of time is almost impossible to deal with unless large amounts of overtime are to be worked. Lack of skills or experience however can be overcome if assistance is sought.

Skills – if the inability to perform a particular task is due a lack of skills or necessary knowledge for that task then there should be no embarrassment about admitting this fact. For example suppose that you have never before performed a bank reconciliation, and a stand-in supervisor in the department has suddenly asked you to prepare the monthly bank reconciliation by the end of tomorrow. Obviously this task is impossible for you. There is no point in attempting it alone as this will simply be an unproductive use of the organisation's time. However it is likely that colleagues in your department, or indeed the supervisor, may be able to instruct you in exactly how to perform a bank reconciliation. Therefore the only practical option for you is to seek assistance.

Lack of experience – it is often the case that an individual is perfectly capable of performing a task but does not have the confidence to do so because of a lack of experience, which leads to a lack of confidence. Perhaps it is the first time that that individual has been required to perform a particular task. In such instances both informal and formal support can be sought. Colleagues may well be able to encourage an individual to feel confident of performing the task. However if the situation is such that an individual truly believes himself or herself to be incapable of performing the task, then it is probably most appropriate to discuss this matter with the supervisor or manager.

1.8   Informal and formal assistance

Many people find it much easier to approach a colleague to ask for help – **informal assistance** – with a problem than to approach a more senior member of staff. This might well be appropriate if it is within the organisation's policies, the colleague is fully skilled in the area concerned and the colleague has the time, ability and inclination to help. In many cases this will be the most satisfactory way of dealing with a problem.

Formal assistance means approaching the supervisor or manager of the department to ask for help in dealing with a lack of skills. Once it has been realised that no training has been given in that particular area then the individual will not be allocated that task again until they are trained.

 KAPLAN PUBLISHING

2 Communication

2.1 Introduction

Communication is the basis of our relationships with other people. It is the means whereby people in an organisation exchange information regarding the operations of the enterprise. It is the interchange of ideas, facts and emotions by two or more persons. To be effective, the manager needs information to carry out management functions and activities. All organisations have formal, acknowledged and often specified communication channels. There will be lists of people who are to attend briefings or meetings, and distribution lists for minutes of meetings or memos. There will be procedures for telling people of decisions or changes, and for circulating information received from outside the organisation.

Communication takes place between various employees of a business and the outside world, in such forms as:

(a)   reports and dividend payments to shareholders

(b)   invoices and correspondence to customers

(c)   orders, payments and queries to suppliers.

For the present purpose, our immediate concern is communication within a business, where the need arises because of:

- day-to-day and periodic control needs
- the incidence of unplanned change
- the introduction of planned change
- the day-to-day interaction in the normal work situation.

2.2 Communication process

Communication is the process of passing information and understanding from one person to another. The communication process involves six basic elements: sender (encoder), message, channel, receiver (decoder), noise and feedback. You can improve your communication skills by becoming aware of these elements and how they contribute to successful communication. Communication can break down at any one of these elements. The process of communication can be modelled as shown in the following diagram.

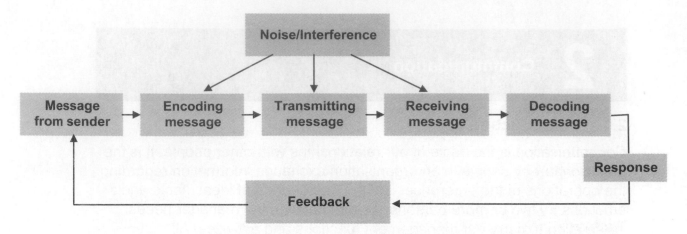

A sender will initiate the communication process. When the meaning has been decided, a channel for transmitting the messages to the receiver is selected and the message is put into words or images. When the receiver has heard the 'message' then they have to 'decode' it to make sure they understand what is being said. For example, the sender may use 'jargon' which the receiver may not understand.

Sometimes the response may result in action taking the form of the receiver asking for clarification in respect of something they do not understand or asking for additional information.

The final stage of the process is feedback which can consist, for example, of the receiver indicating that they understood the message by providing the information requested.

Within the communication process it is also important to note the problem of 'noise'. Anything in the environment that hinders the transmission of the message is significant. Noise here is a word to describe any 'interference' and can arise from many sources, e.g. factors as diverse as loud machinery, status differentials between sender and receiver, distractions of pressure at work or emotional upsets. The effective communicator must ensure that noise does not interfere with successful transmission of the message.

2.3   Noise/interference

 Definition

'Noise' is full or partial loss of communication. It can arise at the collecting and measuring point, or there can be errors or omissions in transmission and/or misinterpretation or misunderstanding, or blatant disregard of communication.

The two principal types of noise are verbal and technical.

Verbal noise is the misunderstanding of words. Examples are:

(a)   the misspelling or omission of an important word in a communication, so as to obscure or alter its meaning

(b)   technical persons (such as accountants, who are some of the worst offenders) using jargon that is incomprehensible to non-technical persons

(c)   the incorrect use of English, written in a style that is difficult to follow.

Technical noise is created by the information itself during communication. Examples are:

(a)   in response to a request for a simple piece of information, a voluminous report may be prepared obscuring the vital information (accountants' monthly reports frequently have this failing)

(b)   a message is left that is not sufficiently clear to convey its meaning when its intended recipient returns

(c)   damage to an organisation's communications centre, such as its telephone exchange, prevents information from being transmitted clearly.

Failure to transmit information can have serious consequences on a company's operations. Some noise can be reduced, if not overcome, by using more than one channel of communication, so that if a message fails to get through by one channel, it may succeed by another. For example, a managing director may need the latest stock figures. To confirm the information from the accountant, the figures from sales and production may be analysed personally to find the relevant stock figures.

2.4   Formal communication channels

Formal communication channels are normally established as part of the organisation's structure. In a hierarchical structure the channels are largely vertical chains designed to allow effective communication between managers and subordinates. Organisational communication establishes a pattern of formal communication channels to carry information vertically and horizontally. (The organisational chart displays these channels.) The channel is the path a message follows from the sender to the receiver.

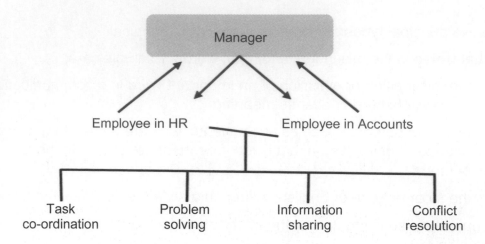

- Managers use downward channels as a basis for giving specific job instructions, policy decisions, guidance and resolution of queries. Such information can help clarify operational goals, provide a sense of direction and give subordinates data related to their performance. Downward communication also helps link levels of the hierarchy by providing a basis for co-ordinated activity.

- Employees use upward channels to send messages to managers. Upward communication provides management with feedback from employees on results achieved and problems encountered. It creates a channel from which management can gauge organisational climate and deal with problem areas, such as grievances or low productivity, before they become major issues.

- Horizontal channels are used when communicating across departmental lines, with suppliers or with customers. Four of the most important reasons for lateral communication are:

  - **task co-ordination** – department heads may meet periodically to discuss how each department is contributing to organisational objectives

  - **problem-solving** – members of a department may meet to discuss how they will handle a threatened budget cut

  - **information sharing** – members of one department may meet with the members of another department to explain some new information or requirement

  - **conflict resolution** – members of one department may meet to discuss a problem, e.g. duplication of activities in the department and some other department.

2.5 Informal communication networks

In every organisation there are informal communication networks as well as the formal channels. This is often referred to as 'the grapevine', which has been defined as 'the network of social relations that arises spontaneously as people associate with one another. It is an expression of people's natural motivation to communicate'.

Grapevine activity is likely to flourish in many common situations, for example:

- where there is a lack of information about a situation and people try to fill in the gaps as best they can

- where there is insecurity in the situation

- where there is a personal interest in a situation e.g. when a supervisor disciplines a friend, people may well gossip about it

- where there is personal animosity in a situation and people seek to gain advantage by spreading rumours

- where there is new information that people wish to spread quickly.

Though the grapevine can pose a threat to management, it can also be useful as a means of making unofficial announcements, 'off-the-record' statements or intentional leaks of future plans.

2.6 Attributes of effective communication

The main attributes of effective communication are promptness and accuracy.

Promptness – if information is essential then it is likely to be urgent. It is therefore important that such information is passed on at the earliest possible opportunity.

In respect of messages, if at all possible you should try to identify how urgent the message is, for example, by asking the following questions (which to ask would depend on the specific situation):

'Jane Smith is in a meeting at the moment and will not be out until 3.00 pm. Would you like me to arrange for this message to be passed to her in the meeting?'

'Jack Little is in the building but I'm not sure where. Would you like me to arrange for him to be paged?'

'Peter Green is currently travelling to a meeting. Would you like his mobile telephone number?'

If the information is contained in a report or in some form of written document, then often couriers are used to ensure that they reach their destination that day or as early as possible the next.

Accuracy – accurate transmission of information is clearly vital. For example suppose that a client leaves a telephone message with you changing his meeting with your manager from 3.00pm until 4.15pm. If you tell your manager that the meeting is about 4.30pm this is likely to leave the client waiting for some considerable amount of time.

Always ensure you read back any messages taken to the person you are talking to. In this way telephone numbers etc. can be checked.

 Test your understanding 1

The following fax has just been received in the accounts department. It has been passed to you, the accounts clerk, as the most appropriate person available.

To: J Patel, Quotations Manager

From: Peter Allan, Sales Manager, East Sussex Materials Ltd

Further to our telephone conversation this morning I am prepared to drop the price of raw material XX5 to £2.42 per kg for the project that you explained to me this morning. I hope this is satisfactory.

Consider what the possible implications might be if you delay passing on this information to the quotations manager.

2.7   Overcoming barriers to communication

A barrier to communication is anything that prevents, or may potentially prevent, communication from being effective.

Some general rules to ensure communication is effective are:

- avoid communication overload

- ensure the right information gets to the right person at the right time

- agree and confirm priorities and deadlines for receipt of information

- keep communication simple

- develop empathy with 'listeners'

- confirm, by repeating back, what has been said

- confirm that what information you have given has been understood.

3 Methods of communication

3.1 Oral communication – face-to-face and telephone

For the rapid interchange of information between people, the principal method of communication is the spoken word. Oral communication is preferable for emotive issues and persuasion since it has the advantage of immediate feedback. It is, however, time consuming and, unless recorded, there can be uncertainty about what was said.

Telephone – for many years the telephone has been most important both for internal and external communications. It is usually used when individuals are not on the same site, or when the conversation may be very short. The telephone can now be used for conference meetings, whereby everyone present at each end of the telephone can hear comments made by the other parties. This means people can convene meetings in two locations at the same time and carry out discussions.

Face-to-face discussions may be used where people need to exchange/ give/obtain information quickly and/or obtain documents. This form of communication is appropriate when working relationships need to be developed or negotiation/persuasion has to take place.

Meetings can be organised to include various departments, or may include outside representatives such as shareholders. They may include various levels of management and can be convened to provide information or discuss a specific topic e.g. year end accounts. In formal meetings minutes may be taken.

Advantages of oral communication	Disadvantages of oral communication
There is the personal touch of seeing the face and/or hearing the voice.	There is no permanent record, so disagreement can easily arise as to what was said.
There is instant feedback with the opportunity to respond quickly to questions of misunderstanding and disagreement.	Vocabulary shrinkage occurs, in that we use only 66% of our full vocabulary when communicating orally – the full vocabulary is available to us only when writing.
Due to the strong personal aspect, it is a good persuasive medium encouraging people to take a certain course of action.	There is no facility, as with writing, to go back and replace an earlier sentence because we wish to amend its meaning.
The message is unique to you – no-one else is likely to select your mix of words or emphasise the same key phrases.	

3.2 Written communication – letters, memos and word-processed documents

Written methods of communication of all sorts – letters, memos, bulletins, files, circulars, e-mails – are the norm in many companies. The dominant characteristic of many managers' working day is paperwork and meetings. They do have the advantage that being in permanent or hard copy form they are less open to misinterpretation. With meetings, for instance, formal minutes may be taken, circulated and agreed to as the definitive written evidence of the meeting. Written methods of communication can be very flexibly used. When trying to reach a number of workers in one place notice-boards are often used, typically to announce meetings, job vacancies, health and safety notices, details of company social events and similar matters which are not of crucial significance.

Most written communications will be word-processed documents nowadays with the exception of memos that are written by hand and placed in the internal mailing system. **Memos** can also be sent by electronic mail on the computer network. They are most useful where the same information has to be given to a number of people e.g. details of the date, time and location of a meeting.

Letters provide a written record and information of matters discussed. These are used mainly for external communication.

Notes – you may need to write notes for a talk or a presentation. Other occasions when note taking is required might be in the preparation of a report or in connection with a meeting or a telephone call. Whatever the context, notes should suit their purpose and be neither so detailed that they resemble an essay, nor too compressed that their meaning is lost.

Notes that are going to be used very soon after they have been written down can afford to be more condensed than notes which will have to wait before they are written in a more acceptable form. Telephone messages tend to suffer from brevity and, with each hour that passes, recollection of the conversation will fade.

Reports may be for internal or external circulation and can take a variety of forms. Reports may contain data, graphs, complex facts and points for and against a variety of situations. This form of communication allows people to study the content in their own time. Some reports are required by law, while other reports may detail progress made in respect of a particular project.

Word-processed documents – word processing programs are now common in the workplace and used to produce a wide variety of written documents, often in a 'house style'. Standard letters and memos can be produced from template files set up on the computer. Mail-merge facilities enable a word processed letter file to import names and addresses from a database and print out a batch for sending out.

 KAPLAN PUBLISHING

Word-processed documents can have sophisticated page layouts and tables. They can import graphics and embody colour elements for illustrative purposes. They are also used in the form of transaction documents, such as payslips, invoices sent to customers, purchase orders sent to suppliers, works orders sent to the factory, day book listings or standard letters. Large numbers of these documents are produced, perhaps in electronic form and displayed on screens or perhaps as 'paperwork'.

Bulletins and newsletters usually provide details on major changes or events that will affect the organisation and may appear in the local or national press; for example a move to a new site or the creation of new jobs.

3.3 Visual communication

Visual methods are preferable where it is necessary for the eye to assist the ear, where the message can be made more vivid, or where distance, environmental or personal factors preclude the use of speech. Examples include films, videos, graphs, traffic signals and sign language.

Graphic displays of data can be an effective way of communicating. For example, sales data comparing this year with last year can often be better illustrated to users by presenting the data on a line graph or bar chart. Data can often appear more meaningful when presented in this way rather than just a list of figures.

Films and slides – allow information to be absorbed in an easily digestible way. Also, if entertaining and well put together, individuals are more likely to listen, concentrate and remember what is being said.

3.4 Electronic methods – fax, e-mail and video conferencing

More and more offices are increasingly reliant on a range of electronic communication equipment. Larger businesses link computers through the telephone network using modems leading to the use of electronic mail and computers 'speaking' to each other, some accessing databanks. Personal computers are being arranged in networks, fax machines, e-mail, value added networks (VANs) and dedicated satellite communication systems are becoming commonplace.

Fax (facsimile) – allows images of documents to be transmitted and then reproduced. It can handle photographs, hand-written notes, drawings, diagrams, charts, etc with no specialist skill to transmit. It is also easy to send the same document to many recipients. Developments include an interface between fax and the computer so that the latter is able to hold, store and process fax transmissions.

The system can 'read' the incoming fax material and relay it to the individual addressee (by displaying on the screen of the terminal).

The development of fax cards for fitting inside desktop and portable personal computers has eliminated much of the need for specialised fax machines. It is now possible to send and receive fax messages using a laptop PC and mobile telephone anywhere in the world.

E-mail – e-mail is very popular as a form of communication that uses the internet.

The following are hints on what to do and what not to do when using e-mail.

- E-mail is meant to be one of the quickest ways to communicate. It is much more efficient than a letter or even a phone call. Some people receive hundreds of e-mails a day, so keep e-mail short and to the point. But be aware – rushed messages can lead to bad grammar, miscommunication and a negative initial impression of the sender.

- You can send e-mail by following three simple steps:

1   Enter the recipient's e-mail address in the 'To' field.

2   Type your message in the large text box. Avoid using a string of capital letters in your correspondence unless absolutely necessary. This is the online equivalent of SHOUTING!

3   Click on the Send button.

You can also use several options when addressing your message, such as:

1   Put additional or secondary recipients in the Cc (carbon copy) or Bcc (blind copy) field.

2   When you are sending a message to many people, a long delivery list may appear at the top of the message. This can annoy readers. It also can make your message seem like junk mail. To hide the distribution list from all recipients, use the Bcc (blind carbon copy) field. Using Bcc also preserves confidentiality for all recipients.

3   If you have created nicknames in the Address Book, you can just type the nickname in the appropriate field. In order to send your message to multiple recipients, separate each recipient by a comma. For example: nickname1, nickname2, recipient3@host.domain.

- Although the **Subject** is an optional field, it is a good idea to enter one. Your recipients may receive many e-mail messages, perhaps even several from you alone. The subject helps distinguish between the different messages. It also helps users when they are trying to locate messages that they have filed away.

- You can attach a file to your message by clicking **Attach**. The attachment area will be opened in a new window. Click **Browse**... and search for the file or type the full path name of the file you wish to attach. Once found, press the **Upload file** button and the file name will appear in the Attachment List. In order to remove an already attached file, select the file from the Attachment List and press the **Remove** button. Finally, press the **OK** button to return to the 'compose' window.

  The file you attach can be of any type, for example: a sound file, an image or even a spreadsheet. Adding attachments to your message can be done at any time while composing the message. All files are scanned for viruses before they are attached to a message. If a file contains a virus that cannot be cleared by the virus scanning software, you will be unable to attach it to the message.

- You can check the spelling of your message by choosing the language from the selection list and pressing the **Spell Checker** button. The Spelling area will be opened in a new window. The first word that is not found in the Spelling Dictionary will appear on the top of the page marked by red text. You will see a list of possible suggestions. Select the appropriate replacement from the list or write the replacement yourself in the change to edit box. Then press the Change button to accept the change or the Ignore button to disregard it. This process will continue until the end of the message is reached.

- Pressing the Cancel button, before completion, will discontinue the spelling process.

- The sender of an e-mail message is not always apparent to the recipient simply by looking at the sender's address. It is good practice to sign your e-mail with your name and what company you are with, if applicable. You may want to include your e-mail address as well. Most e-mail services allow you to write a signature that will automatically be attached to each message you send.

Video conferencing is increasingly used as a medium whereby meetings are convened in two locations simultaneously.

4 Confidential information

4.1 Types of confidential information

You may handle information that is clearly confidential, such as payroll details. Some information may not appear to be confidential at first sight but could cause embarrassment or problems internally or externally if revealed, so it is best always to err on the side of discretion. For example:

(a) reports on purchases of new machinery whose introduction might lead to fewer jobs

(b) details of price rises not yet sent to customers

(c) news of changes in key personnel not yet communicated to customers and suppliers.

When dealing with customers and suppliers, you must also respect their own right to confidentiality. For instance, do not reveal details of a customer's account or type or level of purchases to another customer.

Remember that, if someone appears to be asking for confidential information, or for information which is none of their concern, it is always best to refer them to your supervisor.

In certain limited circumstances students may become aware of confidential information that needs to be passed to the appropriate staff member. This means that it should not be discussed in any circumstances other than with the person for whom the information was meant. The information should not therefore be discussed in passing with colleagues, managers or in social situations. Confidentiality should always be maintained where considered necessary. Your organisation's affairs and those of its clients are confidential and should not be disclosed to others unless the circumstances are appropriate.

If you are leaving a confidential message for someone who is not available it should be written down, and placed in a sealed envelope, marked 'Private and Confidential, Addressee Only'.

Alternatively if you have to send a memo, letter or report, which contains confidential information, then you should ensure it is marked private and confidential and placed in a sealed envelope that is similarly marked.

4.2 Organisational procedures

It is each individual's responsibility to ensure that they are fully aware of the organisation's rules and procedures regarding confidential information. It is equally important that an individual follows them strictly.

For example if the organisation's policy is that documents marked as 'confidential' are kept under lock and key then it is important that such documents are stored in a locked storage cabinet or desk each night. This is reasonably easy to remember to do. It is perhaps harder to remember to keep the information locked away whenever the individual is not using it and is not in their office or at their workstation. Such information should not, under any circumstances, be left unattended on a desk.

When confidential information is considered, individuals should be aware that they are only likely to be able to access confidential information if they have been allocated a particular password. If an individual is given a password in order to access confidential information then under no circumstances should they tell anybody else what their password is.

Disclosure of information could damage the company if it was to fall foul of the data protection legislation and cause embarrassing publicity, or help a competitor by allowing sensitive information to be accessed by outsiders or non-related employees.

4.3 Handling confidential information

The increasing use of computers in all aspects of business has meant that increasingly large amounts of information about individuals is now kept by various organisations. For you to perform some of your tasks it may be necessary to obtain and keep confidential information. This is a great responsibility and should not be taken lightly.

There will be rules and procedures for compliance with the Data Protection Act and with the copyright laws, and to avoid any action that might reflect badly on the reputation of the company.

Under the terms of the Data Protection Act, the need for privacy is recognised by the requirements that all data should be held for clearly designated purposes. Accuracy and integrity must be maintained and data must be open to inspection. Only legitimate parties can access data and information must be secured against alteration, accidental loss or deliberate damage. Furthermore, the Act states that data must be obtained fairly, to precise specifications and must not be kept for longer than required.

Copyright law covers books of all kinds, sound recordings, film and broadcasts, computer programs, dramatic and musical works. Modern software packages are complex and costly to produce, but are often easy to copy and distribute. Manufacturers are increasingly bringing prosecutions to try to reduce the number of pirate copies of their software. There are steep penalties for companies prosecuted for software theft – unlimited damages, legal costs and the cost of legitimising the software.

However, not all information at work is covered by legislation. There will be times when you are told something and asked to 'keep it to yourself', either by a colleague, your supervisor or a visitor. Sometimes this will be in the context of a message you may have to pass on, but at other times it may be in the form of a confidence, which is entrusted to you. It is vital that you keep your word and do not pass it on to others at the earliest opportunity.

Working as part of a team will inevitably mean that you must pass certain information on to other members of the team. This must always be done accurately and promptly.

4.4 Copyright law

It is highly likely that when supplying information a student will use another individual's ideas or information. Is this a breach of copyright law?

Copyright law covers books of all kinds, sound recordings, films and broadcasts, computer programmes, dramatic and musical works etc. Is it possible to legally photocopy or manually copy such information?

It is normally quite acceptable for an individual to copy a few pages of the work of another person. That other person may have signalled his copyright by the international symbol of ©; however, it is still quite acceptable to copy such works in small amounts either for personal or business usage.

Unless you intend to copy an entire book or reproduce a copyright article for the entire organisation, it is unlikely that any copyright law would be infringed.

5 Interpersonal skills

5.1 Definition

Interpersonal skills can sometimes be called interactive, face-to-face or social skills used in establishing and maintaining relationships between people.

If you can answer yes to any of the following questions, it indicates your power is based on interpersonal skills.

- Do you have a sense of relationship – rapport – with other people?

- Are you an 'active listener? Do you make sure you have understood the other person's point of view? Do you make it clear to them that you understand and empathise?

- Do you avoid being either passive or aggressive in formal or informal discussions with others in the organisation?

- Can you persuade or influence another person?

- Are you aware that people admire you in some respects, and do others copy you?

- Do people want to be with you at informal meetings?

5.2 Steps to improve your people skills

Being able to manage your relationships at work, so that they have the effect you want, is a prerequisite of optimum performance. Key interpersonal skills are the building blocks of relationships:

1   **Self-management** – when we think of people skills, we usually think of them in relation to other people, rather than how we handle ourselves, and yet most of us realise that we are better or worse at relating to people depending on our 'mood' or attitude. The reason for the 'mood' is the way we are choosing to react to a particular situation; we can learn to choose consciously, and use a mood to our advantage in any situation. We all know the difference it makes to a working day when we wake up feeling good, rather than feeling that it is 'going to be one of those days'. Make a conscious effort to see the benefits of each situation, to enjoy the process as well as the end results of work. What we tell ourselves is very powerful in affecting our state, we can talk ourselves 'up' or 'down'.

2   **Building rapport** – the word 'rapport' comes from the French word that means carrying something back; rapport is about actively making sure that we have some shared message that we both send and receive. We can build rapport by being aware of the non-verbal messages we communicate. If we make eye contact, use a friendly tone of voice, turn towards them, look relaxed and smile, we create the impression of being someone easy to deal with.

3   **Giving attention** – paying attention is not the same as listening, and if we want to develop good people skills, we need to learn to pay close attention to people. When someone is really paying attention we feel not just that they have listened, but that they have understood where we are coming from and what we really mean.

To pay full attention requires:

- listening with your ears – you pick up the words someone is saying

- listening with the inner ear – we pick up the tone of voice, the meaning behind the words, the emphasis and hesitations

- attending with your eyes – how the person's body language supports or negates what they are saying

- attending with your guts – this is the intuitive level, we get a sense of something not being communicated

- attending with your heart – we view the person sympathetically rather than judgmentally, and get a sense of what it is like from their point of view.

4   **Recognising and working with differences** – most of us have not been brought up to value other people for their difference, often we have to learnt to judge others because of it. By finding out how others are different from us, we gain very useful information to help us to deal with them more effectively. We can find out about other people's approaches or perspectives by asking 'what' and 'how' questions; e.g. How did you do that? What prompted you to handle it in that way? How is that important for you? If you were left to your own devices, how would you deal with this? Once you have found out what really matters to the other person, you can make your communication with them much more effective.

5   **Conveying your message clearly** – if we want to be sure our message is received correctly, it is important that we are sure what our message is! You may wish to tell people about new working practices, but additionally, your tone of voice, body language and choice of words will tell them what sort of person you are, what you feel about your overt message, how you operate in the world and what you think and feel about your listeners. Being clear in our own minds what our message is, and what we want the listener to do or feel as a result helps to ensure that the right message is conveyed.

6   **Using feedback** – this is a term that describes a loop of action and reaction. The most common feedback we receive is that which is given unconsciously, it is the immediate response or reaction to what we have done or said. If you are not sure of someone's reaction, asking them is the simplest way of finding out, but we need to guide the feedback, as most people are not good at giving useful information about their reactions and will tend to rationalise or justify their responses.

7   **Working in a team** – good team skills include respect for each other's viewpoints, sharing information, mutual support and presenting a coherent front.

8   **Dealing with conflict** – when you strongly disagree with someone, it is hard to maintain a good working relationship as we tend to equate the disagreement with the person. It is important in dealing with conflict to step back and assess the situation objectively. Identify the reason for the conflict (misunderstanding, different approaches, different interests?) and where possible find common ground. Changing the language of discussion can improve the situation; notice the difference in feeling these pairs of comments produce:

You make me angry.	I am angry about X.
You're wrong.	I don't agree with what you are saying.
You don't understand.	I haven't made myself clear.

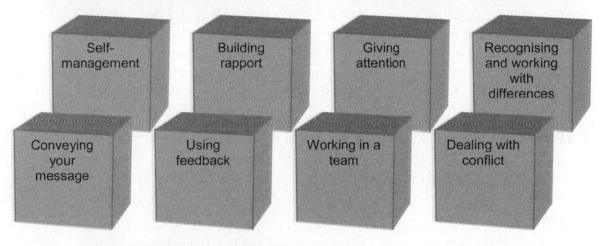

5.3   Responding to requests

To be able to communicate effectively you must have the ability to:

•   pass on information accurately and without delay so that all concerned are aware of the situation and the correct action can be taken

•   talk to a wide range of people with whom you have had little or no previous contact

•   converse with your colleagues in a way which will promote and maintain a harmonious working atmosphere

•   interpret non-verbal communication gestures and their meanings and put people at their ease.

Even if you can schedule a lot of your own work, you will inevitably be asked to do things by your supervisor or other managers. In any job, you will have to do things you do not like. The important thing is to accept that everyone is in the same position and so you should try to carry out unwelcome tasks without complaining.

The way you act is very important. Do you appear disinterested when other people ask you to do something or do you appear attentive? Do you interrupt or do you let the other person finish first?

When dealing with colleagues, it is important to think about not only what you say but also the way you say it.

5.4   Asking for help

Sometimes you will need help from other people, but think carefully before asking. You may waste other people's time if you ask them for simple factual information that you could find elsewhere.

If you do need help, do not be embarrassed to admit that you do not know the answer.

When asking for help it is important that you listen to the help or advice given. Most of us have poor listening skills. We listen to the first part of what we are being told and then spend the next few seconds waiting for the other person to stop speaking so that we can say the next thought that has come into our heads. During this latter part of the other person's speech, we have totally switched off from what is being said.

Without effective listening, there can be no effective communication. It has been discovered that people forget most of what they have heard within a couple of days. This can be improved by better messages, repeated messages and also by helping the receiver to learn to be a more efficient listener.

Among the many ideas for better listening are the following:

(a)   concentrate on what is being said, not on the person saying it

(b)   ask for something to be repeated if you do not understand

(c)   try to concentrate on the meaning of the message

(d)   do not become emotionally involved

(e)   remember that thoughts are quicker than words and you can evaluate what is being said without missing anything

(f)   do not take many notes, just the key points.

Listening is not the same as hearing. It involves a more conscious assimilation of information and requires attentiveness on the part of the interviewer. Failure to listen properly to what someone is saying will mean that probing questions (in an interview) may become a worthless exercise. In preparing to listen you should ask 'What new things can I learn from this person?'

Barriers to listening include the following:

- scoring points – relating everything you hear to your own experience

- mind-reading

- rehearsing – practising your next lines in your head

- cherry-picking – listening for a key piece of information then switching off

- daydreaming – you can think faster than people can talk and there is a temptation to use the 'spare' time to daydream

- labelling – putting somebody into a category before hearing what they have to say

- counselling – being unable to resist interrupting and giving advice

- duelling – countering the other's advances with thrusts of your own, e.g. 'Well at least this department is never over budget'

- side-stepping sentiment – countering expressions of emotion with jokes or hollow clichés, such as 'Well it's not the end of the world'.

There are also health factors that may cause difficulties in concentrating on what is being said. People who are suffering from stress, who are in pain or are anxious about something will not be at their best when it comes to effective communications.

If you are to do your job properly then it is important that you listen carefully to all instructions, help and advice.

6 Teams

6.1 Introduction

A work team can be a department, section or group with a set of common tasks. It is a part of a larger organisation with one person in charge of it, although every member of the team has some input into the way it operates.

Teams are groups of people who show the following characteristics:

- They share a common goal, and are striving to get a common job done.

- They enjoy working together, and enjoy helping one another.

- They have made a commitment to achieve the goals and objectives of the project by accomplishing their particular portion of the project.

- They are very diverse individuals having all kinds of different disciplinary and experiential backgrounds, who must now concentrate on a common effort.

- They have great loyalty to the project as well as loyalty and respect for the project manager, and have a firm belief in what the project is trying to accomplish.

- They have attained a team spirit and very high team morale.

6.2 Team performance

An important aspect of work is that it is usually done in groups or teams. It does not matter whether the work is developing a corporate strategy for an organisation, checking insurance claims in an office or building cars in a factory. A team is quite simply a number of individuals working together to achieve a common task.

There are a number of factors that contribute to the performance of teams; for instance, the organisational structure within which the team works, the type of task to be accomplished, the resources available and the characteristics of the team and the team members.

Many jobs within an organisation are impossible to complete on an individual basis and take place as part of a team or a group. Although it is necessary to have such a group, for example a department such as the accounts department or a production group within the manufacturing area, it is also necessary to recognise that group relationships can be even more complex than individual relationships.

The main factors to take into consideration when working within a group or closely knit department are as follows:

- The varying members of the group are likely to have a wide variety of personalities. You will have to work closely, possibly even constantly, with this group of people and therefore must be prepared to put up with the various types of personality that will be present.

- **Individual aptitudes and skills** – again it is likely that any team will be made up of a group of people with a variety of different aptitudes and skills. The group will need each of these aptitudes and skills and this should be remembered when dealing with other members of the group.

- **Goals** – it is likely that each work group will have particular goals or aims. If the goals or aims of the individual members of the group do not coincide with those of the group as a whole, then there is likely to be conflict and pressures affecting members of the group. Wherever possible a student should try to tie in his/her own goals with those of the group. For example if the group concerned is the accounting department then provision of accurate and relevant information will be the group's goal, and a student studying for AAT levels of competence should also have similar types of goals regarding accuracy and relevance.

- **Communication** – a group can only operate effectively if there is full communication at all levels and between all parties in the group. If you do work as part of a group then you should ensure that you understand exactly what the group is doing, why it is being done and what part you are required to play in this.

- **Deadlines** – deadlines in general have been considered earlier in the study text. In a group or team context you should be even more aware of the importance of deadlines. If you are asked to produce information or a piece of work by a particular time or date then if this deadline is not met it is likely to affect the workings of the entire group.

Organisations are increasingly becoming aware of the importance of teams working effectively, and how in doing so they can contribute to the organisation's success. One way of doing this is by considering how an existing group can be developed into a team. Some organisations use team-building courses to help with this process. The objective of team building is to improve the team's performance by:

- encouraging effective working practices

- reducing difficulties the team encounters

- improving work procedures

- improving interpersonal relationships between team members.

The benefits of team building are:

- it increases the chances of real improvement in performance because the whole team is involved

- it gives the team a chance to stop and think about the way the work is done.

6.3 Teamwork

There are very few jobs in which it is not necessary to work as part of a team.

Being part of a team means dealing with people at all levels within your organisation and building professional relationships with them. It takes time to build this association with people but there are a few guidelines, which might get you off to a good start:

(a) be tactful and courteous

(b) treat with respect people who are your senior in either age or position

(c) have a pleasant and helpful manner

(d) make allowances for others having personal problems which may affect their work, but do not joke about it or expect them to tell you why they might be having a 'bad day'

(e) communicate with people using the correct words and tone.

6.4 Commitments to others

It is firstly necessary to consider what a commitment actually is. 'A commitment is a firm agreement to do something within a particular time scale or at a particular time'.

A commitment is therefore binding, within a business context. The main reason for this is that the person to whom the commitment has been made has probably made corresponding commitments to other parties, either within the organisation or outside of the organisation, based upon your commitment.

We can also describe commitment as something that happens when team members see themselves as belonging to the team instead of as individuals acting on their own initiative. It is evident when the team members are committed to the team goals over and above their own personal goals.

6.5 Agreed time scales

In most organisations if you are required to produce information then the time scale for producing it will be discussed with you rather than simply being imposed. If you believe that the time scale proposed is unrealistic then you should say so, explaining why you hold this belief. You should never make promises that you cannot keep. The consequences of not producing work for a specified deadline are far worse than those of admitting that a deadline currently being set is unrealistic. It is far better to ensure that a reasonable deadline or time scale is set at the outset of the project rather than having to extend the deadline, or indeed not meet it, later in the project.

It is appreciated that it is sometimes difficult to speak up when dealing with those of a higher authority. However the final consequences should be borne in mind in all situations.

6.6 Personality differences

Having a professional relationship with someone is different from a social relationship. In a social relationship you can choose how well you get to know someone, even whether or not you get to know them in the first place.

At work you will inevitably have to deal with people whom you would not necessarily choose as friends. This does not mean that you have to treat them as friends, but as colleagues. This means being polite to other people and speaking to them in an appropriate tone of voice. It also means offering to help them if you can see they need help.

It can be difficult if you do have a personality clash with someone at any level, but you must keep it in proportion. One of the worst things you can do is to dwell on the problem. You will quickly become unpopular with your other colleagues if you talk continually about your problems with another member of staff. It may also mean that the other person hears about your complaints, which makes the matter worse.

6.7 Complaints

Staff morale is very important wherever you work and you can contribute to it. In the short term, everyone likes to complain about things, but in the long term this can cause tensions within the office.

In some cases, however, you may have a genuine cause for complaint. You should discreetly arrange to see your manager or personnel manager to discuss the problem. Remember that they will not necessarily have all the answers but will expect you to suggest solutions. Think carefully first about what you want to say and be positive.

7 Handling disagreements and conflicts

7.1 Disagreements and conflicts

Although one would hope that the vast majority of work time would pass without disagreement between individuals or conflicts within a team there will be circumstances in which such disagreements or conflicts do occur. There is no avoiding such situations and students should think carefully about how to deal with them.

The general rule should be that if there is a disagreement or conflict with a fellow employee then this should be dealt with at a higher level of management rather than between the individual employees. There is little to be gained from two employees losing their tempers with each other if a manager can solve the problem or produce some sort of compromise.

A second important consideration is that it is usually far more constructive to recognise any conflict and discuss this with a manager, rather than try to avoid or simply smooth over the problem.

There are likely to be simple personality conflicts between students and other employees, but these should be dealt with on a polite and professional basis. Any disagreement or conflict on a work matter should normally, however, be taken to a higher authority through the organisation's Grievance Procedure. Grievances can include unfair treatment by managers e.g. being passed over for promotion because of gender or race, unfair pay – men being paid more than women and unfair dismissal (an extreme case).

7.2 Managing disagreements and conflicts

There are many ways of managing conflict and disagreements and the suitability of any particular action will be determined by the situation. Several possible ways of resolving conflicts and disagreements are detailed below:

(i)   **Problem solving** – the individuals/team are brought together to try to find a solution to the particular problem.

(ii) **Common goal** – finding a common goal that is more important than the differences of team members/individuals.

(iii) **Allocating resources** – ending conflict over resources e.g. use of computers, by giving extra resources.

(iv) **Compromise** – finding a solution without there being a defined winner or loser. Each party must 'give' a little.

(v)   **Management decisions** – management making a decision.

(vi) **Altering the team/individual's role** – changing team members and/or their roles; perhaps moving people between departments.

To be successful in resolving conflicts and disagreements you must understand the reason for it, why the team/individual is behaving in such a way and what their expectations are.

7.3   Negotiation

Disagreements and negative conflict lead to:

* the misuse of resources, time, energy and creativity

* an increase in hostility

* a decrease in trust and openness

* a decrease in the ability of groups and the organisation as a whole to achieve the set objectives.

The best way of managing negative conflict is by negotiation, because the potential outcome is much more positive than with any other approach.

The ultimate goal when resolving a conflict is for both parties to be satisfied with the outcome. Ideally, this means that both individuals get what they want. In reality, both individuals may have to compromise and get most of what they want, especially if their goals are mutually exclusive. This type of solution is called WIN-WIN because both individuals feel satisfied with the outcome, they both win. This type of solution involves a commitment by both parties to work out the problem fairly via compromise.

However, there are times when this commitment is absent. When that happens, less ideal solutions are probable. These solutions may take the following forms:

WIN-LOSE – one party gets what it wants but the other does not.

LOSE-WIN – the first party does not get what it wants but the other does.

LOSE-LOSE – neither party gets what it wants.

Everyone negotiates – almost every day – and certain principles seem to be present which anyone can learn.

* **Ask questions** – before stating a position or making proposals, it is very helpful to inquire about the other side's interests and concerns. This will help you understand what is important to the other side and may provide new ideas for mutual benefit. Ask clarifying questions to really understand the other's concerns in this negotiation. This will also help you determine their approach to negotiations: win-lose or win-win. You can then make more realistic proposals.

* **'Win-win' negotiations** involve understanding each other's interests and finding solutions that will benefit both parties. The goal is to co-operate and seek solutions so both parties can walk away winners. If you come to the table thinking only one person can win (win-lose), there won't be an effort to co-operate or problem solve.
By the same token, if you come to the table expecting to lose (lose-win), you play the martyr and resentment builds.

- **Respect** – when the other side feels that you respect him or her, it reduces defensiveness and increases the sharing of useful information, which can lead to an agreement. When people feel disrespect, they become more rigid and likely to hide information you need.

- **Trust** – people tend to be more generous toward those they like and trust. An attitude of friendliness and openness generally is more persuasive than an attitude of deception and manipulation. Being honest about the information you provide and showing interest in the other side's concerns can help.

7.4 The skills of a negotiator

The skills of a negotiator can be summarised under three main headings:

- **Interpersonal skills** – the use of good communicating techniques, the use of power and influence and the ability to impress a personal style on the tactics of negotiation.

- **Analytical skills** – the ability to analyse information, diagnose problems, to plan and set objectives and the exercise of good judgement in interpreting results.

- **Technical skills** – attention to detail and thorough case preparation.

In most situations a negotiation strategy is not an easy option but it is one that has much more of a positive outcome than an imposed solution. The first step is to get the parties to trust you. Next, you can try to find as much common ground as there is between the parties and encourage them to arrive at a middle ground. If neither party get what they want then you have a lose-lose situation. This is a very common situation where compromise comes in. Unfortunately, compromises result in needs not being satisfied.

You are aiming for a win-win situation, where both parties get as close as possible to what they really want. This situation is not always possible but working towards it can achieve mutual respect, co-operation, enhanced communication and more creative problem solving.

You need to start by identifying what both parties really want – as opposed to what they think they want. The parties also need to explain what they want it for and what will happen if they do not get it. This procedure is a severe test of a manager's interpersonal skills, but it could bring about the best solution.

7.5 Negotiating styles

Negotiating styles that can be used are competing, collaborating, compromising, accommodating and avoiding.

Competing – 'hard bargaining' or 'might makes right'

Pursuing personal concerns at the expense of the other party. Competing can mean 'standing up for your rights' defending a position that you believe is correct or simply trying to win.

Collaborating – 'sharing tasks and responsibilities' or 'two heads are better than one'

Working with someone by exploring your disagreement, generating alternatives, and finding a solution that mutually satisfies the concerns of both parties.

Compromising – 'splitting the difference'

Seeking a middle ground by 'splitting the difference', the solution that satisfies both parties.

Accommodating – 'soft bargaining' or 'killing your enemy with kindness'

Yielding to another person's point of view – paying attention to their concerns and neglecting your own.

Avoiding – 'leave well enough alone'

Not addressing the conflict, either by withdrawing from the situation or postponing the issues.

Test your understanding 2

You work in quite a large accounts department. Your manager has three deputies and the rule is that only one of them can be away on holiday or attend a course at a time. All three approach him in March asking for the same two weeks off in June. Tom, who is the most senior of the three, wants to do a sponsored bike ride in Cuba. Dick wants to take his family to Las Vegas for his brother's wedding. Harry has been accepted on a special course that will enhance his promotional prospects.

Each of them hears about the other's applications and they have a furious row and now only talk to each other about work-related matters.

Outline five different ways the manager can deal with this situation.

7.6   Maintaining good relationships

Once you have created a good relationship with other staff, this must be maintained because it is important for the following reasons:

(a)   staff who are happy and co-operate with each other work harder and are more productive

(b)   morale and motivation are improved.

Be the ideal member of staff that everyone appreciates by:

(a)   communicating with people in a mature and professional manner

(b)   thinking through the consequence of your words and actions before you say or do anything that you might later regret

(c)   carrying out requests promptly and willingly, explaining fully and politely when you are not able to help

(d)   asking others for help and assistance politely and only when necessary

(e)   informing others about anything you have said or done on their behalf

(f)   bearing no grudges, not being moody or difficult to work with

(g)   knowing the difference between telling tales and reporting unethical behaviour or problems to your superior

(h)   finding solutions for any conflicts and dissatisfaction that could reduce personal effectiveness and team effectiveness.

Test your understanding 3

Darren is the supervisor of a travel shop. When his staff take a customer booking, they have to add on a charge for airport taxes. The charges are different for each airport but are found in the company's fares manual.

One afternoon Fiona, who has worked in the shop for six weeks, asks Darren for the charge for Oslo airport. Darren gets angry. What could explain his outburst?

 Test your understanding 4

Diana's supervisor is explaining a new accounting procedure to her. Suggest some things that Diana might do which would suggest that she is not listening properly.

How might her supervisor react to these?

 Test your understanding 5

Can you think of any advantages and disadvantages associated with the preparation of office manuals?

 Test your understanding 6

Your boss is currently overseas negotiating an extension of a sales contract with one of your existing customers. You receive the following fax message from him:

'Urgent – we've agreed that the trade discount applying to the future contracts will be based on a formula related to sales volumes over the last two years. Please fax me the details of monthly sales volumes to this customer over that period immediately.'

Outline the likely consequences if you fail to act quickly on this message.

Test your understanding 7

There are various ways in which a business can communicate information electronically. A facility whereby a duplicate copy of a document can be sent electronically is known as:

(i) electronic mail or e-mail

(ii) internet

(iii) telex

(iv) facsimile or fax.

8 Summary

This chapter has demonstrated the need to be sensitive to the responsibilities and commitments of your colleagues' workloads. It has also described how communication between individuals and within teams can be improved, and how communication can be altered according to the goals and context of the situation.

You should now understand how empathy and sensitivity to the needs, background and position of colleagues (both more junior and more senior) will improve professionalism and performance of the whole organisation and how this can help to establish constructive working relationships.

Test your understanding answers

 Test your understanding 1

Scenario 1

The quotations manager is currently in a meeting with a prospective customer. He is presenting a quotation to that customer for a series of contracts; however the price is based upon the existing price of XX5, which is £2.65 per kg.

If this information does not reach the quotation manager during this meeting there is a possibility that the prospective customer will be lost to a competitor, as the price quoted will not be low enough.

Scenario 2

The quotations manager is currently in his office making a number of telephone calls. He is in fact telephoning a variety of alternative suppliers in order to find a lower price than the current £2.65 per kg for XX5.

If this information does not reach the quotations manager promptly then he may agree a price higher than £2.42 with an alternative supplier.

Scenario 3

The quotations manager is just about to enter a meeting with the production manager. At that meeting they will discuss the use of an alternative product to XX5 that can be purchased at a price cheaper than the current £2.65 per kg of XX5. It is suspected that the product is of inferior quality to XX5 but the needs of cost cutting are too great to ignore.

If the information regarding the reduced price of XX5 does not reach the quotations manager then there is a possibility that future production may use an inferior product, which can be purchased at a price cheaper than the current £2.65 per kg.

Test your understanding 2

Your manager you could deal with the situation in the following ways.

- Call them all together and explain they must sort the matter out themselves but, if they fail to do so, you will sort the matter out for them by exercising your right to determine the holiday rota, and that no one will be allowed to go that fortnight anyway. If you go for this option, you are choosing the power route. This is fine if jobs are scarce, but highly risky. If you win, they all lose!

- Call them all together and tell them they must sort the matter out themselves. By choosing this option and letting them sort it out themselves you are avoiding the situation.

- Talk the matter over with each of them separately to discuss the facts with them. Make a decision as to whose need is the most pressing, then get them all together and announce your decision. This option is an attempt at a compromise, although not allowing very much input from them.

- Tell them individually not to be silly, and suggest they take an afternoon off and talk the matter over with their families/friends/training officer. This solution of patting them on the head and telling them to talk to others is trying to defuse the situation.

- Discuss all the problems the situation raises with each fully and, if the matter still cannot be sorted out, go to the training officer and see if there is an alternative course; and the Chief Officer to see if on this occasion two deputies can be allowed on holiday at the same time. Bring them all back to hear the outcome. Only this option begins to address the problems. Even though there is no knowing there will be a successful outcome, you are trying to resolve all the conflicting needs.

A team-building approach can promote openness and discussion of problems like these, meaning that there will be fewer destructive conflicts to cope with.

Test your understanding 3

Darren might be used to giving his staff this information (particularly as Fiona is a new employee) but on this day one of the following may apply:

(a)   he is very busy himself

(b)   he has personal problems.

He might expect all staff to look up information for themselves and several other people might already have asked him.

Test your understanding 4

Diana might:

(a)   look away or out of the window

(b)   play with a pencil or other item

(c)   continue writing

(d)   interrupt unnecessarily.

Her supervisor might assume that she is either not capable of doing the job or not interested. Her supervisor might decide not to give her some more interesting work as a type of punishment.

Test your understanding 5

The advantages and disadvantages associated with the preparation of office manuals include:

Advantages

(i)   To prepare an office manual the systems and procedures must be examined carefully. This close attention can only benefit the organisation, in that strengths and weaknesses are revealed.

(ii)   Supervision is easier.

(iii) It helps the induction and training of new staff.

(iv)   It helps to pinpoint areas of responsibility.

(v)   Having been written down in the first place, systems and procedures are easier to adapt and/or change in response to changing circumstances.

Disadvantages

(i)   There is an associated expense in preparing manuals both in the obvious financial terms and the perhaps less obvious cost of administrative time.

(ii)   To be of continuing use an office manual must be updated periodically, again incurring additional expense.

(iii)   The instructions as laid down in the office manual may be interpreted rather strictly and implemented too rigidly. Within any organisation it is often beneficial for employees to bring a degree of flexibility to their duties to cope with particular circumstances.

 Test your understanding 6

(i)   Your boss would look foolish and the customer will have a poor opinion of your organisation's efficiency.

(ii)   Without detailed and accurate information to base the discounts on, your boss may be forced to defer discussions until a later, and perhaps less opportune, occasion. Alternatively, he could concede an over-generous rate of discount to finalise the deal while he has the opportunity.

(iii)   Your boss will form a poor opinion of your abilities and reliability, with possible damaging consequences to your later career.

 Test your understanding 7

(iv)   A facsimile or fax is a facility for sending a duplicate copy of a document electronically.

Policies, procedures and legislation

5

Introduction

This chapter identifies some of the major risks to the security of computer systems and data, and discusses some controls available to reduce or eliminate those risks. The latter part of the chapter covers the issue of health and safety in the workplace from a general perspective and also the rules and regulations that all businesses must adhere to by law.

ASSESSMENT CRITERIA	CONTENTS
1.2 Demonstrate an understanding of how finance staff contribute to an organisation's success 1.4 Identify the importance of data security	1 Security 2 Protecting data from risks 3 Legislative requirements for Data Protection 4 Health and safety regulations for equipment 5 Health and safety in your workplace 6 Internal policies and procedures

1 Security

1.1 Security risks

Security is defined by the British Computer Society as 'the establishment and application of safeguards to protect data, software and computer hardware from accidental or malicious modification, destruction or disclosure'.

There are five basic types of security risk to an organisation.

1   **Physical intrusion** leading to theft or damage of assets. Theft includes loss and illegal copying.

2   **Physical damage** to hardware or computer media. This includes malicious damage, poor operating conditions, natural disasters and simple wear and tear, any of which can physically damage machinery and storage media such as disks, tapes and diskettes. These possibilities carry a triple threat – the cost of repair or replacement of hardware, the danger of damaged data or program files and the cost of computer down time.

The loss of accounting records could be sufficient to cause the company to fail. Most non-technical users of systems would be surprised that there is an inherent risk to any computer system. Systems failure can mean that data is lost, or physical damage can occur in a manner that is virtually impossible to guard against in a cost-effective way.

3   **Damage to data** – hackers, viruses, program bugs, hardware and media faults can all damage data files. The havoc caused by damaged data is made worse if it is not detected and rectified quickly. Hacking activities can:

-    generate information which is of potential use to a competitor organisation

-    provide the basis for fraudulent activity

-    cause data corruption by the introduction of unauthorised computer programs and processing onto the system, otherwise known as 'computer viruses'

-    alter or delete the files.

4   **Operational mistakes** – due to innocent events such as running the wrong program, or inadvertently deleting data that is still of value to the organisation, can cause significant problems – ranging from the need to resuscitate files and repeat computer runs, to the possibility of losing customers.

Links to the Internet bring extra security risks. Examples include the following:

- corruptions such as viruses can spread through the network

- disaffected employees can cause deliberate damage to data or systems

- hackers may be able to steal data or damage the system

- employees may download inaccurate information or imperfect or virus-ridden software from an external network

- information sent from one part of an organisation to another may be intercepted

- the communications link itself may break down.

5 **Industrial espionage/fraud** – can lead to loss of confidentiality with sensitive information being obtained by outsiders or unauthorised employees. Industrial espionage and sabotage can yield significant advantages to competitors, and fraud and blackmail is a significant threat.

1.2 Software security risks

The effects of poor security on software could be:

- **Deliberate physical attacks**, including theft or damage to the installation in general – with files being taken. This threat can come from inside and/or outside the organisation e.g. access by unauthorised personnel could result in theft, piracy or vandalism.

- **Malicious damage** can also involve individuals from inside or outside the organisation (such as hackers), damaging or tampering with data or information in order to disrupt the organisation's activity for malevolent reasons.

- **Fraudulent attacks** by employees or management, or fraudulent transactions affected by altering programs. Fraudsters can divert funds from an enterprise to their own pockets or can attempt to hold employing companies to ransom by the threat of sabotage to vital computer systems.

- **Loss of confidentiality** – sensitive information obtained by outsiders or unauthorised employees. This could result in an organisation breaching Data Protection laws.

1.3   Risks to information

The increasing use of computers in all aspects of business has led to a lot of information about individuals being kept by various organisations.

Information can be damaged, lost or stolen in the same way that equipment and other assets can be. There are certain types of information that must be protected due to its confidential nature or the value it holds for competitors – for example:

- **Personal and private information** about employees and customers – there is a risk that some of this information is inaccurate which could cause serious problems for the individual concerned (e.g. being refused a loan if they have the wrong credit rating). The Data Protection Acts of 1984 and 1998 were introduced to help reduce this risk. The Acts stipulate that only legitimate parties can access data, and information must be secured against alteration, accidental loss or deliberate damage. Furthermore, the Act states that data must be obtained fairly, to precise specifications and must not be kept for longer than required. Individuals can find out what information is being held about themselves by writing to the organisation and asking for a copy.

- **Critical information** about the business and its products/services, its marketing plans and legal or financial details of intended mergers, takeovers or redundancies. The importance of the organisation's commercial and trade information cannot be underestimated. The leaking of a company's trade secrets, such as production processes, to competitors may seriously affect its performance and profits.

- **Details related to the security** of the organisation such as access codes, passwords and banking schedules. If these details were to be compromised it would be easy for hackers and thieves to steal information.

There are also risks associated with copyright and copying, transmitting, sending and destroying confidential information without authorisation and appropriate security measures.

Remember email is neither secure nor confidential.

1.4   Computer viruses

 Definition

A **computer virus** is a piece of software that piggybacks on real programs and seeks to infest a computer system; hiding and automatically spreading to other systems if given the opportunity.

For example, a virus might attach itself to a program such as a spreadsheet. Each time the spreadsheet program runs, the virus runs too, and it has the chance to reproduce (by attaching to other programs) or wreak havoc. A computer virus passes from computer to computer like a biological virus passes from person to person.

Viruses can be classified using multiple criteria: origin, techniques, types of files they infect, where they hide, the kind of damage they cause, the type of operating system or platform they attack etc.

A single virus, if it is particularly complex, may come under several different categories. And, as new viruses emerge, it may sometimes be necessary to redefine categories or, very occasionally, create new categories.

Types of virus/infection include:

- **File infectors** – this type of virus infects programs or executable files (files with an .EXE or .COM extension). When one of these programs is run, directly or indirectly, the virus is activated, producing the damaging effects it is programmed to carry out. The majority of existing viruses belong to this category, and can be classified depending on the actions that they carry out, as seen below.

- **Overwrite viruses** – this type of virus is characterised by the fact that it deletes the information contained in the files that it infects, rendering them partially or totally useless once they have been infected. Infected files do not change size, unless the virus occupies more space than the original file because, instead of hiding within a file, the virus replaces the content of the file. The only way to clean a file infected by an overwrite virus is to delete the file completely, thus losing the original content.

- **E-mail viruses** – an e-mail virus moves around in e-mail messages, and usually replicates itself by automatically mailing itself to dozens of people in the victim's e-mail address book.

- **Trap doors** – undocumented entry points to systems allowing normal controls to be bypassed by Logic bombs – these are then triggered on the occurrence of a certain event.

- **Time bombs** – which are triggered on a certain date e.g. Friday 13th.

- **Worms** – are not strictly viruses, as they do not need to infect other files in order to reproduce. They have the ability to self-replicate, and can lead to negative effects on the system and most importantly they are detected and eliminated by antiviruses.

- **Trojans** – these are examples of malicious code which, unlike viruses, do not reproduce by infecting other files, nor do they self-replicate like worms. They appear to be harmless programs that enter a computer through any channel. When that program is executed (they have names or characteristics which trick the user into doing so), they install other programs on the computer that can be harmful. A Trojan may not activate its effects at first, but when it does, it can wreak havoc on your system. They have the capacity to delete files, destroy information on your hard drive and open up a backdoor to your system. This gives them complete access to your system allowing an outside user to copy and resend confidential information.

Most computer viruses have three functions – avoiding detection, reproducing themselves and causing damage. The damage caused may be relatively harmless and amusing ('Cascade' causes letters to 'fall' off a screen), but are more often severely damaging.

The potential for the damage a virus can cause is restricted only by the creativity of the originator. Given the mobility between computerised systems and the sharing of resources and data, the threat posed by a viral attack is considerable.

Once a virus has been introduced, the only course of action may be to regenerate the system from back up. However, some viruses are written so that they lie dormant for a period, which means that the backups become infected before the existence of the virus has been detected – in these instances restoration of the system becomes impossible.

1.5   Fraudulent activities

Fraud is criminal deception – essentially it is theft involving dishonesty. It may be opportunistic or organised. The dishonesty may involve suppliers, contractors, competitors, other third parties, employees and ex-employees and, increasingly, organised crime and senior managers. Many frauds involve collusion and sophisticated methods of concealment. With an ever-increasing amount of business being carried out electronically (via 'e-commerce') the opportunities for cybercrime and computer fraud are also growing exponentially.

Fraud normally involves staff removing money or other assets from the company, but other methods of fraud that might affect the data held on a computer system include:

- the creation of fictitious supplier accounts and submission of false invoices, usually for services rather than goods, so that payments are sent to the fictitious supplier

- corruption and bribery, particularly where individuals are in a position of authority as regards making decisions on suppliers or selecting between tenders

- misappropriation of incoming cheques from bona fide customers

- giving unauthorised discounts to customers

- stock losses, including short deliveries by driver

- fictitious staff on the payroll (also known as 'ghost employees').

2 Protecting data from risks

2.1 Security measures

Computer security can be divided into a number of separate functions with different aims:

- **Threat avoidance:** this might mean changing the design of the system.

- **Prevention:** it is practically impossible to prevent all threats in a cost-effective manner.

- **Deterrence:** the computer system should try to both prevent unauthorised access and deter people from trying to access the system. Controls to prevent and detect access include passwords and hardware keys. As an example of possible deterrent computer misuse by personnel could be grounds for dismissal.

- **Detection:** if the computer system is accessed without authorisation, there should be controls to sense the access and report it to the appropriate personnel. Detection techniques are often combined with prevention techniques. Controls will therefore include control logs of unauthorised attempts to gain access and manual reviews of amendments made to program and data files.

- **Recovery:** if the threat occurs, its consequences can be contained e.g. by the use of checkpoint programs. Procedures should be in place to ensure that if the computer system was destroyed or compromised by a virus, then processing could continue quickly. A basic control procedure would be a complete, and regular, backup of all data.

- **Correction:** any unauthorised changes made to the computer systems are corrected as soon as possible. This means that complete backups of all data are available and that staff are properly trained in the procedures necessary for recovery and re-installation of data in an emergency situation.

2.2 Physical security

Physical security includes protection against natural and man-made disasters, e.g. fire, flood, etc. Examples of measures to avoid physical damage to the system include:

- Fire precautions, e.g. smoke and heat detectors, training for staff in observing safety procedures and alarms

- Devices to protect against power surges

- Appropriate positioning of computer hardware.

Physical security also includes protection against intruders and theft. As computers and other hardware become smaller and portable, they are more likely to be taken from the organisation. Burglar alarms should be installed and a log of all equipment maintained. People with official access to the equipment who are taking it off-site should book it out with the appropriate authorisation.

Access to the building may be controlled by security guards, closed circuit TV monitoring access and other mechanical devices such as door locks and electronic devices, e.g. badge readers and card entry systems.

2.3 Data security

Guidelines for data security include keeping files in fireproof cabinets, shredding computer printouts if they include confidential information, controlling access to the data, (e.g. passwords and physical access controls) and taking back-ups of data to minimise the risks of destruction or alteration.

To offset the risk of fraudulent attacks there must be: adequate controls over input/processing/programs, strict division of duties and regular internal audit review of systems and controls.

To prevent loss of confidentiality, there should be controls over input and output. With on-line systems there should be passwords issued only to authorised personnel, restricted access to files at the terminals and a computer log of attempted violations.

All disks containing important information must be backed up on a regular basis. Information on a computer is vulnerable: hard disks can fail, computer systems can fail, viruses can wipe a disk, careless operators can delete files and very careless operators can delete whole areas of the hard disks by mistake. Computers can also be damaged or stolen. For these reasons backing up of data is essential. This involves making copies of essential files, together with necessary update transactions, and keeping them on another computer, or on some form of storage media so that copies can be recreated. Master file copies should be taken at regular intervals and kept at locations away from the main computer installation.

Contingency plans for a disaster should include standby facilities, with a similar computer user or a bureau being available to allow processing to continue.

2.4 Rules for using passwords

If passwords are used for authentication in a computer system, the safety of the access privileges will depend on their correct use and the following rules should be observed:

- It must not be possible to guess the password as easily as names, motor vehicle licence numbers, birth dates or the like.

- The password should consist of at least one non-letter character (special character or number) and have at least six characters. The selection of trivial passwords (BBBBBB, 123456) must be prevented.

- Preset passwords (e.g. set by the manufacturer at the time of delivery) must be replaced by individually selected, unique passwords.

- The password must be kept secret and should only be known personally to the user.

- The password must be changed regularly, e.g. every 90 days. This will ensure that if an unauthorised person has obtained it, he or she will have limited use.

- The password should be altered if it has, or may have, come to the knowledge of unauthorised persons.

- After any alteration of the password, previous passwords should no longer be used and re-use of previous passwords should be prevented by the IT system.

Test your understanding 1

You have been asked for suggestions for a checklist of control procedures to remind authorised users about password security in the computer department. What suggestions would you make?

2.5   Controls to help prevent hacking

Hacking is the gaining of unauthorised access to a computer system. It may form part of a criminal activity or it may be a hobby, with hackers acting alone or passing information to one another. Hacking is often a harmless activity, with participants enjoying the challenge of breaking part of a system's defences, but severe damage can be caused.

Once hackers have gained access to the system, there are several damaging options available to them. For example, they may:

- gain access to the file that holds all of the ID codes, passwords and authorisations

- discover the method used for generating/authorising passwords

- discover maintenance codes, which would render the system easily accessible.

By specifically identifying the risks that the hacker represents, controls can be designed that will help prevent such activity occurring. Examples include:

- **Physical security** – check that terminals and PCs are kept under lock and key and ensure that, where dial-in communication links are in place, a call-back facility is used. (In call-back, the person dialling in must request that the system calls them back to make the connection).

- **Authorisation** – Management often requires that the contents of certain files (e.g. payroll) remain confidential and are only available to authorised staff. This may be achieved by keeping tapes or removable disks containing the files in a locked cabinet and issuing them only for authorised use.

- **Passwords** – the controls over passwords must be stringently enforced and password misuse should represent a serious disciplinary offence within an organisation. Associated with the password is a list of files, and data within files, which the user is allowed to inspect. Attempts to access unauthorised files or data will be prohibited by the operating system and reported at the central computer. For example, an order clerk using a VDU would be allowed access to the stock file, but not to the employee file.

Similarly, the clerk would be allowed access to the customer file for purposes of recording an order, but would not necessarily be able to inspect details of the account. For systems that use passwords and logging on techniques, the workstation should not be left in the middle of editing. A screensaver with password control can be used for short absences, which saves closing down the machine.

- **Data encryption** – files can be scrambled to render them unintelligible unless a decoding password is supplied. Data may be coded so that it is not understandable to any casual observer who does not have access to suitable decryption software. Encryption provides a double benefit. It protects against people managing to gain access to the system, and it protects against the tapping of data whilst being transmitted from one machine to another.

- **System logs** – every activity on a system should be logged and be subject to some form of exception reporting, e.g. unusual times of access could be reported.

- **Random checks** – the 'constable on the beat' approach checks who is doing what at random intervals on the system, and ensures that they are authorised for those activities.

- **Shielding of VDUs** – to protect against people with detection equipment being able to view remotely what is being displayed on VDUs, the units may be shielded to prevent the transmission of radiation that can be detected.

2.6 Preventative steps against computer viruses

It is extremely difficult to guard against the introduction of computer viruses. Even seemingly harmless screen savers have been known to contain deadly viruses that destroy computer systems. You should not download from the Internet or open e-mails that have attachments, unless you know the source of the e-mail and you trust that source. If you are in doubt you should ask your line manager for permission to open documents.

Steps may be taken to control the introduction and spread of viruses, but these will usually only be effective in controlling the spread of viruses by well-meaning individuals. The actions of hackers or malicious employees are less easy to control. **Preventative steps may include:**

- Anti-virus software to prevent corruption of the system by viruses. However, the focus of the program is to detect and cure known viruses, and therefore it will not always restore data or software that has been corrupted by the virus. As new viruses are being detected almost daily, it is virtually impossible for the virus detection software to be effective against all known viruses

- Anti-virus software must therefore be kept up-to-date

- Control on the use of external software (e.g. checked for viruses before use)

- Use of only tested, marked disks/memory sticks within the organisation

- Restricted access to floppy disks, CDs & flash drives on all PCs/workstations

- Passwords and user numbers can be used to limit the opportunities for unauthorised people to access the system via the public communications network.

3 Legislative requirements for Data Protection

3.1 Introduction

Several Acts of Parliament, notably the **Data Protection Act 1998**, the **Copyright, Designs and Patents Act 1988** and the **Computer Misuse Act 1990** regulate the use of computers. Each act identifies a number of prohibited actions which, if proven in a court of law, may lead the perpetrator to face damages and/or a fine or imprisonment or both. Additionally, the use of software may also be subject to the terms of licensing agreements entered into by the organisation you work for, which are enforceable in the civil courts.

3.2 Data Protection Act 1998

People have been keeping records for centuries and it might be considered surprising that concern is only recently being voiced. These concerns arise mainly due to the amount of information that can now be gathered and stored, and the ease with which that information can be manipulated, accessed and exchanged. School records, banking records, itemised telephone bills, medical records, etc. are all now capable of being consolidated to show what purchases someone makes, where they travel, who they talk to and how healthy they are. It is well known that information is traded between organisations for marketing purposes.

The exchange of information itself is not worrying. The concern lies in how such information will be used, or how it may be interpreted. It may be used to decide whether or not to offer a person a job, give somebody credit or call them into the police station for interrogation.

The **1998 Data Protection Act** covers how information about living **identifiable** persons is processed and used. It is much broader in scope than the earlier 1984 act, in that **ALL** organisations that hold or process personal data **MUST** comply. This Act has implications for everyone who processes manual or electronic personal data. It applies to filing systems of records held on computer or manual sets of accessible records e.g. a database of customer names, addresses, telephone numbers and sales details.

Under the terms of the Act, the need for privacy is recognised by the requirements that all data should be held for clearly designated purposes. Accuracy and integrity must be maintained and data must be open to inspection. Only legitimate parties can access data and information must be secured against alteration, accidental loss or deliberate damage. Furthermore, the Act states that data must be obtained fairly, to precise specifications and must not be kept for longer than required.

It reinforces the need for confidentiality in business dealings. A business should not reveal information about one customer to another or information about its employees without their permission. The Act gives a data subject, with some exceptions, the right to examine the personal data that a data controller is holding about him or her. Individuals may write to a data controller to ask whether they are the subject of personal data, and they are entitled to a reply.

The data controller may charge a nominal fee for providing the information, but is required to reply within a certain time.

Where personal data is being held, **the data subject has the right to receive details of:**

(i)   the personal data that is being held about them

(ii) the purposes for which this information is being processed

(iii) the recipients to whom the information might be disclosed.

The data subject is also entitled to receive this information in a form that can be understood. In practice, this usually means providing the data subject with a printout of the data, and an explanation of any items of data (such as codes) whose meaning is not clear.

Any individual who suffers damage as a result of improper use of the data by the data controller is entitled to compensation for any loss suffered.

The **Data Protection Registrar** keeps a register of companies who hold information on computer. Each company that falls into this category must register of its own accord. A copy of the Data Protection Register is held in all major libraries.

Any unregistered data user who holds personal data that is not exempt commits a criminal offence – the maximum penalty for which is an unlimited fine.

3.3   Retention of documents

All businesses need to keep certain records for legal and commercial reasons. The difficulty lies in knowing which documents must be kept and for how long. Your organisation will have a policy that states the retention (and disposal) policy for such documentation. It will outline minimum retention periods for different types of documents based on best practice and, where applicable, the minimum retention periods required by law.

The Data Protection Act stipulates that personal data is kept securely and that it should be accurate.

Business records are normally kept for at least **six years**. Payroll data must be kept for **three years**. There are a number of legal reasons why financial data, which of course includes personal data, should be kept for this time. Accounting records need to be kept for at least **six years** in case they are required as evidence in a legal case. They should also be kept so that they can be inspected by HM Revenue and Customs in case there is a tax or VAT inspection.

Once information becomes out of date, it may be deleted or destroyed but you must be aware that throwing a piece of paper in the waste bin is not destroying it. Even when information is out of date it may still be damaging if it falls into the wrong hands.

 Test your understanding 2

A well-known customer telephones you and asks if you can look up on your screen and let him know if Joe Bloggs (another customer) is paying on time, because he is having trouble getting money out of him and wonders whether he is going bust. Unfortunately, you know from your work that Joe Bloggs is not very good at paying his invoices. What should you say?

3.4   Patent and copyright infringement

Copyright law covers books of all kinds, sound recordings, film and broadcasts, computer programs, dramatic and musical works. Copyright in general terms is the right to publish, reproduce and sell the matter and form of a literary, musical, dramatic or artistic work. The **Copyright Designs and Patents Act 1988** states that the copyright holder has the exclusive right to make and distribute copies. The **Copyright (Computer Software) Amendment Act 1989** indicates that **software is treated as literary work** and provides the same protection to the authors of computer software as it does to literary, dramatic and musical works. An amendment to the 1988 Act made in 1992 allows you to make a copy for back-up purposes.

The Act makes it illegal to steal or to create copies of software. You are not allowed to make copies of software or manuals, or allow copies to be made unless you have a licence from the owner of the copyright that allows you to do so. It is also an offence to run the software on more than one computer at the same time unless that is covered in the licence.

Application packages will always contain an embedded serial number. If a pirate copy is found, the original purchaser can usually be determined.

There are steep penalties for companies prosecuted for software theft – unlimited damages, legal costs and the cost of legitimising the software. However, most breaches of copyright law happen because business users do not know what the law is.

Where a package is intended for use by more than one person, for instance on a network, then a multi-user licence is normally purchased, and this sets a limit on the total number of users. An alternative to this is a site licence, but this can be restrictive if, say, a travelling salesperson or someone working from home connects to the network. Some software can be copied legally – this is known as shareware. The software can be loaded onto a computer and tested, however, if the user decides to keep the software, then a royalty payment is due to the author. Freeware is software that can be copied and used without charge, although the software author retains the copyright to that software. Finally, public domain software is freely available and sharable software that is not copyrighted.

Modern software packages are complex and costly to produce, but are often easy to copy and distribute. Manufacturers are increasingly bringing prosecutions to try to reduce the number of pirate copies of their software. Staff should be made aware of this. Master and back-up copies of packages (usually on diskette or CD-ROM) should be kept in a locked safe. Programs on LAN servers should be given 'execute only' protection to prevent them being copied, and physical access to the server should be restricted. Regular and automatic audits should be made of personal computers to check that they only contain authorised programs.

3.5 Why worry about copyright rules?

The 'moral' reasons for following copyright rules are:

- copyright protection is essential to ensure that authors and publishers receive appropriate remuneration for their work

- acknowledging source and ownership of materials is good academic practice.

The pragmatic reasons for following copyright rules are:

- breaches of copyright can lead to civil prosecution and fines and, in worst cases, criminal prosecution

- licensing bodies make regular checks on certain organisations to ensure rules are being followed.

Note also, that you can infringe copyright, and be prosecuted, not only for making illegal copies yourself, but also as an 'accessory' by providing resources or authorisation (e.g. within a company) for someone else to illegally copy or perform material.

3.6 Computer misuse

Data that has been stored on a computer is, potentially, easier to misuse than that stored on paper. Computer-based data can be altered without leaving any obvious trace that it has changed. For example, an exam score written in a mark book can be changed but you can usually tell that the mark has changed. A mark stored on a computer can be changed and it will look as if nothing has happened.

Malicious (harmful) programs can be introduced to a computer that can damage the data stored on it, copy the data and send it somewhere else or simply change the stored data. The programs are named after the way they get onto different computers – viruses, worms and Trojan horses, as previously detailed.

It is very easy to make copies of computer data without leaving a trace that it has been done. A photocopier will also make copies of paper-based data but electronic copies of data can be smuggled out easily on floppy disks, memory chips or over a network connection.

Many computers are connected to a network or the Internet. If someone is persistent enough it is possible to use this connection to gain access to the computer (and the data on it) from outside. Of course, someone is able to physically break into a room and read data from paper records, however, it is sometimes more difficult to trace someone who has broken into a computer over a network or the Internet.

The Computer Misuse Act 1990 makes it a criminal offence to attempt to access, use or alter any computer data, program or service to which you have not been granted authorised access rights. Therefore any attempt to interfere with or bypass the security controls, to attempt to obtain information such as other people's passwords, or accessing or modifying other people's programs or files without permission are offences under the Act. Amongst other things, this Act makes the activity of hacking illegal as well as the introduction of viruses and worms.

The Act has created three new criminal offences.

(i) **Unauthorised access** – This refers to any hacker who knowingly tries to gain unauthorised access to a computer system. The crime is committed in attempting to gain access, regardless of whether the hacker is successful or not. It includes: using another person's identifier (ID) and password, creating a virus, laying a trap to obtain a password or persistently trying to guess an ID and password.

(ii) **Unauthorised access with the intention of committing another offence** – This crime carries stricter penalties than the crime mentioned above. It seeks to protect against unauthorised entry with the intention of committing a further criminal act such as fraud.

Examples include: gaining access to financial or administrative records, reading or changing confidential information.

(iii) **Unauthorised modification of data or programs** – This makes the introduction of viruses into a computer system a criminal offence. Guilt is assessed upon the intention to disrupt or in some way impair the normal operation and processes of the computer system. Examples include: destroying another user's files, modifying systems files, introducing a local virus, introducing a networked virus or deliberately generating information to cause a system malfunction.

3.7 Enforcement of standards

Observance of standards is more a matter of attitude than policing. When the reasons behind the rules are understood, it is more likely that they will be followed. Training is the main element of enforcement. There are some cases where ignoring standards should automatically lead to disciplinary action:

(i) Standards with legal implications e.g. ignoring a requirement of the Data Protection Act or using an illegal copy of a program.

(ii) Actions which may affect a number of other people, e.g. running a program which might introduce a virus into a network.

(iii) Attempted unauthorised entry, e.g. trying to find someone else's password or unauthorised copying of confidential files (e.g. salaries).

(iv) Any standards to do with safety, e.g. dangerous positioning of cables, particularly power cables, or working alone in an electrically hazardous environment (see below for more detail regarding health and safety legislation).

4 Health and safety regulations for equipment

4.1 The Health and Safety (Display Screen Equipment) Regulations 1992

Ensuring the workplace is safe and healthy for employees can sometimes lead to emphasis on the obvious hazards such as lifting and use of dangerous equipment. However, the health and safety implications of poorly designed workstations is extremely important in today's environment, where more and more people are working at personal computers and desks for long periods of time.

In addition to the **Workplace (Health, Safety and Welfare) Regulations** there are the **Health and Safety (Display Screen Equipment) Regulations**, which relate directly to use of display screen equipment (DSE). In general these are in place to ensure that workstations and jobs are well designed for individuals, and that the risks to health and safety are minimised. The regulations do not cover screens whose main purpose is to show television or film pictures. Workstation equipment includes:

- display screen equipment (DSE) e.g. computers, terminals and accessories such as printers

- desks

- chairs

- accessories – e.g. telephones, foot rests, document holders, wrist rests

- work environment and work organisation.

The Health and Safety (Display Screen Equipment) Regulations 1992 came into effect from January 1993 to implement an EC Directive. They require employers to minimise the risks in VDU work by ensuring that workplaces and jobs are well designed.

The Regulations apply where staff habitually use VDUs as a significant part of their normal work (three hours or more per day) – even if they work from home. Other people, who use VDUs only occasionally, are not covered by these Regulations, but their employers still have general duties to protect them under other health and safety at work legislation.

4.2   Hazards

There are hazards associated with the use of Display Screen Equipment (DSE). They include:

- upper limb disorders (musculoskeletal disorders) – aches and pains in the hands, wrists, arms, neck, shoulders, back, etc

- visual difficulties – eyes can become tired and existing conditions can become more noticeable

- repetitive strain injury (RSI) – appears to arise from making the same movements repeatedly and affects your hands and arms

- fatigue and stress

- headaches

- skin irritation

- back and neck strain.

The likelihood and extent of these harmful outcomes is related to the frequency, duration, pace and intensity of the tasks, the adequacy of the equipment and how it is arranged, the physical environment, the organisational 'climate' of the workplace, the characteristics of the individual and the posture of the user amongst other factors.

It should be noted, however, that only a small percentage of users will experience problems as a result of DSE. Those problems that do occur are generally not due to the equipment itself but the way it is used. The majority of concerns can be prevented by effective workplace and job design, ensuring that workstations and work patterns are designed to suit the individual.

4.3   Problems with Display Screen Equipment (DSE)

If you are a user of display screen equipment:

- Problems with the task, the workstation or its environment that are increasing the risk to your health and safety, and that you cannot resolve yourself, must be reported to your manager.

- You might experience the early signs and symptoms of ill health and identify the cause and the preventative measures to prevent continuing ill health. You must report this to your manager to enable support to be given for the measures you are taking.

- Ill-health problems might have developed to a stage that causes suffering and incapacity from doing all or part of your normal work. This will need to be the subject of an **Accident Report**. The manager's investigation into the accident may need the assistance of a Display Screen Equipment assessor. A long-term remedy might be identified and a short-term adjustment to task, routine and/or workstation might be appropriate. A DSE assessor is not competent to diagnose health conditions or advise on treatment or therapy. If however your doctor recommends certain adaptation of the task or workstation to your condition the assessor might be able to help with implementation.

- In more serious cases the condition might be such that the manager will need to arrange a rehabilitation programme and 'reasonable adjustments' of the work and workstations.

5 Health and safety in your workplace

5.1 The importance of health and safety at work

Of course, health and safety not only relates to computer screen equipment but to the workplace in general. The maintenance of safe working conditions and the prevention of accidents are most important. Top of your list of importance is obviously to protect yourself and others from dangers that might cause injury or sickness.

Health and safety is as important in an office as in a factory. Constant absenteeism through poor working conditions or accidents is costly for any organisation, and people do not work as productively if they are ill, tired or in an unsatisfactory environment. It is therefore in the organisation's interests, as well as the employees', that health and safety procedures are observed. The costs of not having adequate measures to ensure health and safety include the following:

- Cash, cheques, equipment, machinery and stock (i.e. company assets) may be destroyed, lost or damaged. If the losses are serious the organisation may have to close down for a time. It may not be possible to complete orders on time, leading to a loss of customers and the consequent effect on profits and jobs.

- There may be serious injury to employees, customers and/or the general public, which could lead to claims for compensation and damage to the reputation of the organisation.

- Confidential records (e.g. correspondence and information on creditors, debtors and stock) may no longer be available.

Because health and safety at work is so important, there are regulations that require all of us not to put others or ourselves in danger. The regulations are also there to protect the employees from workplace danger.

6 Internal policies and procedures

6.1 The basic requirements

All businesses need policies and procedures to ensure compliance with legislation but also to maintain and improve internal efficiency as mentioned in chapter 1. Staff should be provided with a handbook when they commence their employment which contains these policies and procedures.

These may include:

- Recruitment
- Reporting lines and structure
- Training
- Appraisals
- Holiday cover
- Sickness
- Disciplinary
- Capability

Each function may also have procedures to follow

e.g.

Sale system guide covering – accepting new customers, price queries etc.

 Test your understanding 3

What measures can an organisation take to reduce the risk of equipment being stolen?

 Test your understanding 4

Give examples of the type of fraud that might be perpetrated.

Test your understanding 5

Consider the system at your place of work and list all the security threats to hardware and software. Indicate those risks that might be accidental and those that could be malicious.

What steps can you take to minimise these risks? Consider procedural steps, such as back-up routines, job specifications, physical locations, extra hardware, passwords, etc.

Explore your back-up procedures.

 Test your understanding 6

Copyright law covers:

(a) reference books, sound recordings, film and broadcasts, computer programs, dramatic and musical works

(b) books of all kinds, sound recordings, film and broadcasts, computer programs, dramatic and musical works

(c) books of all kinds, sound recordings, film and broadcasts, computer programs written in the UK, dramatic and musical works

(d) books of all kinds, sound recordings on CD, film and broadcasts, computer programs, dramatic and musical works.

Which one is correct?

 Test your understanding 7

One of your friends at work has told you that she can't remember her password unless it is easy, so she uses her forename, Mary. Can you think of a password that is equally easy but could not be guessed by anyone else?

KAPLAN PUBLISHING

Test your understanding 8

A small company's computer system comprises five desktop personal computers located in separate offices linked together in a local network within the same building. The computers are not connected to a wide area network and employees are not allowed to take floppy disks into or out of the building. Information that the owner of the business wishes to keep confidential to herself is stored in one of the computers.

Which ONE of the following statements can be concluded from this information?

The company's computer system does NOT:

(i)   need a back-up storage system

(ii)   need a password access system

(iii)   receive e-mails from customers and suppliers

(iv)   include virus detection software.

 Test your understanding 9

Mitchell & Co is a partnership of solicitors. They have five offices situated in various parts of the country.

(a)   What information would you expect to find in their health and safety manual, a copy of which is provided for all new employees'?

(b)   What conditions and facilities do you think Mitchell & Co should provide for their employees?

 Test your understanding 10

What do you think are the causes of most accidents in the workplace?

 Test your understanding 11

Describe your actions in the following situations:

(a)   if you discover a fire

(b)   if you hear the fire alarm.

7 Summary

This chapter focused on two important issues: the security of information and data and elements of health and safety. These influence organisational procedures as **business must adhere to various legislation that has an effect upon the workplace** and those engaged in the business activity.

Test your understanding answers

 ### Test your understanding 1

Some of the suggestions that would be included in a checklist for password security are:

- Passwords are meant to be secret and not revealed to anyone else.

- Never write it down.

- Change your password regularly or if you suspect someone knows it.

- Do not choose an obvious password such as your name, or in the case of a PIN, your date or year of birth.

- Try to avoid onlookers seeing you key in your password.

- For keyboard passwords, choose keys that require both hands rather than one or two finger, easy runs along a pattern of the keys.

 ### Test your understanding 2

You should not divulge any confidential information about your customer Joe Bloggs. Apart from it being very unprofessional it would also be breaking the law. Under the Data Protection Act 1998 data should not be made available to outsiders without authorisation.

Test your understanding 3

There are several ways of minimising the risk

- Burglar alarms can be fitted.
- Access to the building can be controlled.
- Smaller items can be locked away securely. Larger pieces of equipment can be bolted to the surface.
- The organisation can maintain a log of all equipment so that its movement can be monitored.
- Disks containing valuable data should not be left lying around.

 Test your understanding 4

Examples include:

- Theft of assets, e.g. computers, stock or software.
- Theft of incoming cheques.
- Invented personnel on the payroll.
- Unauthorised discounts given to customers.
- False supplier accounts.
- Corruption and bribery, e.g. when selecting suppliers.
- Abuse of organisation's credit card facilities, e.g. company car fuel allowance privately.

 Test your understanding 5

The following provide some typical threats and safeguards relating to most systems.

Hardware threats	Software threats
Theft	Hacking into system
Physical damage	Computer virus
Smoke and fire damage	Unathorised access and usage
	Unauthorised amendments

KAPLAN PUBLISHING

Examples of safeguards and precautions that could be adopted include:

- Smoke and fire alarms.

- Assets recorded in an asset register and marked with a company logo and asset number.

- Restricted access to gain access to, and use, hardware e.g. use of personal logins.

- Use of firewalls to prevent access by unauthorised users and/or viruses introduced by malicious emails.

- Controls to ensure that any amendments/updates to software are authorised appropriately and checks to confirm they have been done correctly.

- Back up procedures to minimise risk of loss of data.

 Test your understanding 6

The answer is (b).

 Test your understanding 7

Using your Christian name may be the easiest way to remember your password, but it will also be easy for someone to gain unauthorised access to your files when you are not at your desk. Alternative passwords that are easy to remember are your mother's maiden name or a brother or sister's name. Try to add in a number e.g. year born, to make it even more difficult for someone to guess it.

 Test your understanding 8

(iii) Because the computers are only connected to a local area network they cannot receive e-mail from customers and suppliers.

Test your understanding 9

(a)   It would include information on:

  (i)   the people in charge of health and safety within the firm and their specific responsibilities

  (ii)   safe operating practices (e.g. the operation of electrical equipment)

  (iii)   the system for recording accidents in the accident book

  (iv)   details of first Aid available, including the names of qualified first Aiders and the position of the first Aid box.

(b)   Adequate premises which are structurally sound, have adequate fire exits and safety equipment.

  Suitable accommodation: suitable temperature, enough space for number of people, proper ventilation, blinds for windows, adequate lighting and safe floor surfaces in good condition.

  Appropriate furniture: safety stools to reach items stored on shelves, adjustable chairs for VDU operators and filing cabinets in which only one drawer can be opened at a time.

  Adequate toilet and welfare facilities.

  Separate accommodation for noisy or dangerous equipment (e.g. photocopiers which give out fumes) or substances (e.g. cleaning materials).

  Safe equipment which is serviced regularly by trained technicians.

Test your understanding 10

Most likely causes are:

(a)   people tripping up, slipping or falling off equipment or furniture

(b)   people being hit by falling objects or colliding with equipment, furniture or other people

(c)   people using electrical equipment incorrectly

(d)   people using equipment or materials incorrectly.

Test your understanding 11

(a) Discovering a fire:

   (i)   decide whether or not it can be dealt with using a fire extinguisher or fire blanket – these methods are only successful for small fires

   (ii) ensure that no one else is in immediate danger

   (iii) if the fire is in one room only, close the door

   (iv) raise the alarm and follow company procedure on who must ring the fire brigade

   (v)   leave the building as quickly as possible – do not stop to collect any personal belongings.

(b) Hearing a fire alarm:

   (i)   close all windows and doors and leave the building as quickly as possible – do not stop to collect any personal belongings

   (ii) remain calm and go to the assembly point

   (iii) follow the instructions of your managers or the fire brigade officers – do not re-enter the building until you are authorised to do so.

Improving your own performance

Introduction

The appraisal of performance should identify your strengths and weaknesses and this can be the starting point for a career plan. Your strategy will then be designed to use your strengths and overcome any weaknesses, to help you to take advantage of future career opportunities.

A competence is an observable skill or ability to complete a particular task. It also includes the ability to transfer skills and knowledge to a new situation.

The general purpose of any assessment or appraisal is to improve the efficiency of the organisation, by ensuring that the individual employees are performing to the best of their ability and developing their potential for improvement.

ASSESSMENT CRITERIA
2.3   Identify development needs

CONTENTS

1   Identify your own development needs

2   Career planning

3   Process of competence assessment

4   Learning to improve your performance

5   Methods used to acquire skills and knowledge

6   Review and evaluate your performance and progress

1 Identify your own development needs

1.1 Becoming an accounting technician

There are many reasons for become an accounting technician. If you think you deserve a better career with improved prospects and a higher earning potential, then becoming an accounting technician is an ideal first step to achieving these goals and more.

You will be qualified to work in any number of accounting roles, across a wide range of industries – you do not have to work for an accounting practice.

As an AAT qualified accounting technician you will have an internationally recognised and respected qualification that shows potential employers that you have been trained to a high standard.

In addition, as the AAT's qualification is founded on actually doing the work, they will know that as well as the underpinning knowledge, you have the skills and practical experience not just to perform in an accounting role, but also to excel in it.

And if you are thinking of training to be a chartered or certified accountant then the AAT is an ideal route to these qualifications. All the main UK accountancy bodies offer exemptions to AAT qualified members.

1.2 What is development?

Development is the growth or realisation of a person's ability and potential through the provision of learning and educational experiences.

Organisations often have a training and development strategy based on the overall strategy for the business.

Development activities include:

* career planning
* training – both on and off the job
* appraisal
* other learning opportunities e.g. job rotation.

Training can be described as the planned and systematic modification of behaviour through learning events, programmes and instruction which enable individuals to achieve the level of knowledge, skills and competence that is required to carry out their work effectively.

All training and development is self-development, whether it is provided by the organisation or not. If you do not want to learn, acquire new skills, change attitudes or behaviour or are not sufficiently motivated to do so, you will not achieve it. If the outcome of an appraisal programme or promotion planning incorporates training that is imposed it cannot lead to effective development. The best route to being successful in learning and development is where there is a strong desire for the required outcome.

Some organisations make a commitment to individual development, which requires the setting of individual objectives and the negotiation of a learning contract between the organisation and the employee. It allows the individual to select the way in which learning will take place, the provision of support and guidance by the organisation and joint assessment of the results.

1.3 Development opportunities

Your manager should be able to refer you to others who can assist you in achieving your development, and suggest appropriate referral sources both within and outside the department. E.g. books, journals, professional associations or people who might be willing to act as mentors.

You can undertake research into development opportunities relating to your own job and also relating to the AAT and where it may lead you.

Make a note of useful addresses and look out for publications that keep you up-to-date with development opportunities relating to your job role.

Association of Accounting Technicians (AAT)

140 Aldersgate Street,
London EC1A 4HY

Tel: +44 (0)20 7397 3000

Fax: +44 (0)20 7397 3009

Website: **www.aat.org.uk**

The AAT – ACA fast track is a direct route to qualification as a Chartered Accountant – from the AAT.

For the first two years of the Fast Track, you train for the AAT as normal, making sure you have completed certain units and kept a record of your work experience. After that, if you obtain an ACA training contract and pass a Top Up paper, you effectively bypass the first year of ACA training, leaving you just two years away from a top financial business qualification.

The Institute of Chartered Accountants in England & Wales (ICAEW)

Chartered Accountants' Hall
PO Box 433
London EC2P 2BJ

Tel 020 7920 8100 Fax 020 7920 0547

There are many on-line resources that will give you more information:
AAT – www.accountingtechnician.co.uk

Financial Times Self-Assessment –
http://ftcareerpoint.ft.com/YourCareer/developyourself

Financial Times – Mastering Management – www.ftmastering.com

Financial Times – Business Education – www.ft.com/surveys/businessed

Your People Manager – www.yourpeoplemanager.com

Many colleges will run courses that you might consider. They also have websites or brochures which you might find interesting.

2 Career planning

2.1 Why plan?

Today emphasis is on lifelong learning and multiple job/career transitions. The aim of career development is to help you understand your potential and to help you maximise this potential in the work force today and in the future. From the start, you will need to have a clear idea of the kind of career path you would like to follow. Good career planning can lead to a satisfying career. People who do not career plan sometimes get sick from stress working in fields they are not suited to, and students waste time and money pursuing educational areas in which they have no real interest.

The decisions we make about careers and leisure activities throughout our life are critical to our sense of well being. Satisfaction in our work can be a key ingredient to our feelings of self-worth; happiness can be contingent on a role as a productive and worthwhile employer or employee.

Conversely, excessive stress in a job can interfere with our health and personal relationships. Many believe that a person who maintains a healthy work/life balance can find fulfilment in the workplace, as well as in his or her other roles as citizen, student, parent etc.

When planning your future you need to understand that career development is often a lifetime project and may require continuous learning.

2.2 Preparing a SWOT analysis

It is not easy to take a good look at yourself and to therefore gain insight into yourself – your strengths and weaknesses – yet this is an essential first step in developing a career plan. You need to know whether you are an introvert or an extrovert, and whether you have the right approach towards achievement, work, material things, time and change. Different personal skills are required for interacting with other people, goal planning, self-development, motivation and performance. Many firms evaluate people on such personality factors as aggressiveness, co-operation, leadership and attitude.

Capabilities or skills may be categorised as:

- **technical** –working with tools and specific techniques (often demonstrated by holding specific qualifications).

- **human** – the ability to work with people; co-operative effort; teamwork and the creation of an environment in which people feel secure and free to express their opinions. We may think of this as our 'people skills'.

- **conceptual skill** – is the ability to see the 'big picture', to recognise significant elements in a situation and to understand the relationships among the elements. Being open-minded and recognising the total consequences of all actions.

- **design skill** – is the ability to solve problems in ways that will benefit the organisation.

The relative importance of these skills differs for the various positions in the organisational hierarchy, with technical skills being very important at the supervisory level, conceptual skills being crucial for top managers and human skills being important for all positions.

It is also important to make a careful assessment of the external environment, including its opportunities and threats. For example, joining an expanding company usually provides more career opportunities than working for a mature company that is not expected to grow.

E-learning might make it easier for some people to achieve their qualifications than attending classes at colleges etc.

Some examples of the areas you might look at, and the questions that you might ask yourself, in order to prepare a useful SWOT analysis, are shown below in the sort of grid that is typically used.

Strengths	Weaknesses
– What are your advantages? (colleagues will help identify these) – What do you do well? (competence analysis will identify strengths and development needs)	– What could be improved? (assessment by supervisor will identify any weaknesses) – What is done badly? – What should you avoid?
Opportunities	**Threats**
– What are the interesting trends? (keep up-to-date with courses, colleagues and managers as well as publications) – Does your organisation have high turnover of managerial staff? (appraisals will outline the range of opportunities)	– What obstacles do you face? – Is changing technology threatening your position? – Is your job changing?

2.3 Career strategy

The most successful strategy would be to build on your strengths and take advantage of opportunities. For example, if you have an excellent knowledge of computing and many organisations are looking for accountants who are also computer literate, you should find many opportunities for a satisfying career. On the other hand, if there is a demand for accountants with computing skills and you are interested but lack the necessary skills, the proper approach would be to develop the skills so that you can take advantage of the opportunities.

People do not always choose the most obvious career because it might not be the most fulfilling one. The choice involves personal preferences, ambitions and values. For example, although you might have certain computing skills demanded in the job market, that type of job may not interest you and it might be preferable to broaden your knowledge and skills or deal more with people.

You must also consider whether your choice is realistic and achievable in terms of resources and support from relevant people. You may be thinking of undertaking this course entirely on a distance-learning basis, or you may need to attend college on a day release or full time basis. You may be receiving support from your organisation for this in terms of money and time or you may be entirely self-financing.

The qualification may just be one element in a complex and highly structured development programme. Some accountancy career paths take a long time, are quite expensive and require a lot of spare time to be devoted to study.

If you have a family to consider, this must be discussed thoroughly before you broach the subject at work. An effective career strategy requires that consideration be given to the career of your partner. Dual career couples sometimes have to make very stressful choices, especially when it comes to opportunities for promotion that require relocation.

Even without a family there might be constraints in terms of personal relationships that would suffer if you did not give them your full attention.

Career choices require trade-offs. Some alternatives involve high risks, others low risk. Some choices demand action now, other choices can wait. Your plans are developed in an environment of uncertainty and the future cannot be predicted with great accuracy. Therefore, contingency plans based on alternative assumptions should also be prepared. For example, while you might enjoy working for a fast-growing venture company, it might be wise to prepare an alternative career plan based on the assumption that the venture might not succeed.

2.4   Growth

Your objective should be to ensure 'growth' during your career. This objective can obviously benefit your organisation as well as you. The growth should be triggered by a job that provides challenging goals. The clearer and more challenging the goals, the more effort you will exert, and the more likely it is that good performance will result. If you do a good job and receive positive feedback, you will feel successful (psychological success). These feelings will increase your feelings of confidence and self-esteem. This should lead to you becoming more involved in your work, which in turn leads to the setting of future stretching goals. This career-growth cycle is outlined below:

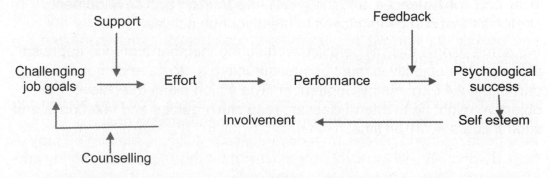

The above cycle can only be successfully completed if you receive support from your supervisor or manager.

2.5   Development goals/objectives

Once the direction of your career has been identified, the strategy has to be supported by objectives and action plans.

Short-term goals should be attainable within **one year**; **medium-term** goals within **three years**; and **long-term goals** within **five years**. Each goal should have a specific target, and the deadlines by which these targets should be achieved should be stated (although flexibility should be retained to allow for unforeseen circumstances).

Your goals and objectives will be aimed at:

- performance in the current job

- future changes in the current role

- moving elsewhere within the organisation – developing specialist expertise.

Your manager can support your career development by informing you about options for improvement and possible barriers to career movement, encouraging you to focus on clear, specific and attainable career goals, or suggesting steps you might take to improve existing skills and knowledge.

Some organisations make a commitment to individual development, which requires the setting of individual objectives and the negotiation of a learning contract between you and the organisation. It allows you to select the way in which learning will take place, the provision of support and guidance by the organisation and joint assessment of the results.

If you are seeking membership of one of the accountancy bodies the selection of the most appropriate qualification and methods of study will have to be determined by discussions between you, the accountant and the training officer (this may have been agreed at the selection interview).

In addition a training programme must be initiated so that the correct practical experience is obtained to satisfy the requirements of the accountancy body. This will include the identification of the necessary skills and competences, and the alternative training and development strategies that can be employed to meet your objectives.

For some people this will be discussed during their performance appraisal process. The objectives must be measurable e.g., to have completed a part of the AAT course by September. The action plans to achieve this objective might be to attend classes, read study guides and text books and submit coursework on time.

2.6 Monitoring progress

Monitoring is the process of evaluating your progress towards career goals and making necessary corrections to the aims or plans. Having embarked on your career path you must demonstrate effective time-management and efficient task-achievement so that you can accomplish your objectives in the time you have allowed yourself.

As well as self-monitoring, you will hopefully be receiving help, encouragement and feedback from your supervisor or manager. During your performance appraisal, your progress will be discussed and you will be encouraged to review your own performance against objectives in the operating areas of your job, and also to review the achievement of milestones in your career path.

3 Process of competence assessment

3.1 Competencies

A competence is an observable ability to complete a specific task successfully. Competencies are the critical skills, knowledge and attitude that a jobholder must have to perform effectively. There are three different types of competence:

- **behavioural** competences include the ability to relate well to others

- **occupational** competences cover what people have to do to achieve the results in the job

- **generic** competences that apply to anyone, e.g. adaptability, initiative.

They are expressed in visible, behavioural terms and reflect the skills, knowledge and attitude (the main components of any job) which must be demonstrated to an agreed standard and must contribute to the overall aims of the organisation.

The term is open to various interpretations because there are a number of competence-based systems and concepts of competence. As a general definition, a competent individual can perform a work role in a wide range of settings over an extended period of time.

Some competence-based systems are achievement-led – they focus on assessment of competent performance – what people do at work and how well they do it. Others are development-led – they focus on the development of competence and are linked to training and development programmes to develop people to a level of performance expected at work.

Actual training needs may be categorised on the basis of the following competencies:

Work quality:

- technical and task knowledge

- accuracy and consistency

- exercise of judgement and discretion

- communication skills

- cost consciousness.

Work quantity:

- personal planning and time management

- capacity to meet deadlines or work under pressure

- capacity to cope with upward variations in work volume.

Supervisory and managerial skills and competencies:

- planning and organising

- communication and interpersonal skills

- directing, guiding and motivating

- leadership and delegation

- co-ordination and control

- developing and retaining staff

- developing teamwork.

3.2 Process

Competences are defined by means of a competence (or capability, or functional) analysis. This process describes:

- the job's main tasks or key result areas

- the types and levels of knowledge and skill that these require

- the acceptable standard of performance in each task or result area and how performance is assessed.

Installing a competence-based system means:

- establishing the elements of competence – activity, skill or ability required by the job holder to perform the job

- establishing the criteria of performance of the skill or ability required and setting standards to measure it by

- measuring the actual performance against the standard

- taking corrective action where there is any deviation from the standard.

The control element of the system allows feedback to change the elements of competence or the criteria of measurement, in the light of actions taken and feedback given by the job-holder.

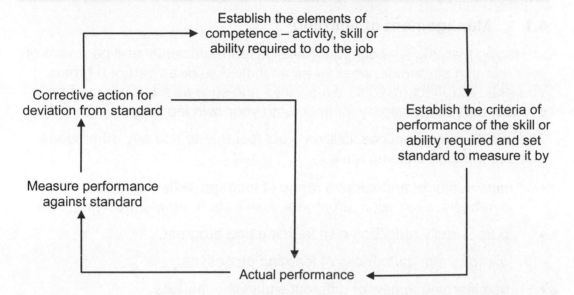

Although it is not a work-based activity, think of the process of passing a driving test. It is an observable skill that is measured against set standards. In the case of failure a list that outlines the failed areas is given to the learner driver and is used to form the basis of any corrective action needed before re-applying for the test.

The Lead Body guidelines for the AAT units that make up your course, are written as statements incorporating:

- elements of competence – specific activities a job holder should be able to perform

- performance criteria – how well it should be performed

- a range statement – in what context and conditions

- the knowledge and understanding that underpins the competence.

Test your understanding 1

After studying this section you should be able to explain the process of competence assessment.

4 Learning to improve your performance

4.1 Management of learning

Managing learning is about your ability to learn efficiently and be aware of your learning strategies, whether as an individual or as part of a group. You need to reflect on your own abilities and style as a learner, and how you can take responsibility for improving your own learning.

These skills represent possibilities – but feel free to use any other ideas and descriptions that you have:

- use, evaluate and adapt a range of learning skills (analysis, synthesis, evaluation, argument, justification, problem-solving, etc)
- purposefully reflect on own learning and progress
- demonstrate awareness of learning processes
- use learning in new or different situations/contexts
- assist/support others in learning and learn from peers
- develop, evaluate and adapt learning strategies
- carry out agreed tasks
- work productively in a co-operative context
- learn through collaboration
- provide constructive feedback to colleagues
- assist/support others in learning
- interact effectively with supervisor/wider group
- develop business awareness
- evaluate own potential for employment.

4.2 Self-management

Self-management is about your personal organisational skills and being able to cope with the demands of managing your work, your studying, your home life and beyond. It might also include addressing your personal values and commitments. You need to ask yourself, whether you:

- manage time effectively
- set realistic objectives, priorities and standards
- listen actively and with purpose

- show intellectual flexibility and creativity

- take responsibility for acting in a professional/ethical manner

- plan/work towards long-term aims and goals

- purposely reflect on own learning and progress

- take responsibility for own learning/personal growth

- demonstrate awareness of learning processes

- clarify personal values

- cope with physical demands/stress

- monitor, evaluate and adapt own performance.

4.3 Communication skills

Communication obviously underpins all aspects of life. At work it will often be oral, but written and visual communication is equally important. How good are you at expressing ideas and opinions, at speaking or writing with confidence and clarity or at presenting yourself to a variety of audiences? You should be able to:

- use appropriate language and form in a range of activities (reports, presentations, interviews, etc)

- present information/ideas competently (oral, written, visual)

- respond to different purposes/contexts/audiences

- persuade rationally by means of appropriate information

- defend/justify views or actions

- take initiative and lead others

- negotiate with individuals/the group

- offer constructive criticism

- listen actively and effectively

- evaluate and adapt strategies for communication

- debate important points rather than argue.

4.4 Team/group work/management of others

Do you fit well into a team? Are you a leader? Have you had wide experience of working with different types of group, whether formal or informal? Have you been on a team development course? Do you work in study groups, project groups or manage meetings for a club or society? Consider your skills of co-operation, delegation or negotiation. How have you worked and learned with others?

The following skills would indicate your group working abilities:

- carry out agreed tasks

- respect the views and values of others

- work productively in a co-operative context

- adapt to the needs of the group/team

- defend/justify views or actions

- take initiative and lead others

- delegate and stand back

- offer constructive criticism

- take the role of chairperson

- learn through collaboration

- negotiate with individuals/the group

- assist/support others in learning from peers

- interact effectively with tutor/wider group

- monitor, evaluate and assess processes of group/team work.

4.5 Problem-solving

Do you like tackling and solving problems? How do you manage your job tasks? Can you identify the main features of a problem and develop strategies for its resolution? Are you able to monitor your performance and improve on strategies? Some subjects may traditionally be perceived as related to problem-solving (say, computing), but, for most of us, in any subject area, assignments such as reports or presentations present us with a variety of problems to be solved.

Problem-solving skills means you need to be able to:

- identify key features of the problem/task

- conceptualise issues **(meaning to think about issues clearly)**

- identify strategic options

- plan and implement a course of action

- organise sub-tasks

- set and maintain priorities

- think laterally about a problem

- apply theory to practical context

- apply knowledge/tools/methods to help solve problems

- manage physical resources (tools/equipment)

- show confidence in responding creatively to problems

- show awareness of issues of health and safety and other regulations

- monitor, evaluate and adapt strategies and outcomes.

5 Methods used to acquire skills and knowledge

5.1 Personal development plan (PDP)
Continuing Professional Development (CPD)

CPD is defined as 'the systematic maintenance enhancement and continuous improvement of knowledge, skills and ability often termed competence, that one needs to work professionally as an accounting technician.'

Your CPD needs are thus expressed in terms of a personal development plan (PDP).

Basically there are four main options you should consider for each of the development needs within your PDP:

- **Education** – this option will most likely lead to a qualification and will provide you with a broad based body of knowledge, which in turn you need to be able to apply in the work place. With the introduction of more flexible delivery methods you can mix and match between taught modules, self-study and open learning and an increasing availability of e-learning facilities.

- **Training** – this option will be most useful when you need to focus on a particular skill or skill set and can be delivered in many ways: in house, off the job, on the job, by instructors or trainers or by self-learning.

- **Development** – this option is a combination of all the other options and should be planned with clear learning goals and measurable outcomes. Ideally the PDP will be aligned with the organisations objectives and your career aspirations.

- **Experience** – we know that there is no substitute for experience, but we also know that many experiences can be painful. Throwing someone in at the deep end may work for some but it is a lot safer if the person doing the throwing knows how deep it is and is on the sideline if difficulties arise.

  Setting stretching goals and objectives and having coaching and mentoring support will provide a really powerful way of growing and developing yourself.

5.2   Training solutions

A training needs analysis addresses the following:

- What skills does my organisation need me to have to perform my current tasks effectively?

- What skills do I need to ensure are maintained?

- What aspects of my work do I enjoy and wish to develop?

- What personal qualities do I need to enhance?

- What training resources are available to me?

- What learning methods suit me best?

- Where do I expect to be in five years' time?

The training plan is constructed from an investigation into training needs and includes the identification of the skills and knowledge required by the labour force, the identification of the skills and knowledge already possessed – the difference between the two providing a picture of the job-centred training needs. This is then incorporated into the organisation's training plan and decisions are taken on priorities, location, duration, timing and content of training.

Training objectives should be specific and related to observable targets that can be measured. They will cover:

- **behaviour** – what you should be able to do

- **standard** – the level of performance

- **environment** – the conditions.

Once the training objectives are identified, the training funds made available and the priorities established in relation to the urgency of the training, the training decisions must be made. These include decisions on the scale and type of training system needed, and whether it can best be provided by the organisation's own staff or by external consultants. Training methods, timing and duration, location and the people actually doing the training also needs to be decided.

Training may be carried out 'in-house' or externally. If any of the training is carried out in-house, decisions will need to be made on such things as:

- training workshops

- location and equipping of classrooms

- selection of training officers.

Colleges, universities, training organisations and management consultants may provide external courses. There are also open and distance learning facilities via the Open University and other programmes.

To make sure that the training needs are being met, separate training and development co-ordinators may be allocated the responsibilities for training within the firm and for any external training. They may also be responsible for reviewing the system on a regular basis to ensure that it is still satisfying those needs.

5.3 Researching training and development methods

Training and development methods vary tremendously depending on the person, the job, the resources, the organisation and the economic environment. You can divide them into on-the-job and off-the-job training methods, structured or unstructured, participatory or self-development, sitting in front of a computer screen or 'sitting with Nellie' (shadowing an experienced staff member).

The methods that you might be looking at include: training courses – both external and in-house, on-the-job training, mentoring, coaching, computerised interactive learning, planned experiences and self-managed learning.

Business games, either in the sophisticated format of the computer based profit-seeking program or as the simple leadership games centred around packs of playing cards, are also effective tools of management development. The list of games available is endless – all involve high participation levels.

5.4 Internal training and development methods

You can research the types of training and development that can take place at work. These include:

- **Job instructions** – are a systematic approach to training for a particular job and are normally used by supervisors when training those who report to them. It can be a cost-effective way of satisfying training needs and can also be linked to a competence-based qualification such as an NVQ, which is supervised by the trainee's immediate superior.

  - Internal training centres are sometimes used to provide customised training programmes e.g. where there would be a risk if the trainee made a mistake.

- **Job rotation** – the training idea of moving an employee from one job to another is that it broadens experience and encourages the employee to be aware of the total activity. It can also help to improve motivation where tasks are repetitive or mundane.

- **Films and closed circuit television** (CCTV) – Films are used to describe company situations, how the different functions of an organisation relate to one another or for presenting an overview of production. CCTV is used increasingly in management training to illustrate how managers behave, and to show how such behaviour can be modified to enable beneficial changes in their interpersonal and problem solving skills.

- **Computer-based training** (CBT) and computer assisted learning (CAL) – user-friendly systems enable trainees to work at their own pace, working on set programmes.

- **Programmed learning** – consists of the presentation of instructional material in small units followed immediately by a list of questions the trainee must answer correctly before progressing to more difficult work.

- **Coaching** – is a specialised form of communication with support being given from the planning stage and continuing during the learning process, with the value of constructive criticism being particularly relevant.

- **Mentoring** – the mentor is expected to guide the new recruit through a development programme and 'socialise' them into the culture of the enterprise. It is a route for bringing on 'high flyers' by allowing them to make mistakes under supervision.

- **Secondments** are temporary transfers to another department or division to gain a deeper understanding or learn more about certain aspects within an organisation.

- **Work shadowing** is a method where one employee shadows another, often more senior, to experience what it is like working at that level.

 Test your understanding 2

What type of training is most suitable for the following people?

- Senior lecturer in a university

- The son of the managing director taking over his father's business in the family firm

- New recruit into the payroll section of the account department

- Bank clerk needing to brush up on selling techniques.

5.5 Internal training and development methods for groups

Group training encourages participants to learn from each other through discussing issues, pooling experiences and critically examining opposite viewpoints. Instructors guide discussions rather than impart knowledge directly. They monitor trainee's understanding of what is going on, ask questions to clarify points and sometimes, but not always, prevent certain members from dominating the group. Some of the most popular methods follow:

1 **The lecture method** – is an economical way of passing information to many people. Lectures are of little value if the aim of training is to change attitudes, or develop job or interpersonal skills.

2 **Discussion methods** – are known ways of securing interest and commitment. They can shape attitudes, encourage motivation and secure understanding and can also underline the difficulties of group problem solving.

3 **Case study method** – learning occurs through participation in the definition, analysis and solution of the problem or problems. It demonstrates the nature of group problem solving activity and usually underlines the view that there is no one best solution to a complex business problem.

4 **Role playing** – This method requires trainees to project themselves into a simulated situation that is intended to represent some relevant reality, say, a confrontation between management and a trade union. The merit of role-playing is that it influences attitudes, develops interpersonal skills and heightens sensitivity to the views and feelings of others.

5 **Business games** – simulate realistic situations, mergers, take-overs, etc in which groups compete with one another and where the effects of the decision taken by one group may affect others.

6 **T-group exercises** (the T stands for training) leave the group to their own devices. The trainer simply tells them to look after themselves and remains as an observer. The group itself have to decide what to do and, understandably, the members feel helpless at first and then they pool their experiences and help each other. They eventually form a cohesive group, appoint a leader and resolve any conflicts within the group. They exercise interpersonal communication skills and learn to understand group dynamics.

5.6   Self development

Self-development is taking personal responsibility for your own learning. This is an ongoing process that takes place wherever you are and that will continue throughout your life.

A very rich ground for learning, however, is in the workplace. You can have significant learning experiences by doing, being thrown in at the deep end, undertaking challenging new projects and even making mistakes! You can:

- learn ways to improve what you do now

- learn new skills to meet the changing needs of your employer or prepare to move on to a new job.

Effective self-development means you need to focus on the following:

- Assess your current skills and interest through paper-and-pencil career tests or through computer programs that analyse skills and interests.

- Maintain a learning log or diary to help you analyse what you are learning from work experiences.

- Develop a personal development plan that identifies your learning needs and goals.

- Consciously seek out learning opportunities to meet your goals e.g. by watching colleagues and asking relevant questions.

- Actively seek feedback on performance/abilities/actions.

- Find a mentor who can provide you with support, advice, and assistance in your career direction.

- Become involved in professional organisations.

- Be opportunistic – look for learning opportunities outside of formal activities e.g. home, social, voluntary, etc.

- Read books, professional journals and trade magazines to keep current on the latest developments in your field.

- Use the Internet to browse for interesting sites and different views on subjects that interest you.

 KAPLAN PUBLISHING

6 Review and evaluate your performance and progress

6.1 Assessment

In all organisations someone assesses the performance of each employee. Often this is a casual, subjective and infrequent activity where the manager or supervisor spontaneously mentions that a piece of work was done poorly or well. The subordinate then responds in an appropriate manner. It encourages desirable performance and discourages undesirable performance before it becomes ingrained. But increasingly, many organisations (particularly larger ones) have decided to formalise the assessment process and use it to improve performance, assess training needs and predict the potential of employees.

If you are studying for the AAT qualification you are assessed on your standards of competence; the focus being on what you have achieved – can you do what is being assessed?

There are only three possible outcomes of an assessment:

- pass
- not yet competent
- insufficient evidence upon which to make a judgement.

For work based assessment the majority of the assessment is done at work and when the student is ready for it. Assessment methods at an NVQ level 3 may be practical, written and oral:

- **practical** – from observing performance within an organisation or department
- **written** – from examining entries in log books
- **oral** – from assessment of oral presentations or observation of leading discussions.

This method of assessment allows you to gain the level of competence required for your jobs in stages. The successful completion of a unit is recorded in the National Record of Achievement.

6.2 Appraisal

Performance appraisal is a formal procedure to ensure that employees receive objective feedback on their performance, in the context of organisational goals and enabling them to improve themselves. It is often used:

- to audit an employee's competences

- to identify potential, agree targets and to review achievements

- to communicate and align plans and priorities, both personal and those of the organisation

- to identify training and development needs and monitor career progression

- to exchange feedback and motivate an employee

- A modern approach to setting goals and objectives for an employee is the application of SMART technique.

  The acronym SMART relates to the characteristics of sound objectives in that they should be:

Specific

Measurable

Achievable

Relevant

Timely

When agreeing objectives set by your manager ensure that they meet all the elements listed above.

6.3 Techniques of appraisal

Appraisal techniques include the following:

- **Employee ranking** – Employees are ranked on the basis of their overall performance. This method is particularly prone to bias and manipulation, and its feedback value is practically zero. It does, however, have the advantage that it is simple to use.

- **Rating scales** – Graphic rating scales consist of general personal characteristics and personality traits such as quantity of work, initiative, co-operation and judgement. The judges rate the employee on a scale whose ratings vary, for example from low to high or from poor to excellent. It is called 'graphic' because the scale visually graphs performance from one extreme to the other.

- **Description/Report** – This is a qualitative method of assessment where the manager writes a brief description of the employee under a number of headings.

6.4   Self-appraisal

Self-appraisal is assessing your own capabilities and personal characteristics. Occupational Standards and Key/Core Skills provide a framework and language to describe them.

It is a vital component in managing your own professional development and will help you:

- plan and manage your career

- improve your job performance, by being able to understand your own capabilities and shortfalls

- improve your capacity to learn

- increase your self confidence and present yourself more effectively

- identify and take advantage of job and learning opportunities

- obtain support from mentors and managers

- manage and provide support to others.

With a realistic self-appraisal you are more likely to be loyal to a supportive environment and committed to improving your own and colleagues' performance. It will enable you to develop yourself to your full potential, reliably managing your work and career. You are also more likely to make use of your training, development and experience as lifelong learning and provide good role models to others.

Steps to self-appraisal:

1   **Clarify personal aims** – focus on your objectives – how much is your self-appraisal for: improved work performance, enhanced career development or personal growth? Record your aims.

2   **Manage the appraisal** – find sources of help. Use the professional guidelines to identify relevant standards and key/core skills. Gather insights from others inside and outside the organisation according to personal circumstances. Record the results.

3   **Review personal experience** – look at your CV, performance appraisal records, portfolios of evidence and significant events. Assess values, interests, competences, motivation and contacts. Know yourself.

4   **Assess your own competencies** – assess yourself against occupational standards and key/core skills. Identify strengths, weaknesses, opportunities and threats. Analyse your job. Use diagnostic tools. Identify your priority competences in terms of relative importance of career competence needs and ease of access/opportunities for achieving.

5   **Assess what helps and hinders your development** – identify your learning style and forces for/against personal change.

6   **Review self-appraisal process** – identify the benefits. Record the results and improve the process.

Test your understanding 3

Draw up your own SWOT analysis using the following type of cruciform diagram.

Strengths	Weaknesses
Opportunities	Threats

Test your understanding 4

Why are staff appraisals important?

Test your understanding 5

You work in the bought ledger department of a large company – Global Supplies Ltd. The purchasing manager is due to meet a potential new supplier of product PF123. In preparation for the meeting you have been asked to provide an analysis of Global Supplies' purchases of this product over the last few months, showing the unit price charged by two different suppliers the company has used in the past.

(i)   What sources of information would you be likely to access to fulfil this request?

(ii)   The meeting is scheduled for 4pm this Friday coming. It is now 5pm on Wednesday and you have not been able to begin assembling the information because you have had to cover for a colleague who is off sick. You begin to doubt whether you will be able to produce the information on time. What action should you take?

7   Summary

This chapter has looked at ways of improving your own performance at work. Now that you have studied this chapter you should be able to identify your development needs and research appropriate ways of acquiring skills and knowledge.

Training and development need to be reviewed from time to time, just as any other procedures. Some organisations have continuous assessment of training in general; others will have annual appraisals to monitor performance and review achievements.

Test your understanding answers

 Test your understanding 1

Your explanation should include the fact that it is a way of measuring what people do at work and how well they do it.

After analysing a job, there should be a statement drawn up by the supervisor or manager establishing both the specific activities a jobholder should be able to perform and the performance criteria detailing how well it should be performed.

The assessment is predominantly by observation – the jobholder demonstrating how well he or she performs the activity. Feedback is given and assistance with corrective actions required where the performance does not match the standard set.

 Test your understanding 2

The type of training that is most suitable:

- Secondment might be considered for a senior lecturer in a university.

- Mentoring or coaching could be the best solution for the son of the managing director taking over his father's business in the family firm.

- Job instructions might be the quickest way to get the new recruit up to scratch on the payroll system.

- Programmed learning or computer-based training could give the bank clerk the ability to brush up on selling techniques.

 Test your understanding 3

There is no printed answer for this question.

Test your understanding 4

The appraisal is important in staff counselling and development. This would involve such matters as:

- Feedback on performance and problems encountered – they establish an individual's current level of performance and identify strengths and weaknesses.

- Career development – they identify training and development needs.

- Identifying job interests and likely development areas – they can motivate individuals.

- Defining performance targets – they provide a basis for rewarding staff in relation to their contribution to organisational goals.

- Reviewing promotion potential – they assess potential and provide information for succession planning.

- Enabling individuals to appreciate where their jobs fit in the overall company scheme.

 Test your understanding 5

(i)   Possible sources of information include:

    (a)   the bought ledger accounts of the two current suppliers

    (b)   invoices from the two current suppliers

    (c)   costing records showing purchasing costs over the last six months.

(ii)   You should immediately contact the purchasing manager and explain the problem. It may be possible to take action to salvage the meeting by asking for help from someone who has not such a heavy workload. Alternatively, the meeting may be postponed.

Ethics and sustainability

7

Introduction

You should be able to identify, explain and apply in business situations, the fundamental ethical principles. In addition you should be able to identify potential conflicts of interest and the requirement, in particular, to maintain confidentiality.

You should also be able to explain sustainability, and consider the types of policies and procedures that could be adopted by business in order to support sustainability.

ASSESSMENT CRITERIA	CONTENTS
4.1 Demonstrate an understanding of corporate social responsibility (CSR)	1 Ethics – The principles
4.2 Identify how finance staff can support ethical business practices	2 Threats to principles (conflicts of interest)
4.3 Establish the features and benefits of sustainable business practices	3 Sustainability and corporate social responsibility (CSR)

1 Ethics – The principles

In the UK we have a principles-based approach rather than a rules-based approach.

1.1 Why?

If people are provided with a set of rules to follow they will apply them but may try to find loopholes, e.g. if the rules state that gifts of over £5 cannot be accepted as it may be regarded as a bribe, then 10 gifts of £4.50 may be given instead of one gift of £45, in order to get around the rule.

Alternatively, if you establish a principle not to accept gifts that may be regarded as a bribe then people should comply with the principle. They cannot simply state that they accepted a gift of £45 simply because 'it was within the rules'. Judgement therefore needs to be exercised before a gift of any value is accepted.

The idea behind a principles-based approach is that people should not be given a set of rules, but rather they should learn to behave properly and do the right thing.

The fundamental ethical principles you need to learn and understand are as follows:

- confidentiality
- objectivity
- professional competence and due care
- integrity
- professional behaviour.

1.2 Confidentiality

You should, in accordance with the law, respect the confidentiality of information acquired as a result of professional and business relationships, and not disclose any such information to third parties without proper and specific authority, unless there is a legal or professional right or duty to disclose.

Confidential information acquired as a result of professional and business relationships should not be used for the personal advantage of you or any third parties.

In your working life you are likely to deal with a broad range of information which should remain confidential between you and those to whom the information belongs or from whom it originates. Put simply, you must ensure that you do not share any privileged information with anyone who does not have the right to receive or know such information.

This includes, but is not limited to, details of contracts, sales and purchases transactions with customers and suppliers as well as any details pertaining to employees, such as personal addresses and telephone numbers, salary or contract agreements.

The need to maintain confidentiality and protect the details of those who have dealings with your company is enshrined within the law via the Data Protection Act.

As such failure to maintain confidentiality could lead to the possibility of prosecution and fines for any organisation that has breached the requirements of the Act.

1.3 Objectivity

You should not allow bias, conflict of interest or undue influence of others to override your professional or business judgements. For example, any work you undertake should be fairly stated and presented, so that it can be relied upon by others.

1.4 Professional competence and due care

You have a professional duty to maintain professional knowledge and skill at a level required to ensure that you are able to provide a competent service based on current developments in practice, legislation and techniques. For example, you shod have technical competence for the work that you undertake. This may be obtained from a combination of passing relevant examinations, having practical experience, or working under the supervision of another to gain experience.

You should act diligently and in accordance with applicable technical and professional standards. This means that you should not be negligent or careless in the performance of your work. If necessary, you should seek guidance from an appropriate colleague or supervisor to ensure that you are dealing with things appropriately.

1.5 Integrity

You should be straightforward and honest in the performance of your work duties and responsibilities.

1.6 Professional behaviour

You should comply with relevant laws and regulations and avoid any action that could bring you or your profession into disrepute. You should behave in a manner that would be expected from a professional person carrying out their work duties and responsibilities.

2 Threats to principles (conflicts of interest)

2.1 Why?

There can be a number of threats that may affect how easy it is to adhere to the ethical principles. In particular, the principle of objectivity is subject to several threats, any one of which has the capacity to create a conflict of interest for you.

Self interest – A threat to objectivity may derive from a financial or other self-interest conflict. This could arise, for example, from a direct or indirect interest in a customer, supplier or client, or from fear of having your employment terminated as a consequence of undue commercial pressure from within or outside of the organisation.

Self review – There may be a threat to objectivity if any product or judgement of the member or the organisation needs to be reconsidered at some later date. This may arise, for example, if you have been asked to recheck information you have already prepared. You should not try to hide or disguise the fact that you may have made an error previously.

Advocacy – There is a threat to objectivity if you were to become an advocate for or against the position taken by the client or employer in any adversarial proceedings or situation. The degree to which this presents a threat to objectivity will depend on the individual circumstances. For example, if you are asked to explain why there is a difference between a suppliers' statement of account and the balance on the purchase ledger account. You should provide all relevant information, not just some of it. The presentation of only one side of the case may be compatible with objectivity provided that it there is full, accurate and truthful explanation.

Familiarity – A threat that you may become influenced by any one of a number of factors, such as:

- prior knowledge of the issue, so that you do not retain objectivity

- any relationship with your customer, supplier or employer, including personal relationships with individuals

- undue reliance upon the judgement of ethical standards of a customer, supplier, client or colleague to the extent that you become too trusting.

Intimidation – The possibility that you may become intimidated by threat, by a dominating personality or by other pressures, actual or feared, applied by the customer, supplier, client, colleague, employer or other third party. This could lead to you behaving in a manner that was not in the best interests of your employer or client. For example, a supplier may threated not to supply your organisation with further goods unless they are allowed discount to which they are not entitled based upon agreed terms of business between you. In the worst case scenario it could lead to you breaking the law.

If you considered that you were in a position where a conflict of interest could arise, it is important that you communicate this to a supervisor or manager in your organisation at the earliest opportunity. This will enable others to take appropriate action to avoid or minimise any potential problem.

If a conflict of interest has already arisen it is important that you take the same action, i.e. report the matter to the most appropriate person within your organisation immediately.

You may also be able to minimise the potential for conflict of interest by, for example, immediately referring friends or family to a work colleague if they approach you for assistance – this would mean that you would not be involved in any way with any transactions or activities they entered into with your organisation.

Test your understanding 1

Review each of the practical situations below, and match each situation with the ethical principle from the drop-down menu below relates to it. You may use an ethical principle more than once.

	Practical situation	Ethical principle
1	A family member has advised you that they will purchase goods from the organisation you work for only if you obtain a discounted price for them. You are unsure whether or not to try to arrange this.	
2	You have been asked by your manager to calculate depreciation on motor vehicles for the year, and then to reduce the calculated amount by 10% to reduce the expense and increase profit for the year.	
3	Your supervisor has asked that you resolve any payroll queries from other employees that arise during the week ahead in the absence of the payroll clerk. Whilst you are willing to help, you have no experience of dealing with accounting for payroll or dealing with payroll queries from other employees.	
4	A friend has asked you to disclose salary details of a mutual friend who also works with you as they believe the friend is living beyond their means and wants to try to help them if possible.	
5	A work colleague arrived late on the first day of a course and didn't bother to apologise to the course leader, and nor did they engage in the course activities during the day, explaining to you, "It's not really important and it's better than being in work for the day".	

KAPLAN PUBLISHING

| 6 | You are reconciling the sales ledger control account balance with the total of the sales ledger account balances as at 30 June 20X5 and are having problems agreeing the totals. You have experience of preparing this reconciliation on numerous occasions, and any previous problems have related to discount allowed not being included in the relevant sales ledger accounts. As it is nearly the end of the working day, and your manager needs the completed reconciliation before you finish work, you intend to pass the reconciliation to your manager which includes the statement "reconciliation complete, except for inclusion of discount allowed in sales ledger accounts," without actually confirming that is that case. | |

Drop-down menu choices:

- Competence and due care
- Integrity
- Professional behaviour
- Objectivity
- Confidentiality

3 Sustainability and corporate social responsibility (CSR)

Sustainability is about meeting the needs of the present without compromising the ability of future generations to meet their own needs.

It is the practice of doing business in a way that balances economic, environmental and social needs, and as such is often referred to as **'The Three P's' – People, Planet, Profit**.

Corporate social responsibility (CSR) is a business approach that contributes to sustainable development by delivering economic, social and environmental benefits for all stakeholders.

As a result many companies now consider how their operations affect the environment and future generations.

Ways in which this may be manifested include:

- introduction of a paper recycling policy within an office building

- adoption of 'paperless' office procedures

- reduction of business-related travel, perhaps by use of 'virtual' meetings, via Skype or other telecommunication tools

- introduction of schemes to encourage employees to use public transport, cycle or even walk to work – such as a 'bike to work' scheme whereby a bicycle can be hired or purchased from the company at a low rate and space is provided for it to be kept at work during the day

- introduction of energy saving schemes – whereby lights and heating are turned off when not required

- choosing to deal only with suppliers that have similar CSR values.

This list is not exhaustive and you may well be able to think of other methods by which firms can operate in a more sustainable way.

Sustainability may well have a cost at the outset of implementing CSR policies, and indeed it was originally considered to represent an additional cost to a business. This may explain why some organisations choose not to adopt CSR policies.

However, over time, and as the values of society itself have changed, many organisations recognise that they can reap benefits by following a sustainable path. This includes the recognition, by customers and potential customers, of the stance they are taking in trying to 'do the right thing'. This is now acknowledged by many to be a key driver to increase sales and business activity over time.

For instance an organisation may decide to use only recyclable packaging from now on. There will clearly be a cost to the organisation to source new packaging supplies and, perhaps, paying more for their packaging. However, this should be offset by the positive effect their actions will have on the environment, and the resulting improved image that they can project to their customers and potential customers, who may well switch from a competitor.

Test your understanding 2

Review each of the practical situations below, and match each situation with the corporate social responsibility (CSR) objective of an organisation from the drop-down menu below relates to it. You may use a CSR objective more than once.

	Practical situation	CSR objective
1	An organisation has a policy of recruiting new employees from within a fifteen-mile radius of its location.	
2	An organisation has a policy of ensuring that all employees attend one personal development training course each year.	
3	An organisation has recently installed solar panels to the factory roof to generate energy that can be used in the production process.	
4	Employees are permitted two days leave of absence each year to volunteer their time for a charitable good cause.	

Drop-down menu choices:

- Ethical employment practices
- Environmentally-friendly policies
- The local community

 4 Summary

In this chapter we have seen the importance of maintaining confidentiality of information, behaving professionally within the finance function, acting with honesty and ensuring we have up to date professional knowledge to perform our job role.

The importance of corporate social responsibility in the workplace has also been reviewed and ensuring that we balance the three pillars of sustainability.

Test your understanding answers

Test your understanding 1

	Practical situation	Ethical principle
1	A family member has advised you that they will purchase goods from the organisation you work for only if you obtain a discounted price for them. You are unsure whether or not to try to arrange this.	Objectivity
2	You have been asked by your manager to calculate depreciation on motor vehicles for the year, and then to reduce the calculated amount by 10% to reduce the expense and increase profit for the year.	Integrity
3	Your supervisor has asked that you resolve any payroll queries from other employees that arise during the week ahead in the absence of the payroll clerk. Whilst you are willing to help, you have no experience of dealing with accounting for payroll or dealing with payroll queries from other employees.	Competence and due care – specifically competence
4	A friend has asked you to disclose salary details of a mutual friend who also works with you as they believe the friend is living beyond their means and wants to try to help them if possible.	Confidentiality
5	A work colleague arrived late on the first day of a course and didn't bother to apologise to the course leader, and nor did they engage in the course activities during the day, explaining to you, "It's not really important and it's better than being in work for the day".	Professional behaviour

6	You are reconciling the sales ledger control account balance with the total of the sales ledger account balances as at 30 June 20X5 and are having problems agreeing the totals. You have experience of preparing this reconciliation on numerous occasions, and any previous problems have related to discount allowed not being included in the relevant sales ledger accounts. As it is nearly the end of the working day, and your manager needs the completed reconciliation before you finish work, you intend to pass the reconciliation to your manager which includes the statement "reconciliation complete, except for inclusion of discount allowed in sales ledger accounts," without actually confirming that is that case.	Competence and due care – specifically due care

Test your understanding 2

	Practical situation	CSR objective
1	An organisation has a policy of recruiting new employees from within a fifteen-mile radius of its location.	The local community
2	An organisation has a policy of ensuring that all employees attend one personal development training course each year.	Ethical employment practices
3	An organisation has recently installed solar panels to the factory roof to generate energy that can be used in the production process.	Environmentally-friendly practices
4	Employees are permitted two days leave of absence each year to volunteer their time for a charitable good cause.	The local community

Question Bank

Introduction

The Test your understanding questions in this chapter are arranged in Assessment Objective (AO) order. Each Test your understanding consists of more than one requirement, including some written requirements, to prepare you for the synoptic assessment. Note that each Test your understanding is longer than you would expect to encounter in the real synoptic assessment, but should help you to 'see the bigger picture' of how different activities contribute to the recording and reconciliation of transactions. It is also important to be aware that individual activities from different parts of the synoptic assessment syllabus may be combined within any task in the synoptic assessment.

AO1 Demonstrate an understanding of the finance function and the roles and procedures carried out by members of an accounting team

Based upon the specimen assessment, AO1 was assessed by parts of Task 1 and 5, and all of Task 2.

Test your understanding 1 and 2 deal with elements of AO1 to demonstrate an understanding of the finance function and the roles and procedures carried out by members of an accounting team.

 Test your understanding 1

You have been asked by the head of the finance department to help a new trainee accountant to settle in to their new job. They are due to join the department next month.

Required:

(a) In preparation for their first day as a member of the department, list the practical issues relevant to your department that the new trainee should be made aware of when you have a meeting with them for one hour.

Note that the new trainee will be attending a separate induction course organised by the human resources department, so your answer should focus upon practical issues relating to your department.

(b) You have also been asked to prepare a brief memorandum for the new trainee to list the practical skills and competences that the new trainee could expect to develop over a period of time.

Test your understanding 2

You have been nominated as a representative of the finance function to join a team with responsibility to improve communication and understanding throughout the organisation. As an initial task, each team member has been asked to identify the role of the department or function they represent.

Required:

Explain the role of a typical finance function and identify its key responsibilities.

Test your understanding 3 and 4 deal with elements of AO1 to understand corporate social responsibility, ethics and sustainability within organisations which is based upon Work Effectively in Finance LO4. It does require some practical thought and application, rather than restatement of rote learning.

 Test your understanding 3

Gymco Ltd is trying to adopt positive corporate social responsibility (CSR) policies and uphold good ethical principles in all that it does.

Required:

(a) Review each of Gymco Ltd's situations and suggest how it could improve its corporate social responsibility (CSR).

	Practical situation	CSR policy
1	Gymco Ltd currently has a café in each of its leisure centres. Currently, it leaves the choice of food and drink available in the cafe to the local centre manager.	
2	Gymco Ltd does not currently monitor the fitness programmes used by its personal trainers with members on a 'one-to-one' basis. There is no way of knowing whether any individual session is safe or effective.	

3	Gymco Ltd currently charges a standard annual membership fee for each individual, irrespective of their personal circumstances.	
4	Gymco Ltd currently makes paper hand towels available in its wash rooms and food preparation areas.	

(b) Review each of the practical situations below and, for each situation, identify the ethical principle that appears to have been breached or compromised by either Gymco Ltd or its employees.

	Practical situation	**Ethical principle**
1	Some personal trainers sell health supplements to gym members without approval from Gymco Ltd.	
2	Some of the personal trainers have stopped using their regulation trainer uniform and occasionally cancel sessions at short notice without apparently having a good reason to do so.	
3	The receptionist at one leisure centre regularly admits friends who are not members so that they can use the facilities free of charge.	
4	Gymco Ltd puts pressure on personal trainers to recruit new members by withholding part of their salary if they do not recruit at least two new members each month.	

KAPLAN PUBLISHING

5	One leisure centre manager has provided the list of members' names and addresses to a local call centre so that they can contact people about car insurance. He did not accept any payment or gift in exchange for this information.	
6	Some personal trainers do not insist on members doing proper 'warm-up' and 'warm-down' activities at the start and end of a fitness session.	

 Test your understanding 4

Goodco Ltd is trying to adopt positive corporate social responsibility (CSR) policies and uphold good ethical principles in all that it does.

Required:

(a) Review each of the practical situations below, and match each situation with the appropriate corporate social responsibility (CSR) objective of Goodco Ltd from the drop-down menu. You may use a CSR objective more than once.

	Practical situation	**CSR objective**
1	Goodco Ltd is considering introducing a policy of paying its employees at least 5% more than the legal minimum wage.	
2	Goodco Ltd may introduce a policy of donating surplus paper and card to a local nursery for use in its activities.	
3	Goodco Ltd may purchase delivery vehicles that are powered by electricity, rather than petrol or diesel.	
4	Goodco Ltd may permit its office staff to work from home one day per week.	

Drop-down menu choices:

- Environmentally-friendly policies
- The local community
- Ethical employment practices

(b) State the procedures that Goodco Ltd could introduce to ensure confidentiality of data.

AO2 Process transactions, complete calculations and make journal entries

Based upon the specimen assessment, AO2 was assessed by parts of Tasks 1 and 4, and all of Task 3.

This Test your understanding deals with elements of AO2 to process supplier transactions by coding each item and recording them in the daybook, before moving on to prepare a summary of day book totals for posting into the general ledger.

Test your understanding 5

Nethan Builders code all purchase invoices and credit notes with a supplier code and a general ledger code. Extracts of the codes used are as follows:

Supplier	Supplier Account Code
Haddow Bros	HAD29
AJ Broom & Company Ltd	AJB14
Jenson Ltd	JEN32
JM Bond & Co	JMB33

Item	General Ledger Code
Softwood	GL110
Hardwood	GL112
Sand	GL130
Steel	GL140
Brick	GL145

Below are the purchases invoices received by Nethan Builders on 22 April 20X1.

SALES INVOICE

Haddow Bros

Invoice to:
Nethan Builders
Brecon House
Stamford Road
Manchester
M16 4PL

Deliver to:
As above

The White House, Standing Way, Manchester
M13 6FH
Tel: 0161 560 3140
Fax: 0161 560 5140

Invoice no: 033912
Tax point: 22 April 20X1
VAT reg no: 460 3559 71
Purchase order no:: 7166

Code	Description	Quantity	VAT rate %	Unit price £	Amount excl of VAT £
PLY8FE1	Plywood Hardwood 2440 × 1220 mm	12 sheets	20	17.80	213.60
					213.60
VAT at 20%					42.72
Total amount payable					256.32

Deduct discount of 2% if paid within 10 days

SALES INVOICE

Invoice to:
Nethan Builders
Brecon House
Stamford Road
Manchester
M16 4PL

Deliver to:
As above

Jenson Ltd

30 Longfield Park, Kingsway, M45 2TP

Invoice no:	47792
Tax point:	22 April 20X1
VAT reg no:	641 3229 45
Purchase order no::	7162

Code	Description	Quantity	VAT rate %	Unit price £	Amount excl of VAT £
PL432115	Steel rods 32 × 115 mm	14	20	30.25	423.50
PL432140	Steel rods 32 × 138 mm	8	20	33.15	265.20

	688.70
Trade discount 15%	103.30
	585.40
VAT at 20%	117.08
Total amount payable	702.48

Deduct discount of 3% if paid within 14 days

SALES INVOICE

Invoice to:
Nethan Builders
Brecon House
Stamford Road
Manchester
M16 4PL

Deliver to:
As above

A J Broom & Company Limited

59 Parkway, Manchester, M2 6EG
Tel: 0161 560 3392
Fax: 0161 560 5322

Invoice no:	046123
Tax point:	22 April 20X1
VAT reg no:	661 2359 07
Purchase order no:	7164

Code	Description	Quantity	VAT rate %	Unit price £	Amount excl of VAT £
DGS472	SDG Softwood	9.6 m	20	8.44	81.02
CIBF653	BIC Softwood	7	20	12.30	86.10

	167.12
Trade discount 10%	16.71
	150.41
VAT at 20%	30.08
Total amount payable	180.49

CREDIT NOTE
J M Bond & Co

Credit note to:
Nethan Builders
Brecon House
Stamford Road
Manchester
M16 4PL

North Park Industrial Estate, Manchester, M12 4TU
Tel: 0161 561 3214
Fax: 0161 561 3060

Credit note no: 06192
Tax point: 22 April 20X1
VAT no: 461 4367 91
Invoice no: 331624

Code	Description	Quantity	VAT rate %	Unit price £	Amount excl of VAT £
DGSS4163	Structural softwood untreated	6m	20	6.85	41.10

	41.10
Trade discount 20%	8.22
	32.88
VAT at 20%	6.57
Total amount of credit	39.45

Required:

(a)   For each invoice and credit note shown above select the appropriate supplier account code and general ledger code to be used for each item and include it in the summary grid below.

Invoice from:	Supplier account code	General ledger code
Haddow Bros		
Jenson Ltd		
AJ Broom & Company Ltd		
JM Bond & Co		

(b) Complete the recording of each invoice or credit note in the purchases day book, and total the columns in the purchases day book. You should include any credit notes as negative amounts.

PURCHASES DAY BOOK

Date 20X1	Supplier	A/C Ref	Inv No.	Total £	VAT £	GL110 £	GL112 £	GL140 £
22/4	Haddow							
22/4	Jenson Ltd							
22/4	AJ Broom							
22/4	JM Bond							
			TOTALS					

(c) Complete the posting summary to record the accounting entries in the general ledger from the purchases day book totals.

POSTING SUMMARY – 22 April 20X1

	Debit/ Credit	Total £	VAT £	GL110 £	GL112 £	GL140 £
General Ledger title						
Purch – Softwood						
Purch – Hardwood						
Purch – Steel						
Purch – Sand						
Purch – Brick						
VAT						
Purchase ledger control account						

(d) If Nethan Builders took advantage of the discount offered by Jenson Ltd of 3% for payment within 14 days, state the date by when payment must be received by Jenson Ltd and the amount of that payment.

Payment must be received by Jenson Ltd:

The amount of the payment:

(e) Use the drop-down menu below choose the ledger accounts required to record the prompt payment discount on the sales invoice issued by Jenson Ltd in the general ledger of Nethan Builders and complete the accounting entries required.

Account name	Amount £	Dr ✓	Cr ✓

Drop-down menu choices:

- Purchase ledger control account
- Discount received
- VAT
- Discount allowed
- Purchases

Test your understanding 6 deals with elements of AO2 to prepare a sales invoice and record the invoice in an analysed sales day book, before moving on to prepare a summary of day book totals for posting into the general ledger. Although this Test your understanding may be larger than you may face in the synoptic assessment, it is a good learning exercise and revisits content from earlier units.

Test your understanding 6

You are an accounts assistant for Smith Shirts. You are required to prepare a sales invoice to be sent to a customer, Clobber. You have been provided with the delivery note and an extract of Smith Shirts' price list.

Delivery note: 165

To: Clobber
10 Main Street
Prestwick
South Ayrshire
KA9 4BB

Smith Shirts

**4 Booth Road
Newton Mearns
G2 1PW
Tel: 0141 333 989
Email: admin@smithshirts.co.uk**

Delivery date: 20 September 20X6

Quantity	Code	DESCRIPTION	Colour
20	POL01	Polo shirt	Assorted
12	TAR04	Tartan shirt	Green
20	STR09	Stripe shirt	Red/white

Received by: ....

Signature: .... Date: ....

Extract of price list:

Code	Shirt description	Colour	Unit price £	VAT rate
POL01	Polo shirt	Assorted	20.00	Standard
TAR04	Tartan shirt	Green	12.50	Standard
STR09	Stripe shirt	Red/white	30.00	Standard

The customer file shows that Clobber's account number is CL02 and that no trade discount is offered to this customer.

The last invoice number used was 1586.

Today's date is 22 September 20X6.

Required:

(a)   Complete the sales invoice below.

SALES INVOICE

Invoice to: **Smith Shirts**
Clobber   **4 Booth Road**
10 Main Street   **Newton Mearns**
Prestwick   **G2 1PW**
South Ayrshire   **Tel: 0141 333 989**
KA9 4BB   **Email: admin@smithshirts.co.uk**

Deliver to:

As above

Invoice no:
Tax point:
VAT reg no: 488 7922 26
Delivery note no:
Account no:

Code	Shirt description	Quantity	VAT rate	Unit price	Total
			%	£	£
			20		
			20		
			20		

Net amount of goods	
Trade discount @	
Net amount of goods after discount	
VAT	
Total amount payable	

(b) Complete the recording of the invoice in the sales day book, and total the columns in the sales day book.

SALES DAY BOOK

Date 20X6	Customer	Ref No	Inv No.	Total £	VAT £	POL 01 £	TAR 04 £	STR 09 £
20/9	Myshirt	MYS06	1584	316.32	52.72		263.60	
21/9	Joeshirtz	JOE32	1585	738.48	123.08			615.40
21/9	Shirtu	SHI14	1586	180.48	30.08	150.40		
			TOTAL					

(c) Complete the posting summary to record the accounting entries in the general ledger from the sales day book totals.

POSTING SUMMARY – 22 September 20X6

	Debit/ Credit	Total £	VAT £	POL01 £	TAR04 £	STR09 £
General Ledger title						
Sales – Polo						
Sales – Tartan						
Sales – Stripe						
VAT						
Sales ledger control account						

(d) If Clobber was offered a prompt payment discount of 5% in exchange for payment received by Smith Shirts within seven days of the invoice date, state the date by which Smith Shirts should receive payment and the amount of that payment.

Payment must be received by

Amount of payment

(e) State the accounting entries required to account for the prompt payment discount in the general ledger of Smith Shirts.

Account name	Amount £	Dr ✓	Cr ✓

Test your understanding 7 deals with elements of AO2 to process transactions, complete calculations and make journal entries. Specifically, Test your understanding 7 requires you to prepare sales transactions and record the transactions in the books of prime entry, before moving on to record transactions in the cash receipts book and recording discount on a transaction. The final part of Test your understanding 7 requires you to update the general ledger and the sales ledger accounts.

Test your understanding 7

Ellis Electricals makes the following credit sales on 17 June to A and B giving a 20% trade discount plus a 5% prompt payment discount if customers pay their invoices within 5 days.

	Customer A £	Customer B £
Sales value	1,000	4,000
Trade discount (20%)	200	800
Net sales value	800	3,200
VAT		
Customer A: (800 × 20%)	160	
Customer B: (3,200 × 20%)		640
Total invoice value	960	3,840

On the same day Ellis Electricals also makes a cash sale to C for £300 plus VAT at 20%.

Prompt payment discount is only deducted upon the receivable making payment within the discount period.

Customer A paid his invoice in full within 5 days and takes the prompt payment discount. Customer B paid £2,000 on account.

Required:

Write up the sales day book (SDB), the cash receipts book (CRB) and the discounts allowed book (DAB) and post the entries to the general and sales ledgers. Finally, confirm that the total of the sales ledger control account agrees with the total of sales ledger balances.

Write up the sales day book.

SALES DAY BOOK				
Date June	Customer	Total £	VAT £	Sales £
	A			
	B			
	Total			

Write up the cash receipts book and the discounts allowed book.

CASH RECEIPTS BOOK					
Date June	Customer	Total £	VAT £	SLCA £	Cash sales
	A (W1)				
	B				
	C				
	Total				

DISCOUNTS ALLOWED BOOK				
Date June	Customer	Total £	VAT £	Net £
	A (W1)			
	Total			

(W1) Calculation of cash received from customer

Cash paid by A:

	£
Sale value net of VAT	
Less: prompt payment discount	
	_____
VAT	
	_____
	_____

The prompt payment discount is:

Net

VAT

Gross

Post the totals to the general ledger and calculate the balance carried down (c/d) on each account. For this example, use the source of the data (e.g. daybook references) as the cross-reference.

Sales		VAT	
£	£	£	£
_____	_____	_____	_____

SLCA		Discount allowed	
£	£	£	£
		_____	_____
_____	_____		

Post individual amounts from the SDB, DAB and CRB to the individual sales ledger accounts.

A		B	
£	£	£	£
_____	_____	_____	_____

Confirm that the total of the sales ledger control account agrees with the total of the sales ledger account balances.

£

Sales ledger account balances:

A

B

_____

Total of sales ledger control account

_____

AO3 Compare, produce and reconcile journals and accounts

Based upon the specimen assessment, AO3 was assessed by parts of Tasks 4, 5 and 6 and all of Task 7.

This Test your understanding deals with elements of AO2 and AO3 to record transactions and update the cash account, prepare a posting summary to the general ledger following update of the cash account, and finally, to prepare a bank reconciliation.

 Test your understanding 8

Graham

The cash account of Graham showed a debit balance of £204 on 31 March 20X3. A comparison with the bank statements revealed the following:

		£
1	Cheques drawn but not presented	3,168
2	Amounts paid into the bank but not credited	723
3	Entries in the bank statements not recorded in the cash account	
	(i) Standing order – insurance	35
	(ii) Interest on bank deposit account	18
	(iii) Bank charges	14
4	Balance on the bank statement at 31 March 20X3 (credit)	2,618

Required:

(a) Show the appropriate adjustments required in the cash account of Graham carrying down the correct balance at 31 March 20X3.

Cash account

	£		£
Balance b/d	204	Sundry accounts:	
	——		——
	——		——
Balance b/d			

(b) Prepare a posting summary of entries into the general ledger as a result of adjustments required to the cash account.

General Ledger title	Debit £	Credit £
TOTAL		

(c) Prepare a bank reconciliation at 31 March 20X3.

	£
Balance per bank statement	
Outstanding lodgements	——
Unpresented cheques	——
Balance per cash account	——

Test your understanding 9 deals with elements of AO2 and AO3 to clear a suspense account, make adjustments to ledger account balances and prepare a trial balance. Although this Test your understanding may be larger than you may face in the synoptic assessment, it is a good learning exercise and revisits content from earlier units.

Test your understanding 9

Kara's Vans has provided a list of general ledger account balances at 31 May 20X5 which includes a suspense account with a balance of £2,800 as shown below:

	£
Receivables	33,440
Bank (debit balance)	2,800
Sales	401,300
Inventory	24,300
Wages	88,400
Telephone	2,200
Motor car	12,000
VAT (credit balance)	5,300
Electricity	3,800
Rent	16,200
Purchases	241,180
Purchases returns	1,600
Sales returns	4,200
Office equipment	5,000
Capital	49,160
Motor expenses	5,040
Discounts allowed	4,010
Discounts received	2,410
Payables	20,000
Drawings	40,000
Suspense (credit balance)	2,800

The following errors were discovered:

- Rent of £200 had been debited to the motor expenses account.

- An electricity payment of £800 had been debited to both the electricity and the bank account.

- The balance on the discounts received account had been incorrectly extracted to the TB – the actual balance on the ledger account was £4,210.

- The balance on the miscellaneous expenses account of £500 was omitted from the TB.

- The purchase returns day book for 22 May 20X5 was incorrectly totalled, as shown below.

Purchase returns day book					
Date	Details	Credit note number	Total £	VAT £	Net £
22 May	Todd Ltd	578	4,320	720	3,600
22 May	Fallon Ltd	579	720	120	600
22 May	Dean's plc	580	960	160	800
	Totals		6,000	1,100	5,000

Required:

(a)   Produce journal entries to correct each of the errors above.

Account name	Amount £	Dr ✓	Cr ✓

Account name	Amount £	Dr ✓	Cr ✓

Account name	Amount £	Dr ✓	Cr ✓

Account name	Amount £	Dr ✓	Cr ✓

Account name	Amount £	Dr ✓	Cr ✓

(b) Complete the suspense account to demonstrate that, after correcting the errors, it has been cleared.

Suspense account

	£		£
		Per TB	2,800
	_____		_____
	_____		_____

(c) Re-draft the trial balance using the balances above and your journal entries.

	£	£
Receivables		
Bank		
Sales		
Inventory		
Wages		
Telephone		
Motor car		
Sales tax		
Electricity		
Rent		
Purchases		
Purchases returns		
Sales returns		
Office equipment		
Capital		
Motor expenses		
Discounts allowed		
Discounts received		
Payables		
Drawings		
Miscellaneous expenses		

Test your understanding 10 deals with elements of AO3 to provide actual and budgeted cost information, and then A04 to provide a written explanation of the difference between a fixed and a variable cost. Although this Test your understanding may be larger than you may face in the synoptic assessment, it is a good learning exercise and revisits content from earlier units.

 Test your understanding 10

ABC Ltd is costing a product which has the following cost details:

Variable costs per unit:

Materials	£3
Labour	£10
Total overheads	£120,000

Required:

(a) Complete the following table of budgeted total cost and unit cost for a production level of 12,000 units. Each unit takes 0.5 machine hours to make, and overheads are to be absorbed into units using a rate per machine hour.

Element	Total cost	Unit cost
	£	£
Materials		
Labour		
Overheads		
Total		

The actual costs incurred for the production costs of 12,000 units were as follows:

Element	Total cost
	£
Materials	33,500
Labour	124,000
Overheads	120,000
Total	**277,500**

(b) Prepare a summary of budgeted and actual total costs, calculate the variances and state whether each variance is favourable or adverse.

Element	Budgeted cost	Actual cost	Variance	Fav/Adv
	£	£	£	£
Materials				
Labour				
Overheads				
Total				

(c) Explain the difference between a fixed cost and a variable cost.

AO4 Communicate financial information effectively

Based upon the specimen synoptic assessment, AO4 was assessed by parts of Task 4 and Task 6. It assesses Learning Outcome 3 of Work Effectively in Finance.

This assessment objective may require you to produce accurate work in an appropriate format, and to communicate that information effectively. You could also be required to plan your workload to meet the needs of the organisation.

Test your understanding 11

The aged receivables analysis for Richwel plc shows that a customer, J Oliver, has an outstanding balance of £8,570.51. The credit limit for J Oliver is £8,600 and he has just placed another order for goods with an order value of £1,200.

Required:

Review the draft letter below to J Oliver, which explains the situation with his account and find SEVEN errors. Errors may be incorrectly spelt, incorrectly used or technically incorrect.

Dear Mr Oliver,

Please find enclosed a current statement of your account, which shows the account balance owed to you. Your current account balance is £8,570.15 and you have recently placed a order for goods to the value of £1,200. This order cannot be processed as the order will result in your credit limit being exceeded.

I would like to arrange a meeting with you to discuss your crdit limit. It may be possible to increase your credit limit as you be one of our highly valued customers and your account is due for review.

Please could you contact me as soon as possible to let me know you're availability for a meeting to discuss the above?

I look forward to hearing from you.

Yours faithfully

 Test your understanding 12

Below is a draft letter to Okidoke plc, a supplier, to advise them of the results of your reconciliation. You returned goods to the value of £856.25 to them on 12 August 20X6 and you have not received a credit note for this return. It is now mid-September 20X6 and, due to this omission, Okidoke Plc is chasing you to settle your account when actually they owe money to you.

Required:

Review the draft letter below to Okidoke plc, which explains the situation with your account and find TEN errors. Errors may be incorrectly spelt, incorrectly used or technically incorrect.

Deer Sir/Madam,

Please find enclosed a copy of my recent sales ledger account reconciliation showing our account with you. We returned goods to you on 12 August 20X6 to the value of £865.25 and we are still awaiting a credit not for this return.

Thank you for sending your statement of acount to us but we believe it to be incorrect due to the omission of the above credit note. In fact, when the credit note is applied to our account, this will result in our account being in credit and amounts being owed to you.

Plaese could you apply the credit note to our account as soon as possible and forward a updated statement of account?

I look forward to sending the updated statement.

Yours sincerely

 Test your understanding 13

Suzy, a Management Accountant, has been asked by the Finance Director to prepare a sales report for the first quarter of 20XY. The sales report needs to be split into product type and the location of sale where possible. Suzy has identified all variances and highlighted those over £500 as they will need explanations to be added by the finance director.

Required:

Choose ONE first paragraph and ONE second paragraph for Suzy's email to the finance director from the options below:

	First paragraph	Second paragraph
Please find attached the sales report for the first month of 20XY, as requested last week. They have been split into product type and location to allow clear analysis.		
I would appreciate it if you could add comments to column F of the spreadsheet, giving reasons for the variances exceeding £500. On completion of this, please email it back to me so I that can discuss it with the relevant sales managers.		
Please could you add comments to column F of the spreadsheet, giving reasons for all of the variances which I have noted. On completion of this, please email it back to me so I can discuss it with the relevant sales managers.		

Attached is the sales report for the first quarter of 20XY, as requested last week. The sales have been split into product type and location to allow clear analysis.		
Please could you add comments to column F of the spreadsheet, giving reasons for all of the variances I have noted. On completion of this, please email it back to me so I can discuss it with the relevant purchase managers.		
The sales attached have been split into product type and colour to allow clear analysis.		

5 Summary

The questions in this chapter should prepare you for the range of tasks that you are likely to encounter in the synoptic assessment. You may find that the content of each task relates to more than one assessment objective.

Test your understanding answers

 Test your understanding 1

(a) Practical issues for a new trainee

There are numerous practical issues upon which you should be able to advise the new trainee of, such as:

- a brief introduction to team members and responsibilities – perhaps with a seating plan

- more information re colleagues who the new trainee is expected to work closely with, e.g. will they be assisting the purchase ledger clerk to process purchase invoices

- health and safety – location of fire alarms, fire escape routes etc

- location of drinks and snacks machines, canteen etc

- location of photocopier, stationery cupboard etc

- who maintains the petty cash float and how to complete a petty cash claim form

- who to contact if they have any particular queries e.g. someone in HR, someone in the finance function and yourself.

(b) Practical skills and competences

MEMORANDUM

FROM: A Clerk

TO: A Trainee

SUBJECT: SKILLS AND COMPETENCES

DATE: XX/XX/XX

This memorandum lists the practical skills and competences that you could expect to develop as a member of the finance department.

- Numeracy – building up speed, familiarity and confidence using basic mathematical skills.

- Written skills – communication with others using emails, memoranda and letters, perhaps with supporting diagrams, charts or spreadsheets.

- Verbal communication skills – working with colleagues and face-to-face or video meetings with varying degrees of formality.

- Technology skills, such as keyboard skills and use of software.

- Technical accounting knowledge – understanding and use of technical accounting terms and concepts.

- Professional qualifications – you may commence studies for a professional accounting qualification.

- Teamwork – shared values, complementary skills and mutual support to achieve combined objectives within appropriate timescales.

 Test your understanding 2

The finance function is established to meet a variety of requirements and responsibilities that will differ from one organisation to another. However, it is generally recognised that a typical finance function will have the following responsibilities:

- responsibility for preparation of statutory financial statements

- provision of information to a range of internal stakeholders, for example:

    - preparation and provision of financial accounting information e.g. providing reconciled bank and cash balances at the end of each week to the finance director

    - preparation and provision of cost and revenue summaries e.g. comparing budget and actual costs and revenues, with identification of variances for department heads

    - guidance and advice to other departments e.g. the cost of recruiting a new employee, or the cost of purchasing a new machine

- activities to comply with legal and regulatory matters, such as accounting for income tax deducted from employees' salaries and subsequent payment to HM Revenue & Customs

- updating, maintaining and preserving accounting information to enable the finance function to discharge its responsibilities effectively

- performance of ad hoc tasks, e.g. investigation of potential fraud or systems hacking problems

- provision of information to a range of external stakeholders, for example:

  - communication with customers e.g. information to credit customers relating to trade and prompt payment discount terms

  - communication with suppliers e.g. agreeing amounts outstanding and when they will be paid

  - information provided to banks and other providers of finance at their request, subject to having appropriate authority to disclose information.

Test your understanding 3

(a) Review each of Gymco Ltd's situations and suggest how it could improve its corporate social responsibility (CSR). Note: the suggested list of CSR policy initiatives is not exhaustive – you may be able to think of others.

	Practical situation	CSR policy
1	Gymco Ltd currently has a café in each of its leisure centres. Currently, it leaves the choice of food and drink available in the cafe to the local centre manager.	• Source ethically-produced drinks and snacks. • Source 'healthy option' drinks and snacks, such as those with reduced sugar and/or reduced salt content. • Source locally produced food and drinks to minimise the adverse effects caused by transportation e.g. pollution, greenhouse gases.

2	Gymco Ltd does not currently monitor the fitness programmes used by its personal trainers with members on a 'one-to-one' basis. There is no way of knowing whether any individual session is safe or effective.	• Fitness programmes should be reviewed to ensure that they are safe and effective. • Introduce a number of standardised programmes which have been approved by a qualified and experienced personal trainer. • Hold 'refresher courses' to remind and update personal trainers of best practice.
3	Gymco Ltd currently charges a standard annual membership fee for each individual, irrespective of their personal circumstances.	• Introduce family memberships to encourage family health and fitness. • Introduce concessions to encourage use of the facilities by other groups e.g. unwaged, students etc. • Introduce corporate memberships to encourage local employers to take an interest in the health and welfare of their employees.
4	Gymco Ltd currently makes paper hand towels available in its wash rooms and food preparation areas.	• Install hot air hand dryers in all wash rooms and food preparation areas to reduce paper waste.

(b) Review each of the practical situations below and, for each situation, identify the ethical principle that appears to have been breached or compromised by either Gymco Ltd or its employees.

	Practical situation	Ethical principle
1	Some personal trainers sell health supplements to gym members without approval from Gymco Ltd.	Integrity – the personal trainers are breaking the rules and are therefore dishonest in their behaviour.
2	Some of the personal trainers have stopped using their regulation trainer uniform and occasionally cancel sessions at short notice without apparently having a good reason to do so.	Professional behaviour of the trainers is compromised by the lack of attention to club regulations and the cancellation of scheduled sessions at short notice without good reason.
3	The receptionist at one leisure centre regularly admits friends who are not members so that they can use the facilities free of charge.	Integrity – the receptionist is effectively cheating Gymco Ltd out of membership fees.
4	Gymco Ltd puts pressure on personal trainers to recruit new members by withholding part of their salary if they do not recruit at least two new members each month.	Objectivity is threatened as Gymco Ltd is putting financial pressure on personal trainers to recruit new members. In turn, this may lead them to use unethical practices to recruit members, such as misrepresenting the range and extent of facilities at the leisure centre.

5	One leisure centre manager has provided the list of members' names and addresses to a local call centre so that they can contact people about car insurance. He did not accept any payment or gift in exchange for this information.	Breach of confidentiality – it is irrelevant that the manager in question did not accept any payment or gift in exchange for providing this information.
6	Some personal trainers do not insist on members doing proper 'warm-up' and 'warm-down' activities at the start and end of a fitness session.	This would appear to be a lack of competence and due care by the personal trainers as members may suffer injury if they do not perform proper 'warm-up' and 'warm-down' activities.

Test your understanding 4

(a)   CSR objectives

	Practical situation	**CSR objective**
1	Goodco Ltd is considering introducing a policy of paying its employees at least 5% more than the legal minimum wage.	Ethical employment practices
2	Goodco Ltd may introduce a policy of donating surplus paper and card to a local nursery for use in its activities.	The local community
3	Goodco Ltd may purchase delivery vehicles that are powered by electricity, rather than petrol or diesel.	Environmentally-friendly policies
4	Goodco Ltd may permit its office staff to work from home one day per week.	Ethical employment practices

(b) Procedures that Goodco Ltd could introduce to ensure confidentiality of data could include any of the following items:

- inclusion of a clause in employees' contracts of employment stating the requirement for confidentiality of data

- staff training and awareness courses to explain why confidentiality of data is important

- restrict access to confidential data to authorised staff only e.g. by use of passwords

- restrict access to data by use of security and physical controls e.g. by keeping relevant documents and files under lock and key, codes to access data cupboards and cabinets

- have named individuals responsible for specified data e.g. the financial accountant is responsible for the safe custody and confidentiality of accounting data

- adoption of anti-hacking procedures and firewalls in computer systems.

Test your understanding 5

(a) For each invoice and credit note shown below select the appropriate supplier account code and general ledger code to be used for each item and include it in the summary grid below.

Invoice from:	Supplier account code	General ledger code
Haddow Bros	HAD29	GL112
Jenson Ltd	JEN32	GL140
AJ Broom & Company Ltd	AJB14	GL110
JM Bond & Co	JMB33	GL110

(b) Complete the recording of each invoice or credit note in the purchases day book, and total the columns in the purchases day book. You should include any credit notes as negative amounts.

PURCHASES DAY BOOK

Date 20X1	Supplier	A/C Ref	Inv No.	Total £	VAT £	GL110 £	GL112 £	GL140 £
22/4	Haddow	HAD 29		256.32	42.72		213.60	
22/4	Jenson Ltd	JEN 32		702.48	117.08			585.40
22/4	AJ Broom	AJB 14		180.49	30.08	150.41		
22/4	JM Bond	JMB 33		(39.45)	(6.57)	(32.88)		
			TOTALS	1,099.84	183.31	117.53	213.60	585.40

(c) Complete the posting summary to record the accounting entries in the general ledger from the purchases day book totals.

POSTING SUMMARY – 22 April 20X1

	Debit/ Credit	Total £	VAT £	GL110 £	GL112 £	GL140 £
General Ledger title						
Purch – Softwood	Debit			117.53		
Purch – Hardwood	Debit				213.60	
Purch – Steel	Debit					585.40
Purch – Sand	Debit					
Purch – Brick	Debit					
VAT	Debit		183.31			
Purchase ledger control account	Credit	1,099.84				

(d) Payment must be received by Jenson Ltd: 6 May 20X1

The amount of the payment: £681.41

Calculated as follows: £702.48 – (£702.48 × 3%) = £681.41

(e) State the accounting entries required in the general ledger of Nethan Builders to account for the prompt payment discount on the sales invoice issued by Jenson Ltd.

Account name	Amount £	Dr ✓	Cr ✓
Discount received	17.56		✓
VAT	3.51		✓
Purchase ledger control account	21.07	✓	

 Test your understanding 6

(a) Completed sales invoice.

SALES INVOICE

Invoice to:
Clobber
10 Main Street
Prestwick
South Ayrshire
KA9 4BB

Smith Shirts
4 Booth Road
Newton Mearns
G2 1PW
Tel: 0141 333 989
Email: admin@smithshirts.co.uk

Deliver to:

As above

Invoice no: **1587**
Tax point: **22 September 20X6**
VAT reg no: 488 7922 26
Delivery note no: **165**
Account no: **CL02**

Code	Shirt description	Quantity	VAT rate %	Unit price £	Total £
POL01	Polo	20	20	20.00	400.00
TAR04	Tartan	12	20	12.50	150.00
STR09	Stripe	20	20	30.00	600.00
Net amount of goods					1,150.00
Trade discount @					
Net amount of goods after discount					1,150.00
VAT					230.00
Total amount payable					1,380.00

(b)   Complete the recording of the invoice in the sales day book, and total the columns in the sales day book.

SALES DAY BOOK

Date 20X6	Customer	Ref No	Inv No.	Total £	VAT £	POL 01 £	TAR 04 £	STR 09 £
20/9	Myshirt	MYS06	1584	316.32	52.72		263.60	
21/9	Joeshirtz	JOE32	1585	738.48	123.08			615.40
21/9	Shirtu	SHI14	1586	180.48	30.08	150.40		
22/9	**Clobber**	**CLO2**	**1587**	**1,380.00**	**230.00**	**400.00**	**150.00**	**600.00**
			TOTAL	**2,615.28**	**435.88**	**550.40**	**413.60**	**1,215.40**

(c)   Complete the posting summary to record the accounting entries in the general ledger from the sales day book totals.

POSTING SUMMARY – 22 September 20X6

	Debit/ Credit	Total £	VAT £	POL01 £	TAR04 £	STR09 £
General Ledger title						
Sales – Polo	Credit			550.40		
Sales – Tartan	Credit				413.60	
Sales – Stripe	Credit					1,215.40
VAT	Credit		435.88			
Sales ledger control account	Debit	2,615.28				

(d)   Payment must be received by 29 September 20X6

Amount of payment £1,311.00

Calculated: £1,380.00 – (£1,380,00 × 5%) = £1,311.00

(e)   State the accounting entries required to account for the prompt payment discount in the general ledger of Smith Shirts.

Account name	Amount £	Dr ✓	Cr ✓
Discount allowed	57.50	✓	
VAT	11.50	✓	
Sales ledger control account	69.00		✓

Test your understanding 7

Write up the sales day book.

SALES DAY BOOK

Date June	Customer	Total £	VAT £	Sales £
17	A	960.00	160.00	800.00
17	B	3,840.00	640.00	3,200.00
	Total	4,800.00	800.00	4,000.00

Write up the cash receipts book and the discounts allowed book.

CASH RECEIPTS BOOK

Date June	Customer	Total £	VAT £	SLCA £	Cash sales £
17	A (W1)	912.00		912.00	
17	B	2,000.00		2,000.00	
17	C	360.00	60.00		300.00
	Total	3,272.00	60.00	2,912.00	300.00

DISCOUNTS ALLOWED BOOK

Date June	Customer	Total £	VAT £	Net £
17	A (W1)	48.00	8.00	40.00
	Total	48.00	8.00	40.00

(W1)

Cash paid by A:

	£
Sale value net of VAT	800.00
Less: prompt payment discount (£800 × 5%)	(40.00)
	760.00
VAT (760 × 20%)	152.00
	912.00

The prompt payment discount is allocated as follows:
Net £800 × 5% = £40
VAT £160 × 5% = £8
Gross £48

Post the totals to the general ledger. Note that for this example the source of the data (day book references have been used for the narrative). The opposite account posted to is also acceptable.

Sales	£		£
		SDB	4,000.00
Bal c/d	4,300	CRB	300.00

VAT	£		£
DAB	8.00	SDB	800.00
Bal c/d	852.00	CRB	60.00

SLCA	£		£
SDB	4,800.00	CRB	2,912.00
		DAB	48.00
		Bal c/d	1,840.00

Discount allowed	£		£
DAB	40.00	Bal c/d	40,00

Post individual amounts from the SDB and CRB to the individual sales ledger accounts.

A	£		£
SDB	960.00	CRB	912.00
		DAB	48.00

B	£		£
SDB	3,840.00	CRB	2,000.00
		Bal c/d	1,840.00

Finally, confirm that the total of the sales ledger control account agrees with the total of the sales ledger account balances.

	£
Sales ledger account balances:	
A	Nil
B	1,840.00
Total of sales ledger control account	1,840.00

Test your understanding 8

(a) Prepare the cash account

Cash account

	£		£
Balance b/d	204	Sundry accounts:	
Interest on deposit account	18	Insurance	35
		Bank charges	14
		Balance c/d	173
	222		222
Balance b/d	173		

(b) Prepare a posting summary of entries into the general ledger as a result of adjustments required to the cash account.

General Ledger title	Debit £	Credit £
Bank charges	14	
Insurance	35	
Bank interest received		18
Cash account		31
TOTAL	49	49

(c) Prepare a bank reconciliation at 31 March 20X3.

	£
Balance per bank statement	2,618
Add Outstanding lodgements	723
	3,341
Less Unpresented cheques	(3,168)
Balance per cash account	173

Test your understanding 9

Account name	Amount £	Dr ✓	Cr ✓
Rent	200	✓	
Motor expenses	200		✓

Account name	Amount £	Dr ✓	Cr ✓
Bank	1,600		✓
Suspense	1,600	✓	

Account name	Amount £	Dr ✓	Cr ✓
Discounts received	1,800		✓
Suspense	1,800	✓	

Account name	Amount £	Dr ✓	Cr ✓
Miscellaneous expenses	500	✓	
Suspense	500		✓

Account name	Amount £	Dr ✓	Cr ✓
Sales tax	100	✓	
Suspense	100		✓

(b) **Complete the suspense account**

Suspense account

	£		£
Bank	1,600	Per TB	2,800
Discount received	1,800	Misc expenses	500
		Sales tax	100
	3,400		3,400

(c) Re-draft the trial balance

	£	£
Receivables	33,440	
Bank (2,800 – 1,600)	1,200	
Sales		401,300
Inventory	24,300	
Wages	88,400	
Telephone	2,200	
Motor car	12,000	
Sales tax (5,300 – 100)		5,200
Electricity	3,800	
Rent (16,200 + 200)	16,400	
Purchases	241,180	
Purchases returns		1,600
Sales returns	4,200	
Office equipment	5,000	
Capital		49,160
Motor expenses (5,040 – 200)	4,840	
Discounts allowed	4,010	
Discounts received (2,410 + 1,800)		4,210
Payables		20,000
Drawings	40,000	
Miscellaneous expenses (per adjs)	500	
	481,470	481,470

Test your understanding 10

(a) Completion of total cost and unit cost

Element	Total cost	Unit cost
	£	£
Materials	36,000	3.00
Labour	120,000	10.00
Overheads (W1)	120,000	10.00
Total	276,000	23.00

(W1)

Total overheads (given) £120,000

Machine hours required for 12,000 units × 0.5 hr per unit = 6,000 hours

Overhead per machine hour = £120,000/6,000 = £20

Overhead per unit = 0.5 × £20 = £10

(b) Summary of budgeted and actual total costs and calculation of variances

Element	Budgeted cost	Actual cost	Variance	Fav/Adv
	£	£	£	
Materials	36,000	33,500	2,500	Fav
Labour	120,000	124,000	4,000	Adv
Overheads	120,000	120,000	Nil	N/A
Total	276,000	277,500	1,500	Adv

(c) Explain the difference between a fixed cost and a variable cost.

A fixed cost does not change with the level of production. Examples of costs that do not change with the level of production include factory rent and insurance.

A variable cost will change with the level of production. Materials costs are a good example of a variable cost. If labour costs are incurred per unit of production, for example on a piecework basis, they will also be a variable cost.

Test your understanding 11

Errors are shown in bold type below:

Dear Mr Oliver,

Please find enclosed a current statement of your account, which shows the account balance owed **(to)** by you. Your current account balance is **(£8,570.15)** £8,570.51 and you have recently placed **(a)** an order for goods to the value of £1,200. This order cannot be processed as the order will result in your credit limit being exceeded.

I would like to arrange a meeting with you to discuss your **(crdit)** credit limit. It may be possible to increase your credit limit as you **(be)** are one of our highly valued customers and your account is due for review.

Please could you contact me as soon as possible to let me know **you're** your availability for a meeting to discuss the above?

I look forward to hearing from you.

Yours **(faithfully)** sincerely

 Test your understanding 12

Errors are shown in bold type below:

(Deer) Dear Sir/Madam,

Please find enclosed a copy of my recent **(sales)** purchases ledger account reconciliation showing our account with you. We returned goods to you on 12 August 20X6 to the value of **(£865.25)** £856.25 and we are still awaiting a credit **(not)** note for this return.

Thank you for sending your statement of **(acount)** account to us but we believe it to be incorrect due to the omission of the above credit note. In fact, when the credit note is applied to our account, this will result in our account being in credit and amounts being owed to **(you)** us.

(Plaese) Please could you apply the credit note to our account as soon as possible and forward **(a)** an updated statement of account?

I look forward to **(sending)** receiving the updated statement.

Yours **sincerely**

Test your understanding 13

	First paragraph	Second paragraph
Please find attached the sales report for the first month of 20XY, as requested last week. They have been split into product type and location to allow clear analysis.	Unsuitable as it refers to the first month – it should be the first quarter.	
I would appreciate it if you could add comments to column F of the spreadsheet, giving reasons for the variances exceeding £500. On completion of this, please email it back to me so that I can discuss it with the relevant sales managers.		✓
Please could you add comments to column F of the spreadsheet, giving reasons for all of the variances which I have noted. On completion of this, please email it back to me so I can discuss it with the relevant sales managers.	Unsuitable as it requests explanation for all variances, not just those over £500.	
Attached is the sales report for the first quarter of 20XY, as requested last week. The sales have been split into product type and location to allow clear analysis.	✓	
Please could you add comments to column F of the spreadsheet, giving reasons for all of the variances I have noted. On completion of this, please email it back to me so I can discuss it with the relevant purchase managers.	Unsuitable as the paragraph refers to purchase managers.	
The sales attached have been split into product type and colour to allow clear analysis.	Unsuitable as it does not clearly explain what has been prepared for the finance director and what the finance director has been requested to do.	

Walkthrough of the synoptic assessment

Introduction

This chapter walks through the sample synoptic assessment which consists of seven tasks.

Overview

1.1 Introduction

The specimen synoptic assessment comprises four assessment objectives which are assessed by seven tasks. The assessment objectives are as follows:

Assessment objective (AO)		*Weighting*
A01	Demonstrate an understanding of the finance function and the roles and procedures carried out by members of an accounting team	24%
A02	Process transactions, complete calculations and make journal entries	24%
A03	Compare, produce and reconcile journals and accounts	34%
A04	Communicate financial information effectively	18%
		100%

If the seven tasks are mapped against the assessment objectives, it can be seen that each of the tasks may cover more than one assessment objective as follows:

	Task							
	1	**2**	**3**	**4**	**5**	**6**	**7**	**Weighting**
AO1	(a) 4 (b) 2	(a) 4 (b) 4 (c) 4			(a) 6			24%
AO2	(c) 4 (d) 2		(a) 4 (b) 6 (c) 1 (d) 1	(a) 4 (b) 2				24%
AO3				(c) 2 (d) 2	(b) 6	(a) 12	(a) 3 (b) 3 (c) 4 (d) 2	34%
AO4				(e) 6		(b) 12		18%
Total	12	12	12	16	12	24	12	100%

It is important that you have a thorough understanding of all synoptic assessment syllabus areas and that you are also ready to manage different syllabus areas within any individual task. Note that all of the tasks have more than one requirement, so it is important that you attempt all parts of a task.

As there is no separate assessment of Work Effectively in Finance, do bear in mind that a significant proportion of the synoptic assessment will be based upon Work Effectively in Finance content.

It is also important to remember that the assessment objectives (including their relative weightings) and the specimen synoptic assessment are indicative only and that a real synoptic assessment may vary to some extent from the specimen assessment.

The synoptic assessment includes some written content and therefore the assessment will be marked partially by computer and partially human marked.

1.2   The synoptic assessment scenario

It is likely that the scenario will be broadly based to enable the assessment to cover a range of task activities which encompass working in a finance environment. Therefore, the scenario could be based upon working in an accounting function which has both financial accounting and management accounting responsibilities, or working for a consultancy business which deals with a range of financial accounting and management accounting assignments on behalf of clients. It may also be based upon working in an organisation with separate financial accounting and management accounting functions, where you could be transferred or seconded between the two functions.

The assessment scenario is likely to identify other relevant information to provide a context or setting for the tasks you are required to complete. For example, you may be advised whether VAT should be accounted for and, if so, at what rate. The scenario is unlikely to assume or require that you have direct knowledge or experience of a particular industry or business sector.

The assessment scenario may incorporate aspects of daily, weekly, monthly or year-end financial and management accounting tasks. For example, there may be daily routines for recording transactions, monthly routines for reconciling control accounts and year-end routines to identify and record adjustments to accounting information. Similarly, costing information could be prepared annually, and subject to monthly review.

The specimen synoptic assessment is set in the context of you working as an accounts assistant in an accounting function which has both financial accounting and management accounting responsibilities. All tasks are independent of each other and require a range of skills and knowledge to be able to complete them.

Scenario:

The tasks are set in a business situation where the following conditions apply:

- You are employed as an accounts assistant in the finance function at SCM Products.

- The finance function includes the financial and management accounting teams.

- SCM Products uses a manual bookkeeping system.

- Double entry takes place in the general ledger. Individual accounts of trade receivables and trade payables are kept in the sales and purchases ledgers as subsidiary accounts.

- The cash book and petty cash book should be treated as part of the double entry system unless the task instructions state otherwise.

- The VAT rate is 20%.

Task 1.1

Introduction

Task 1.1 assesses elements of AO1 and AO2 as follows:

Assessment objective 1	Demonstrate an understanding of the finance function and the roles and procedures carried out by members of an accounting team
Related learning outcome	**Work Effectively in Finance** LO3 Produce work effectively
Assessment objective 2	Process transactions, complete calculations and make journal entries
Related learning outcome	**Bookkeeping Transactions** LO4 Process receipts and payments

Task 1.1 is primarily about Work effectively in Finance along with some Bookkeeping Transactions content. In this task you should therefore expect to be given scenarios where you need to combine your Work Effectively in Finance knowledge with knowledge from another unit.

Task 1.1 has four requirements, the first two relating to Work Effectively in Finance and the final two relating to Bookkeeping Transactions. It is worth a total of 12 marks so you should allocate no more than 14 minutes to it.

Task 1.1(a)

Task 1.1(a) starts by presenting a monthly management accounts schedule and a weekly financial accounts schedule. The first requirement of the task is then as follows:

> Complete your to-do list for today, Friday of week 4. Refer to the management and financial accounts schedule and place the tasks to be completed into the to-do list below.   (4 marks)
>
> Note: You may put each task into the to-do list more than once if the task takes more than one hour to complete.

The answer prioritises the financial accounting tasks as they need to be completed by a specified time within the given day, with the management accounting task completed before the end of the day, which is within the required time. Note also that the financial accounting tasks are also prioritised based upon the time by which each task needs to be completed.

Friday, week 4 to-do list	Time
Cash book	09.00 – 10.00
Process invoices	10.00 – 11.00
Post cheques	11.00 – 12.00
Reconcile statements	12.00 – 13.00
Cost coding	13.00 – 14.00

Task 1.1(b)

Task 1.1(b) develops this task by requiring you to think about your workload for the month ahead. The second requirement of the task is:

Identify on which day in which week you will be the busiest with routine tasks from the management and financial accounts schedules.   (2 marks)

The answer identifies Thursday of week one as the busiest day. This is based upon two management accounting activities that will take a total of three hours, plus financial accounting activities which include the weekly requirement on Thursday to contact customers. Don't forget to include posting cheques which must be done every day.

Day of the week	Week number
Thursday	Week 1

Task 1.1(c) and (d) are based upon extracts of a cash book presented in the assessment and are related. The cash book incorporates both cash and bank transactions.

Task 1.1(c)

Task 1.1(c) requires you to balance the cash and bank columns of the cash book to calculate and state the balances carried down and identify whether each is a debit or credit balance.

What will be the cash and bank balances carried down?   (4 marks)

Task 1.1(d)

Task 1.1(d) requires you to state the total of the cash and bank columns in arriving at the balances carried down in your answer to 1.1(c).

What will be the totals of the cash and bank columns once the balances have been inserted?   (2 marks)

Be careful with you answers to parts (c) and (d) as the requirement is for the balances carried down, not brought down, on both accounts.

The answer – figures in bold identify the information required for tasks 1.1(c) and 1.1(d).

Cash book

Details	Cash (£)	Bank (£)	VAT (£)	Trade receivables (£)	Cash sales (£)
Jaz Shatna	1,110		185		925
Cory Mac		2,150		2,150	
P James		1,525		1,525	
Cash		850			
Bal c/d		**4,012**			
	1,110	**8,537**			

Details	Cash (£)	Bank (£)	VAT (£)	Trade payables (£)	Cash purchases (£)
Balance b/f		6,542			
P Brady Ltd		1,365		1,365	
S Simmons		396	66		330
Cox and Co		234	39		195
Bank	850				
Bal c/d	**260**				
	1,110	**8,537**			

Balances	Amount (£)	Debit	Credit
Cash balance carried down	260		✓
Bank balance carried down	4,012	✓	

Task 1.2

Introduction

Task 1.2 assesses elements of AO1.

Assessment objective 1	Demonstrate an understanding of the finance function and the roles and procedures carried out by members of an accounting team
Related learning outcomes	**Work effectively in Finance** LO1 Understand the finance function within an organisation LO2 Use personal skills development in finance

Task 1.2 focuses upon Work Effectively in Finance and has three requirements, with each considered in turn. The context for this task is that there will be a new trainee starting in the finance function of the organisation and you need to prepare for their arrival. You may be able to relate this to your own experience or perhaps to the experience of a work colleague in your own organisation.

This task is worth 12 marks, so you should spend no more than 14 minutes on this task in the assessment.

Task 1.2(a)

Task 1.2(a) starts by asking you to identify four main roles from a list of eight possibilities prior to the arrival of the new starter. The requirement is as follows as follows:

From the list below, identify the FOUR main roles of the finance function at SCM Products by placing them into your notes. (4 marks)
Ensuring the security of financial data
Ensuring the security of the production process
Managing funds effectively
Managing staff in other internal departments
Producing monthly bank statements
Producing statutory financial statements
Providing accounting information to other internal departments
Providing IT support to other internal departments

The answer is as follows:

Notes for Simon
Main roles of the finance function:
Ensuring the security of financial data
Managing funds effectively
Providing accounting information to other internal departments
Producing statutory financial statements

When you are faced with making choices from a list, try to ensure that you identify the required number of items from those available (in this case choose four from the eight options available). If you are unsure about your choices, try to eliminate some of the options available as being wrong or inappropriate as this may help you to identify correct answers from the remaining items.

Task 1.2(b)

Task 1.2(b) develops this task by considering the situation after the new trainee has started work in the accounting function and requires you to do the following:

From the list below, identify FOUR policies or procedures Simon should familiarise himself with by placing them in your notes. (4 marks)

Holiday entitlement policy
Research and development policy
Product grading procedures
Petty cash claiming procedures
Vehicle maintenance checking procedures
Warehouse storage procedures
Staff development policy
Cheque banking procedures

The answer below identifies the four policies or procedures that are most relevant to the new trainee's situation. The other items, whilst they may be of some relevance or interest to the new trainee, would not be regarded as a priority.

Notes for Simon

Policies and procedures you need to be familiar with:

Holiday entitlement policy

Petty cash claiming procedures

Staff development policy

Cheque banking procedures

Task 1.2(c)

Task 1.2(c) continues to focus upon Work Effectively in Finance and requires you identify ways in which the new trainee could develop their skills. The requirement is as follows:

Identify FOUR ways Simon could develop the necessary skills to help him in his role. **(4 marks)**

Ways for Simon to develop his skills	
Interrupt the speaker to ask questions during meetings.	
Make eye contact with the speaker.	
Wait until the person speaking has finished before asking questions.	
Cough loudly to indicate to the speaker that the meeting has overrun.	
Complete the work tasks at your own pace, focussing on the accuracy of the work.	
Discuss difficulties in meeting deadlines with your supervisor at the earliest opportunity.	
Complete work tasks as quickly as possible, relying on your supervisor to check the accuracy of the work.	
Ask as many questions as you need until you fully understand what you are being asked to do.	

The answer identifies four ways for the new trainee to develop his skills as follows:

Ways for Simon to develop his skills	
Interrupt the speaker to ask questions during meetings.	
Make eye contact with the speaker.	✓
Wait until the person speaking has finished before asking questions.	✓
Cough loudly to indicate to the speaker that the meeting has overrun.	
Complete the work tasks at your own pace, focussing on the accuracy of the work.	
Discuss difficulties in meeting deadlines with your supervisor at the earliest opportunity.	✓
Complete work tasks as quickly as possible, relying on your supervisor to check the accuracy of the work.	
Ask as many questions as you need until you fully understand what you are being asked to do.	✓

Some of the possible ways for the new trainee to develop skills do have some merit, but need to be considered carefully. For example, asking questions during a meeting is a way of gaining knowledge and understanding, but interrupting a speaker would normally be regarded as unprofessional. Similarly, completing work at one's own pace to ensure that work is complete and accurate would help to develop knowledge and understanding, but ignores any other considerations, such as any time deadlines for the work to be completed.

Task 1.3

Introduction

Task 1.3 assesses elements of AO2.

Assessment objective 2	Process transactions, complete calculations and make journal entries
Related learning outcome	**Bookkeeping Transactions** LO2 Process customer transactions

Task 1.3 is about preparing an invoice and then recording it in the daybook. The task then requires you to calculate the amount due from a credit customer if they take advantage of a prompt payment discount, and then to identify the date by which payment must be received for the discount to be applicable.

Task 1.3 is worth 12 marks, so you should spend no more than 14 minutes on this task in the assessment.

Task 1.3(a)

Task 1.3(a) begins by requiring you to complete the preparation of a sales invoice based upon the price list made available in the task data. The task requirement states that there are four boxes that need to be completed, so ensure that you complete all four boxes. Ensure that you do the arithmetic to achieve the correct net, VAT and total amounts as the partially completed invoice identifies that 120 units of the product have been sold to the customer.

The answer is as follows, with the data required shown in bold:

SCM Products
14 London Road
Parton, PA21 7NL
VAT Registration No. 298 3827 04
Invoice No. 3912

To:	Invoice date: 15 May 20XX
Peppers Ltd	Delivery date: 13 May 20XX
121 New Street	Customer account code: PEP003
Grangeton, GX12 4SD	

Quantity of units	Product code	Price each (£)	Net amount (£)	VAT amount (£)	Total amount (£)
120	BXC20	**3.85**	**462.00**	**92.40**	**554.40**

Terms of payment: Net monthly account

Task 1.3(b)

Task 1.3(b) then requires you to record the invoice in the correct daybook by making a choice from a drop-down menu. There are two items that must be selected from drop-down menus, and a further four items that require data to be entered. Ensure that you complete all six items required to record the invoice in the daybook. The task information is as follows:

∇ Drop down menus for task 1.3(b):

Cash book
Discounts allowed daybook
Discounts received daybook
Petty cash book
Purchases daybook
Purchases returns daybook
Sales daybook
Sales returns daybook

Peppers Ltd
SCM Products

Date 20XX	Details ▽	Account code	Invoice number	Total (£)	VAT (£)	Net (£)
15 May			3912			

The completed answer is as follows with the required information in bold:

Sales daybook ▽						
Date 20XX	Details	Account code	Invoice number	Total (£)	VAT (£)	Net (£)
15 May	**Peppers Ltd** ▽	**PEP003**	3912	**554.40**	**92.40**	**462.00**

Task 1.3(c)

Task 1.3(c) then requires you to deal with calculation of a prompt payment discount as follows:

> Calculate the amount that would be paid by Peppers Ltd if a 2.5% prompt discount was offered on the invoice in (a) and the invoice paid within five days.   (1 mark)
>
> | £ | |
> |---|---|

Remember that the discount is calculated based upon the total value of the invoice. The discount can be calculated and deducted from the total amount, or the reduced amount can be calculated directly. Either approach will achieve the correct answer as follows:

(i)   £554.40 – (£554.40 × 0.025) = £540.54

(ii) £554.40 × 97.5/100 = £540.54

£	540.54

Task 1.3(d)

Task 1.3(d) requires you to determine the date by which payment must be received from the customer if they are to be eligible to receive the discount and choose the correct option from the drop-down menu provided.

Remember that the discount terms are based upon the invoice date, and not the delivery date. The answer is:

20 May 20XX ▽

Task 1.4

Introduction

Task 1.4 assesses your knowledge and understanding of two assessment objectives, AO2 and AO3.

Assessment objective 2	Process transactions, complete calculations and make journal entries
Related learning outcome	**Bookkeeping Transactions** LO5 Process transactions through the ledgers to the trial balance
Assessment objective 3	Compare, produce and reconcile journals and accounts
Related learning outcome	**Bookkeeping Controls** LO3 Use control accounts
Assessment objective 4	**Communicate information effectively**
Related learning outcome	**Work Effectively in Finance** **LO3 Produce work effectively**

Task 1.4 considers period-end tasks such as the update and reconciliation of control accounts. When updating or reconciling control accounts, errors may be identified or notified to you, which could require the use of the journal to record adjustments required.

The task is divided into five requirements to progress through the various stages of updating, reconciling and using the journal to record adjustments.

Task 1.4 is worth 16 marks, so you should spend no more than 19 minutes on this task in the assessment.

Task 1.4(a)

Task 1.4(a) begins by identifying that it is the end of June and you have a partially completed sales ledger control account, together with extracts from the sales daybook and sales returns daybook.

What will be the entries in the sales ledger control account? (4 marks) Tick whether each amount will be debit or credit.			
Balances	**Amount (£)**	**Debit**	**Credit**
Entry from the sales daybook			
Entry from the sales returns daybook			

The task answer is below, with the inserted data in bold. Remember to indicate whether each item is a debit or a credit balance.

Balances	**Amount (£)**	**Debit**	**Credit**
Entry from the sales daybook	**43,308**	✓	
Entry from the sales returns daybook	**2,634**		✓

Task 1.4(b)

Task 1.4(b) continues with the reconciliation of the sales ledger control account and requires you to answer the following question:

What will be the balance carried down on the sales ledger control account? (2 marks)		
Amount (£)	**Debit**	**Credit**

The answer is given below:

Amount (£)	**Debit**	**Credit**
53,526		✓

Sales ledger control account

	£		£
Balance b/d	46,803	Bank	32,886
Sales daybook	43,308	Sales returns daybook	2,634
		Irrecoverable debt	1,065
		Balance c/d	53,526
	90,111		90,111
Balance c/d	53,526		

Having dealt with the sales ledger control account, you now need to deal with a reconciliation of the purchase ledger control account with the total of the purchase ledger balances.

The following list of ledger balances was provided.

Credit suppliers	Balances	
	Amount (£)	Debit/Credit
TT Thomas	8,066	Credit
Cope and Croydon	3,197	Credit
Yeltz	17,954	Credit
Marlo plc	365	Debit
Holton and Partners	11,746	Credit

Task 1.4(c)

Task 1.4(c) provides a list of purchase ledger balances, which you need to total, and complete the reconciliation statement.

Complete the reconciliation statement by:

- Inserting the total of the balances in the purchases ledger
- Calculating any difference   (2 marks)

Reconciliation statement	Amount (£)
Purchase ledger control account balance	40,840
Total of the purchases ledger balances	
Difference	

When totalling the list of purchase ledger balances, watch out for debit balances so that your casting of the list of balances is correct. Similarly, if you were dealing with a list of sales ledger balances, be alert to identify any credit balances that may be present. If you make an error here, it is likely to affect the reconciliation and possible identification or explanation of what may have caused any difference between the control account total and the total of the list of ledger balances.

The answer is given below, with the required information in bold.

Reconciliation statement	Amount (£)
Purchase ledger control account balance	40,840
Total of the purchases ledger balances	**40,598**
Difference	**242**

Task 1.4(d)

Task 1.4(d) then asks you to consider the result of your reconciliation exercise and identify possible reasons for the difference between the control account balance and the total list of ledger balances.

On a practical level, this could be a task requirement for a reconciliation of the sales ledger control account with the list of sales ledger balances, or an activity based upon a bank reconciliation.

Which TWO of the reasons below could explain the difference you calculated in (c) above? (2 marks)

Reasons	
A credit note was entered twice in the purchases ledger control account.	
An invoice was entered twice in a supplier's account in the purchase ledger.	
A payment was entered twice in a supplier's account in the purchases ledger.	
A discount received was entered twice in the purchases ledger control account.	
An invoice was entered twice in the purchases ledger control account.	
A discount received was not entered in a supplier's account in the purchases ledger.	

The two possible reasons for the difference are identified in bold in the answer below.

Reasons	
A credit note was entered twice in the purchases ledger control account.	
An invoice was entered twice in a supplier's account in the purchase ledger.	
A payment was entered twice in a supplier's account in the purchases ledger.	✓
A discount received was entered twice in the purchases ledger control account.	
An invoice was entered twice in the purchases ledger control account.	✓
A discount received was not entered in a supplier's account in the purchases ledger.	

Task 1.4(e)

The final part of the task requires you to review a draft letter and identify errors. You have been advised that there are six errors in the draft letter, so ensure that you identify the required number of errors in your answer.

Review the draft letter and highlight SIX errors. Errors may be wrongly spelt, incorrectly used or technically incorrect.   (6 marks)

> Dear Mrs Rodgers,
>
> Our sales ledger shows an erroneous overpayment made earlier in the year has resulted in an amount of £356 owing to us. We would be grateful if you could confirm agreement of the amount and provide us with a cheque so that we can correct the error in preparation for our year-end. If you require me to provide further details of the underpayment please do not hesitate to contact me and I will be happy to forward documentation to you.
>
> Many thancks in anticipation of your co-operation in this matter.
>
> Yours faithfully,

The answer below identifies the errors in bold.

Dear Mrs **Rodgers**,

Our **sales** ledger shows an erroneous overpayment made earlier in the year has resulted in an amount of **£356** owing to us. We would be grateful if you could confirm agreement of the amount and provide us with a cheque so that we can correct the error in preparation for our year-end. If you require me to provide further details of the **underpaymen**t please do not hesitate to contact me and I will be happy to forward documentation to you.

Many **thancks** in anticipation of your co-operation in this matter.

Yours **faithfully**,

The errors consist of spelling mistakes, transposition errors and mis-used words. The important thing is that you should to pay attention to detail so that you identify the relevant items.

Task 1.5

Introduction

Task 1.5 is in two parts. The first part places you in the situation of being part of a team to consider corporate social responsibility (CSR) issues, and the second part requires you to prepare a statement of actual and budgeted costs related to CSR.

This two assessment objectives covered by this task are noted below.

Assessment objective 1	Demonstrate an understanding of the finance function and the roles and procedures carried out by members of an accounting team
Related learning outcomes	**Work Effectively in Finance** LO4 Understand corporate social responsibility (CSR) within organisations
Assessment objective 3	Compare, produce and reconcile journals and accounts
Related learning outcomes	**Bookkeeping Controls** LO3 Provide information on actual and budgeted costs and income

Task 1.5 is worth 12 marks, so you should spend no more than 14 minutes on this task in the assessment.

Task 1.5(a)

Put THREE appropriate initiatives into EACH section of the Corporate Social Responsibility report below. (6 marks)

Initiatives:

Ensuring staff use public transport rather than their own vehicles when travelling for business purposes.
Ensuring production processes maximise energy consumption.
Ensuring all staff minimise costs and expenses to the organisation.
Introducing flexible working conditions so staff can work and still meet personal commitments.
Ensuring all staff complete overtime each month.
Imposing a weekend working requirement on all staff.
Increasing senior management salaries by 10%.
Offering free membership to a local gymnasium for all staff.
Ensuring emissions from our delivery vehicles are minimised.
Allowing staff to complete overseas projects which bring water to communities in developing countries.
Installing energy saving equipment in our production plant.
Offering staff training and supporting those wishing to gain further qualifications.

The answer template provides the following two report headings:

1   Our commitment to minimising the environmental impact of our activities.

2   Our commitment to improving the welfare of our employees.

Many students will be able to use their knowledge of CSR to identify relevant activities from the available list. However, you need to ensure that the activities you identify are allocated under an appropriate report heading as illustrated in the answer.

SCM Products
Corporate Social Responsibility Report
Our commitment to minimising the environmental impact of our activities.
Initiatives planned:
Ensuring staff use public transport rather than their own vehicles when travelling for business purposes.
Ensuring emissions from our delivery vehicles are minimised.
Installing energy saving equipment in our production plant.
Our commitment to improving the welfare of our employees.
Initiatives planned:
Introducing flexible working conditions so staff can work and still meet personal commitments.
Offering free membership to a local gymnasium for all staff.
Offering staff training and supporting those wishing to gain further qualifications.

Task 1.5(b)

Task 1.5(b) requires you to provide some information on budgeted and actual costs relating to an event arranged for CSR purposes.

To complete the task, knowledge of how to calculate budgeted costs is required, along with calculation of a variance and identification of whether the variance calculated is adverse or favourable. There are two drop-down boxes to complete, along with four monetary value boxes.

The scenario provided is as follows:

In line with a previous commitment to improving the local environment, SCM Products recently held an event to raise funds to renovate a local community centre. The CSR team is responsible for reporting on the costs of the event.

The budget costs were:

Food: £1.75 per person

Entertainment: £50 per hundred people

1,500 people attended the event.

The actual costs are shown in the table below and you have been asked to compare these with the budgeted costs.

Complete the table below by:

- Inserting the total budgeted amount for each cost
- Inserting the variance for each cost
- Selecting whether each variance is adverse or favourable.

(6 marks)

∇ Drop down menu for task 1.5 (b):

| Adverse |
| Favourable |

Event cost performance report				
Cost	Budget (£)	Actual (£)	Variance (£)	Adverse/ Favourable
Food		2,200		∇
Entertainment		1,150		∇

The answer is as follows, with the required information in bold.

Event cost performance report				
Cost	Budget (£)	Actual (£)	Variance (£)	Adverse/ Favourable
Food	**2,625**	2,200	**425**	**Favourable**∇
Entertainment	**750**	1,150	**400**	**Adverse** ∇

Ensure that you are able to calculate the total of the variable costs based upon the information presented. Note that there are no fixed costs identified in the task information.

The total of variable costs will change depending upon the level of activity, in this case, the food and entertainment costs respectively. The total of the food and entertainment costs should be calculated separately as they each vary in a different way as follows:

Food: 1,500 × £1.75 = £2,625.00

Entertainment: 1,500/100 × £50 = £750

The actual costs can then be compared with the budgeted costs as calculated. The food cost variance is favourable because the actual costs were less than budgeted. The entertainment cost variance is adverse as the actual costs exceed the budgeted cost.

Task 1.6

Introduction

Task 1.6 is in two parts. The first part places you in the situation of being required to prepare some costing information, and the second part develops this this theme by requiring you to prepare a report comprising three elements of costing. Although the two parts are not directly related, you may be able to use some of your work for the first part to help your thought processes to deal with the second requirement.

This two assessment objectives covered by this task are noted below.

Assessment objective 3	Compare, produce and reconcile journals and accounts
Related learning outcomes	**Bookkeeping Controls** LO3 Provide information on actual and budgeted costs and income
Assessment objective 4	Communicate financial information effectively
Related learning outcomes	**Work Effectively in Finance** LO3 Produce work effectively

Task 1.6 is worth 24 marks, so you should spend no more than 29 minutes on this task in the assessment.

You are provided with the following scenario that sets the scene for the task.

Your manager at SCM Products is interested in how costs behave at different levels of output. She has asked you to prepare a cost analysis at different levels of output for a product. You are told that fixed costs are £20,000 and variable costs are £5 per unit.

Task 1.6(a)

Complete the table below to show fixed, variable and total and unit costs for each of the three levels of output. (12 marks)

Level of output	Fixed costs (£)	Variable costs (£)	Total costs (£)	Unit cost (£)
2,000 units				
5,000 units				
8,000 units				

To complete this task, knowledge of how to calculate fixed and variable costs is required, and then to use that information to determine total cost at each level of output. The final part of the table to complete is to calculate the total cost per unit.

The completed table is set out below with the required information in bold.

Level of output	Fixed costs (£)	Variable costs (£)	Total costs (£)	Unit cost (£)
2,000 units	**20,000**	**10,000**	**30,000**	**15.00**
5,000 units	**20,000**	**25,000**	**45,000**	**9.00**
8,000 units	**20,000**	**40,000**	**60,000**	**7.50**

Remember that fixed costs do not change if the level of output changes, so they remain fixed at £20,000 for each level of output.

The total variable cost can be calculated by using the unit variable cost of £5 per unit and multiplying that by the relevant output level. Total cost is calculated by adding the fixed costs and variable cost for each level of output. Unit cost is calculated by dividing total cost by the number of units produced at each activity level.

Task 1.6(b)

This is a report writing exercise as follows:

In the box below, write a short report for non-finance staff containing:

- A brief introduction outlining the areas you will be covering in the report

- An explanation of what a fixed cost is, giving an example

- An explanation of what a variable cost is, giving an example

- A description of what happens to the unit cost as output increases and the reason for this. (12 marks)

You should use the bullet points as a guide to providing the report structure and content required as presented in the answer below.

Introduction

This report:

- Explains and gives examples of fixed and variable costs.

- Describes the effect of increased output on unit costs.

Fixed cost

A fixed cost is one that remains the same irrespective of the level of output. An example of a fixed cost for a factory would be the cost of rent.

Variable cost

A variable cost is one which changes in relation to the level of output. An example of a variable production cost would be the direct materials used in a product.

Description of what happens to the cost per unit as output increases

The cost per unit deceases as output increases. This is because fixed costs do not change with output so are shared between an increased number of units when output increases.

Note that the format of the report follows that required by the task. It starts with a brief introduction, which is then followed by an explanation of what a fixed cost and variable cost is. The final part of this requirement is to then explain what happens to cost per unit as output increases. You should explain what happens to fixed costs in this situation (i.e. no change) and what happens to variable costs (i.e. they increase at a constant rate per unit). Overall, total cost per unit will fall as output increases.

Task 1.7

Introduction

Task 1.7 is based upon a month-end scenario and is in four parts. The first two parts deal with updating the purchase ledger from information in the purchases daybook. The second two parts focus upon use of the journal.

Assessment objective 3	Compare, produce and reconcile journals and accounts
Related learning outcomes	**Bookkeeping Controls**
	LO3 Use control accounts
	L04 Use the journal

There are 12 marks allocated to this task, which means that you should spend no more than 14 minutes on this task during the assessment.

You have been provided with the following scenario information for this task.

You are preparing for the accounting month-end at SCM Products.

Your first task is to transfer data from the purchases daybook to the ledgers. An extract from the purchases daybook is shown below.

Date 20XX	Details	Invoice number	Total (£)	VAT (£)	Net (£)
31 Aug	Carstairs Ltd	C1673X	474	79	395

Task 1.7(a)

Show whether the entries in the general ledger will be debit or credit entries. (3 marks)

Account name	Debit	Credit
Purchases		
VAT		
Purchases ledger control		

The answer is shown below and should be relatively straightforward for most students using knowledge from Bookkeeping Transactions and Bookkeeping Controls.

Account name	Debit	Credit
Purchases	✓	
VAT	✓	
Purchases ledger control		✓

Task 1.7(b)

This task requires you to complete the entry to the purchase ledger by selecting from the drop-down menu and using information from the purchase daybook.

∇ Drop down list for task 1.7 (b):

Carstairs Ltd
Purchases
Purchases ledger control
Purchases returns
Sales
Sales ledger control
Sales returns
VAT
<empty>

What will be the entry in the purchases ledger?			(3 marks)
Account name	Amount (£)	Debit	Credit
∇			

The answer is shown below and should be quite straightforward for most students applying knowledge from Bookkeeping Transactions and Bookkeeping Controls.

Account name	Amount (£)	Debit	Credit
Carstairs Ltd ∇	474		✓

Parts (c) and (d) of this task deal with adjustments required as a result of identifying errors or omissions in the ledger accounts.

Task 1.7(c)

This part of the task provides the following information:

You have found an error in the accounting records. A cheque payment of £4,206 to a credit supplier has been recorded as £4,260.

You have partially prepared journal entries to correct the error in the general ledger.

Complete the journals below by:

Removing incorrect entries, and

Recording the correct entries.   (4 marks)

Journal to remove the incorrect entries

Account name	Debit (£)	Credit (£)
Bank		
Purchases ledger control		

Journal to record the correct entries

Account name	Debit (£)	Credit (£)
Purchases ledger control		
Bank		

Journal adjustments may require some thought, particularly in this situation, where you are required to remove the incorrect entries and then to record the correct entries, rather than simply making one journal adjustment to correct the error. Knowledge from Bookkeeping Transactions and Bookkeeping Controls will be relevant here.

The journals required are noted below. The original accounting entries were: Debit PLCA, and Credit Bank, so they must be reversed to remove the incorrect entries as follows:

Journal to remove the incorrect entries

Account name	Debit (£)	Credit (£)
Bank	**4,260**	
Purchases ledger control		**4,260**

The correct accounting entries can then be recorded as follows:

Journal to record the correct entries

Account name	Debit (£)	Credit (£)
Purchases ledger control	**4,206**	
Bank		**4,206**

Task 1.7(d)

This part of the task provides the following information:

You have also identified that discounts received were omitted from the general ledger. You have prepared the journal entries below to correct the omission.

Journal

Account name	Debit (£)	Credit (£)
Purchases ledger control	120	
Discounts received		120

Record the journal in the general ledger by dragging the appropriate entry into each account below. (2 marks)

Discounts received

Details	Amount (£)	Details	Amount (£)
		Balance b/f	993

Purchases ledger control

Details	Amount (£)	Details	Amount (£)
		Balance b/f	37,721

Entries:

Discounts received 120

Purchases ledger control 120

The answer is stated below, with the accounting entries in bold.

Discounts received

Details	Amount (£)	Details	Amount (£)
		Balance b/f	993
		Purchase ledger control	**120**

Purchases ledger control

Details	Amount (£)	Details	Amount (£)
Discounts received	**120**	Balance b/f	37,721

SPECIMEN ASSESSMENT

1 Specimen Assessment Questions

Scenario: The tasks are set in a business situation where the following conditions apply:

- You are employed as an accounts assistant in the finance function at SCM Products.

- The finance function includes the financial and management accounting teams.

- SCM Products uses a manual bookkeeping system.

- Double entry takes place in the general ledger. Individual accounts of trade receivables and trade payables are kept in the sales and purchases ledgers as subsidiary accounts.

- The cash book and petty cash book should be treated as part of the double entry system unless the task instructions state otherwise.

- The VAT rate is 20%.

Task 1

You work from 09.00 until 14.00, Monday to Friday of each week. Each finance period is four weeks in duration so you plan your work in a four-week cycle.

The work schedules below show the days when routine tasks must be completed and the amount of time each task takes to complete. It is very important that you complete the management accounts tasks by the end of the identified day and the financial accounts tasks by the day and time indicated.

Monthly work schedules – management accounts					
	Monday	Tuesday	Wednesday	Thursday	Friday
Week 1	Material cost report (2 hours)		Material cost report (2 hours)	Budget report (2 hours)	Product cost analysis (1 hour)
Week 2	Labour cost report (2 hours)	Labour cost report (1 hour)	Labour cost report (2 hours)		
Week 3			Material cost report (1 hour)		Product cost analysis (1 hour)
Week 4	Data gathering (2 hours)			Variance analysis (1 hour)	Cost coding (1 hour)

Weekly work schedule – financial accounts			
Task	Task to be completed each week by:		Task duration
	Day	Time	
Reconcile statements	Friday	13.00	1 hour
Contact customers	Thursday	13.00	2 hours
Process invoices	Friday	11.00	1 hour
Post cheques	Every day	12.00	1 hour
Contact suppliers	Monday	11.00	1 hour
Departmental report	Wednesday	12.00	1 hour
Departmental charges	Tuesday	12.00	2 hours

You are planning your work at the start of the day on Friday of week 4. You have been asked to complete a non-routine cash book task by 10am, which is already included in your to-do list.

1.1

(a) **Complete your to-do list for today, Friday of week 4. Refer to the management and financial accounts schedule and place the tasks to be completed into the to-do list below.** **(4 marks)**

Note: You may put each task into the to-do list more than once if the task takes more than one hour to complete.

Tasks:

Budget report	Departmental report	Reconcile statements
Contact customers	Labour cost report	Variance analysis
Contact suppliers	Material cost reports	
Cost coding	Post cheques	
Data gathering	Process invoices	
Departmental charges	Product cost analysis	

Friday, week 4 to-do list	**Time**
Cash book	09.00 – 10.00
	10.00 – 11.00
	11.00 – 12.00
	12.00 – 13.00
	13.00 – 14.00

You are often asked to complete non-routine tasks. However, on one day in each four week cycle you are too busy with routine tasks to accept non-routine work.

(b) **Identify on which day in which week you will be the busiest with routine tasks from the management and financial accounts schedules.**

Place the day of the week and the week number into the table below. **(2 marks)**

Days and weeks:

Monday, Tuesday, Wednesday, Thursday, Friday

Week 1, Week 2, Week 3, Week 4

Day of the week	**Week number**

The non-routine cash book task in today's to-do list is finalising the cash book below for a colleague who has been taken ill.

Cash book

Details	Cash (£)	Bank (£)	VAT (£)	Trade receivables (£)	Cash sales (£)
Jaz Shatna	1,110		185		925
Cory Mac		2,150		2,150	
P James		1,525		1,525	
Cash		850			

Details	Cash (£)	Bank (£)	VAT (£)	Trade payables (£)	Cash purchases (£)
Balance b/f		6,542			
P Brady Ltd		1,365		1,365	
S Simmons		396	66		330
Cox and Co		234	39		195
Bank	850				

(c) **What will be the cash and. bank balances carried down?**

(4 marks)

Tick whether each amount will be debit or credit.

Balances	Amount (£)	Debit	Credit
Cash balance carried down			
Bank balance carried down			

(d) **What will be the totals of the cash and bank columns once the balances have been inserted?** **(2 marks)**

Totals	Amount (£)
Cash total	
Bank total	

(Total: 12 marks)

Task 2

SCM Products has recruited Simon, who has recently left school, to work in the finance function as the trainee. In his first year, Simon will spend time helping you with general tasks such as postal duties, photocopying and filing and he will also work with the cashiers and the management accounting and financial accounting teams.

As Simon is due to start work next week, you have been asked to provide some notes to help him settle into his role. You have decided to begin the notes with the main roles of the finance function.

1.2

(a) **From the list below, identify the FOUR main roles of the finance function at SCM Products by placing them into your notes.**

(4 marks)

List of roles:

Ensuring the security of financial data
Ensuring the security of the production processes
Managing funds effectively
Managing staff in other internal departments
Producing monthly bank statements
Producing statutory financial statements
Providing accounting information to other internal departments
Providing IT support to other internal departments

Notes for Simon
Main roles of the finance function:

It is Simon's first week and you are helping with his induction into the organisation. You have been asked to highlight important policies and procedures on SCM Products' intranet that Simon should familiarise himself with.

(b) From the list below, identify FOUR policies or procedures Simon should familiarise himself with by placing them into your notes.

(4 marks)

List of policies and procedures:

Holiday entitlement policy
Research and development policy
Product grading procedures
Petty cash claiming procedures
Vehicle maintenance checking procedures
Warehouse storage procedures
Staff development policy
Cheque banking procedures

Notes for Simon

Policies and procedures you need to be familiar with:

Simon has been working with you for a few weeks now and you are aware of some concerns in relation to his performance. During meetings, Simon appears uninterested and does not participate. There have also been instances of Simon misunderstanding instructions and not meeting deadlines. You decide to help Simon develop the skills which are important in his role.

(c) **Identify FOUR ways Simon could develop the necessary skills to help him in his role** **(4 marks)**

Ways for Simon to develop his skills	
Interrupt the speaker to ask questions during meetings.	
Make eye contact with the speaker.	
Wait until the person speaking has finished before asking questions.	
Cough loudly to indicate to the speaker that the meeting has overrun.	
Complete the work tasks at your own pace, focussing on the accuracy of the work.	
Discuss difficulties in meeting deadlines with your supervisor at the earliest opportunity.	
Complete work tasks as quickly as possible, relying on your supervisor to check the accuracy of the work.	
Ask as many questions as you need until you fully understand what you are being asked to do.	

(Total: 12 marks)

Task 3

SCM Products has supplied goods to Peppers Ltd. You have been asked to complete the invoice by calculating the invoice amounts.

1.3

(a) **Refer to the price list and complete the FOUR boxes in the invoice below.** **(4 marks)**

Price list:

Product code	Price each (£)
ACG10	5.53
BCF15	2.75
BXC20	3.85
CXC20	1.52
DFJ15	3.75
DFJ20	4.98

Invoice:

SCM Products
14 London Road
Parton, PA21 7NL
VAT Registration No. 298 3827 04

Invoice No. 3912

To: Invoice date: 15 May 20XX
Peppers Ltd   Delivery date: 13 May 20XX
121 New Street   Customer account code: PEP003
Grangeton, GX12 4SD

Quantity of units	Product code	Price each (£)	Net amount (£)	VAT amount (£)	Total amount (£)
120	BXC20				

Terms of payment: Net monthly account

Your next task is to enter the invoice into the appropriate daybook.

(b) **Record the invoice in the correct daybook by:**

- **Selecting the correct daybook title and**

- **Making the necessary entries.** **(6 marks)**

∇ Drop down list for task 1.3 (b):

Cash book
Discounts allowed daybook
Discounts received daybook
Petty cash book
Purchases daybook
Purchases returns daybook
Sales daybook
Sales returns daybook

▽ Drop down list for task 1.3 (b):

Peppers Ltd
SCM Products

		▽				
Date 20XX	Details	Account code	Invoice number	Total (£)	VAT (£)	Net (£)
15 May	▽		3912			

SCM Products is considering offering its customers a 2.5% prompt payment discount for payment within five days of date of invoice.

(c) **Calculate the amount that would be paid by Peppers Ltd if a 2.5% prompt discount was offered on the invoice in (a) and the invoice paid within five days.** **(1 marks)**

£	

(d) **What is the latest date by which SCM Products should receive the payment from Peppers Ltd if the prompt payment discount was taken?** **(1 marks)**

▽ Drop down list for task 1.3 (d):

13 May 20XX
15 May 20XX
18 May 20XX
20 May 20XX
30 June 20XX

	▽

(Total: 12 marks)

Task 4

It is the end of June and you have partially prepared SCM Products' sales ledger control account, as shown below.

Sales ledger control

Details	Amount (£)		Detail	Amount (£)
Balance b/f	46,803		Bank	32,886
			Irrecoverable debt	1,065

You now have the totals of the sales and sales returns daybooks and must record the appropriate amounts in the sales ledger control account.

Sales daybook extract

Date 20XX	Details	Total (£)	VAT (£)	Net (£)
30 Jun	Totals	43,308	7,218	36,090

Sales returns daybook extract

Date 20XX	Details	Total (£)	VAT (£)	Net (£)
30 Jun	Totals	2,634	439	2,195

1.4

(a) **What will be the entries in the sales ledger control account?**

(4 marks)

Tick whether each amount will be debit or credit.

Balances	Amount (£)	Debit	Credit
Entry from the sales daybook			
Entry from the sales returns daybook			

(b) **What will be the balance carried down on the sales ledger control account?** **(2 marks)**

Amount (£)	Debit	Credit

Your next task is to reconcile the purchases ledger with the purchases ledger control account. These are the balances in the purchases ledger on 1 July.

Credit suppliers	Balances	
	Amount (£)	Debit/Credit
TT Thomas	8,066	Credit
Cope and Croydon	3,197	Credit
Yeltz Ltd	17,954	Credit
Marlo plc	365	Debit
Holton and Partners	11,746	Credit

You have inserted the balance of the purchase ledger control account in the reconciliation statement below.

(c) **Complete the reconciliation statement by:**

- **Inserting the total of the balances in the purchases ledger**
- **Calculating any difference** **(2 marks)**

Reconciliation statement	Amount (£)
Purchase ledger control account balance	40,840
Total of the purchases ledger balances	
Difference	

Your manager wants to know what may have caused the difference shown in the reconciliation statement.

(d) Which TWO of the reasons below could explain the difference you calculated in (c) above? (2 marks)

Reasons	
A credit note was entered twice in the purchases ledger control account.	
An invoice was entered twice in a supplier's account in the purchase ledger.	
A payment was entered twice in a supplier's account in the purchases ledger.	
A discount received was entered twice in the purchases ledger control account.	
An invoice was entered twice in the purchases ledger control account.	
A discount received was not entered in a supplier's account in the purchases ledger.	

The list of balances in the purchases ledger in (c) above shows the account of Marlo plc has a debit balance. Your colleague has prepared a draft letter to be sent to Mrs Odgers at Marlo plc requesting a cheque.

(e) Review the draft letter and highlight SIX errors. Errors may be wrongly spelt, incorrectly used or technically incorrect.

(6 marks)

Dear Mrs Rodgers,

Our sales ledger shows an erroneous overpayment made earlier in the year has resulted in an amount of £356 owing to us. We would be grateful if you could confirm agreement of the amount and provide us with a cheque so that we can correct the error in preparation for our year end. If you require me to provide further details of the underpayment please do not hesitate to contact me and I will be happy to forward documentation to you.

Many thancks in anticipation of your co-operation in this matter.

Yours faithfully,

(Total: 16 marks)

Task 5

SCM Products is committed to improving its Corporate Social Responsibility (CSR) activities. You are part of a team that has been asked to assist in the preparation of an annual report detailing the CSR initiatives planned.

1.5

(a) **Put THREE appropriate initiatives into EACH section of the Corporate Social Responsibility report below.** **(6 marks)**

Initiatives:

Ensuring staff use public transport rather than their own vehicles when travelling for business purposes.
Ensuring production processes maximise energy consumption.
Ensuring all staff minimise costs and expenses to the organisation.
Introducing flexible working conditions so staff can work and still meet personal commitments.
Ensuring all staff complete overtime each month.
Imposing a weekend working requirement on all staff.
Increasing senior management salaries by 10%.
Offering free membership to a local gymnasium for all staff.
Ensuring emissions from our delivery vehicles are minimised.
Allowing staff to complete overseas projects which bring water to communities in developing countries.
Installing energy saving equipment in our production plant.
Offering staff training and supporting those wishing to gain further qualifications.

SCM Products
Corporate Social Responsibility Report

Our commitment to minimising the environmental impact of our activities.

Initiatives planned:

Our commitment to improving the welfare of our employees.

Initiative planned:

In line with a previous commitment to improving the local environment, SCM Products recently held an event to raise funds to renovate a local community centre. The CSR team is responsible for reporting on the costs of the event.

The budget costs were:

Food: £1.75 per person

Entertainment: £50 per hundred people

1,500 people attended the event. The actual costs are shown in the table below and you have been asked to compare these with the budgeted costs.

(b) **Complete the table below by:**

- **Inserting the total budgeted amount for each cost**

- **Inserting the variance for each cost**

- **Selecting whether each variance is adverse or favourable.**

(6 marks)

∇ Drop down list for task 1.5 (b):

Adverse
Favourable

Event cost performance report				
Cost	Budget (£)	Actual (£)	Variance (£)	Adverse/ Favourable
Food		2,200		∇
Entertainment		1,150		∇

(Total: 12 marks)

Task 6

Your manager at SCM Products is interested in how costs behave at different levels of output. She has asked you to prepare a cost analysis at different levels of output for a product. You are told that fixed costs are £20,000 and variable costs are £5 per unit.

1.6

(a) **Complete the table below to show fixed, variable and total and unit costs for each of the three levels of output.** (12 marks)

Level of output	Fixed costs (£)	Variable costs (£)	Total costs (£)	Unit cost (£)
2,000 units				
5,000 units				
8,000 units				

(b) **In the box below, write a short report for non-finance staff containing:**

- **A brief introduction outlining the areas you will be covering in the report**

- **An explanation of what a fixed cost is, giving an example**

- **An explanation of what a variable cost is, giving an example**

- **A description of what happens to the unit cost as output increases and the reason for this.** (12 marks)

Your report must be clear and structured appropriately.

(Total: 24 marks)

Task 7

You are preparing for the accounting month-end at SCM Products.

Your first task is to transfer data from the purchases daybook to the ledgers. An extract from the purchases daybook is shown below.

Date 20XX	Details	Invoice number	Total (£)	VAT (£)	Net (£)
31 Aug	Carstairs Ltd	C1673X	474	79	395

1.7

(a) **Show whether the entries in the general ledger will be debit or credit entries.** **(3 marks)**

Account name	Debit	Credit
Purchases		
VAT		
Purchases ledger control		

(b) **What will be the entry in the purchases ledger?** **(3 marks)**

▽ Drop down list for task 1.7 (b):

Carstairs Ltd
Purchases
Purchases ledger control
Purchases returns
Sales
Sales ledger control
Sales returns
VAT
<empty>

Account name	Amount (£)	Debit	Credit
▽			

You have found an error in the accounting records. A cheque payment of £4,206 to a credit supplier has been recorded as £4,260.

You have partially prepared journal entries to correct the error in the general ledger.

(c) **Complete the journals below by:**

- **Removing the incorrect entries, and**

- **Recording the correct entries.** **(4 marks)**

Do not enter a zero in unused debit or credit column cells.

Journal to remove the incorrect entries

Account name	Debit (£)	Credit (£)
Bank		
Purchases ledger control		

Journal to record the correct entries

Account name	Debit (£)	Credit (£)
Purchases ledger control		
Bank		

You have also identified that discounts received were omitted from the general ledger. You have prepared the journal entries below to correct the omission.

Journal

Account name	Debit (£)	Credit (£)
Purchases ledger control	120	
Discounts received		120

(d)   **Record the journal in the general ledger by dragging the appropriate entry into each account below.**   **(2 marks)**

Discounts received

Details	Amount (£)	Details	Amount (£)
		Balance b/f	993

Purchases ledger control

Details	Amount (£)	Details	Amount (£)
		Balance b/f	37,721

Entries:

Discounts received	120

Purchases ledger control	120

(Total: 12 marks)

2 Specimen Assessment Answers

Task 1

1.1

(a) Complete your to-do list for today, Friday of week 4. Refer to the management and financial accounts schedule and place the tasks to be completed into the to-do list below. **(4 marks)**

Note: You may put each task into the to-do list more than once if the task takes more than one hour to complete.

Friday, week 4 to-do list	Time
Cash book	09.00 – 10.00
Process invoices	10.00 – 11.00
Post cheques	11.00 – 12.00
Reconcile statements	12.00 – 13.00
Cost coding	13.00 – 14.00

(b) Identify on which day in which week you will be the busiest with routine tasks from the management and financial accounts schedules. **(2 marks)**

Day of the week	Week number
Thursday	Week 1

(c) What will be the cash and bank balances carried down? **(4 marks)**

Tick whether each amount will be debit or credit.

Balances	Amount (£)	Debit	Credit
Cash balance carried down	260		✓
Bank balance carried down	4,012	✓	

(d) What will be the totals of the cash and bank columns once the balances have been inserted? **(2 marks)**

Totals	Amount (£)
Cash total	1,110
Bank total	8,537

(Total: 12 marks)

Task 2

1.2

(a) From the list below, identify the FOUR main roles of the finance function at SCM Products by placing them into your notes.

(4 marks)

> **Notes for Simon**
>
> **Main roles of the finance function:**
>
> Ensuring the security of financial data
>
> Managing funds effectively
>
> Producing statutory financial statements
>
> Providing accounting information to other internal departments

(b) From the list below, identify FOUR policies or procedures Simon should familiarise himself with by dragging them into your notes.

(4 marks)

> **Notes for Simon**
>
> **Policies and Procedures you need to be familiar with:**
>
> Holiday entitlement policy
>
> Petty cash claiming procedures
>
> Staff development policy
>
> Cheque banking procedures

(c) **Identify FOUR ways Simon could develop the necessary skills to help him in his role** (4 marks)

Ways for Simon to develop his skills	
Interrupt the speaker to ask questions during meetings.	
Make eye contact with the speaker.	✓
Wait until the person speaking has finished before asking questions.	✓
Cough loudly to indicate to the speaker that the meeting has overrun.	
Complete the work tasks at your own pace, focussing on the accuracy of the work.	
Discuss difficulties in meeting deadlines with your supervisor at the earliest opportunity.	✓
Complete work tasks as quickly as possible, relying on your supervisor to check the accuracy of the work.	
Ask as many questions as you need until you fully understand what you are being asked to do.	✓

(Total: 12 marks)

Task 3

1.3

(a) Refer to the price list and complete the FOUR boxes in the invoice below. **(4 marks)**

Invoice:

SCM Products
14 London Road
Parton, PA21 7NL
VAT Registration No. 298 3827 04

Invoice No. 3912

To: Invoice date: 15 May 20XX
Peppers Ltd   Delivery date: 13 May 20XX
121 New Street   Customer account code: PEP003
Grangeton, GX12 4SD

Quantity of units	Product code	Price each (£)	Net amount (£)	VAT amount (£)	Total amount (£)
120	BXC20	3.85	462.00	92.40	554.40

Terms of payment: Net monthly account

(b) Record the invoice in the correct daybook by:

- **Selecting the correct daybook title and**

- **Making the necessary entries.** **(6 marks)**

Sales daybook ▽

Date 20XX	Details	Account code	Invoice number	Total (£)	VAT (£)	Net (£)
15 May	Peppers Ltd ▽	PEP003	3912	554.40	92.40	462.00

(c) Calculate the amount that would be paid by Peppers Ltd if a 2.5% prompt discount was offered on the invoice in (a) and the invoice paid within five days. **(1 marks)**

£	540.54

(d) What is the latest date by which SCM Products should receive the payment from Peppers Ltd if the prompt payment discount was taken? **(1 marks)**

20 May 20XX ▽

(Total: 12 marks)

Task 4

1.4

(a) What will be the entries in the sales ledger control account? **(4 marks)**

Tick whether each amount will be debit or credit.

Balances	Amount (£)	Debit	Credit
Entry from the sales daybook	43,308	✓	
Entry from the sales returns daybook	2,634		✓

(b) What will be the balance carried down on the sales ledger control account? **(2 marks)**

Amount (£)	Debit	Credit
53,526		✓

(c) Complete the reconciliation statement by:

- Inserting the total of the balances in the purchases ledger

- Calculating any difference **(2 marks)**

Reconciliation statement	Amount (£)
Purchase ledger control account balance	40,840
Total of the purchases ledger balances	40,598
Difference	242

(d) Which TWO of the reasons below could explain the difference you calculated in (c) above? **(2 marks)**

Reasons	
A credit note was entered twice in the purchases ledger control account.	
An invoice was entered twice in a supplier's account in the purchase ledger.	
A payment was entered twice in a supplier's account in the purchases ledger.	✓
A discount received was entered twice in the purchases ledger control account.	
An invoice was entered twice in the purchases ledger control account.	✓
A discount received was not entered in a supplier's account in the purchases ledger.	

(Total: 16 marks)

(e) Review the draft letter and highlight SIX errors. Errors may be wrongly spelt, incorrectly used or technically incorrect. **(6 marks)**

Dear Mrs **Rodgers**,

Our **sales** ledger shows an erroneous overpayment made earlier in the year has resulted in an amount of **£356** owing to us. We would be grateful if you could confirm agreement of the amount and provide us with a cheque so that we can correct the error in preparation for our year-end. If you require me to provide further details of the **underpayment** please do not hesitate to contact me and I will be happy to forward documentation to you.

Many **thancks** in anticipation of your co-operation in this matter.

Yours **faithfully**,

(Total: 16 marks)

KAPLAN PUBLISHING

Task 5

1.5

(a) Put THREE appropriate initiatives into EACH section of the Corporate Social Responsibility report below. **(6 marks)**

SCM Products
Corporate Social Responsibility Report
Our commitment to minimising the environmental impact of our activities. **Initiatives planned:** Ensuring staff use public transport rather than their own vehicles when travelling for business purposes. Ensuring emissions from our delivery vehicles are minimised. Installing energy saving equipment in our production plant.
Our commitment to improving the welfare of our employees. **Initiative planned:** Introducing flexible working conditions so staff can work and still meet personal commitments. Offering free membership to a local gymnasium for all staff. Offering staff training and supporting those wishing to gain further qualifications.

(b) Complete the table below by:

- Inserting the total budgeted amount for each cost
- Inserting the variance for each cost
- Selecting whether each variance is adverse or favourable.

(6 marks)

Event cost performance report				
Cost	Budget (£)	Actual (£)	Variance (£)	Adverse/ Favourable
Food	2,625	2,200	425	Favourable ▽
Entertainment	750	1,150	400	Adverse ▽

(Total: 12 marks)

Task 6

1.6

(a) Complete the table below to show fixed, variable and total and unit costs for each of the three levels of output.   **(12 marks)**

Level of output	Fixed costs (£)	Variable costs (£)	Total costs (£)	Unit cost (£)
2,000 units	20,000	10,000	30,000	15.00
5,000 units	20,000	25,000	45,000	9.00
8,000 units	20,000	40,000	60,000	7.50

(b) In the box below, write a short report for non-finance staff containing:

- A brief introduction outlining the areas you will be covering in the report

- An explanation of what a fixed cost is, giving an example

- An explanation of what a variable cost is, giving an example

- A description of what happens to the unit cost as output increases and the reason for this.   **(12 marks)**

Your report must be clear and structural appropriately.

Introduction

This report:

- explains and gives examples of fixed and variable costs
- describes the effect of increased output on unit costs.

Fixed cost

A fixed cost is one that remains the same irrespective of the level of output. An example of a fixed cost for a factory would be the cost of rent.

Variable cost

A variable cost is one which changes in relation to the level of output. An example of a variable production cost would be the direct materials used in a product.

Description of what happens to the cost per unit as output increases

The cost per unit deceases as output increases. This is because fixed costs do not change with output so are shared between an increased number of units when output increases.

(Total: 24 marks)

Task 7

1.7

(a) Show whether the entries in the general ledger will be debit or credit entries. **(3 marks)**

Account name	Debit	Credit
Purchases	✓	
VAT	✓	
Purchases ledger control		✓

(b) What will be the entry in the purchases ledger? **(3 marks)**

Account name	Amount (£)	Debit	Credit
Carstairs Ltd ▽	474		✓

(c) Complete the journals below by:

- Removing the incorrect entries, and

- Recording the correct entries. **(4 marks)**

Do not enter a zero in unused debit or credit column cells.

Journal to remove the incorrect entries

Account name	Debit (£)	Credit (£)
Bank	4,260	
Purchases ledger control		4,260

Journal to record the correct entries

Account name	Debit (£)	Credit (£)
Purchases ledger control	4,206	
Bank		4,206

(d) Record the journal in the general ledger by dragging the appropriate entry into each account below. **(2 marks)**

Discounts received

Details	Amount (£)	Details	Amount (£)
		Balance b/f	993
		Purchases ledger control	120

Purchases ledger control

Details	Amount (£)	Details	Amount (£)
Discounts received	120	Balance b/f	37,721

Entries:

Discounts received	120

Purchases ledger control	120

(Total: 12 marks)

KAPLAN PUBLISHING

MOCK ASSESSMENT

1 Mock Assessment Questions

Scenario: The tasks are set in a business situation where the following conditions apply:

- You are employed as an accounts assistant in the finance function at MM Manufacturing (MM).

- The finance function includes the financial and management accounting teams.

- MM uses a manual bookkeeping system.

- Double entry takes place in the general ledger. Individual accounts of trade receivables and trade payables are kept in the sales and purchases ledgers as subsidiary accounts.

- The cash book and petty cash book should be treated as part of the double entry system unless the task instructions state otherwise.

- The VAT rate is 20%.

Task 1 (12 marks)

You work from 09.00 until 16.00, with one hour for lunch, Monday to Friday of each week. Each finance period is four weeks in duration and you therefore plan your work in a four-week cycle.

The work schedules below show the days when routine tasks must be completed and the amount of time each task takes to complete. It is very important that you complete the management accounts tasks by the end of the specified day and the financial accounts tasks by the day and time indicated.

Weekly work schedule – financial accounts			
Task	Task to be completed each week by:		Task duration
	Day	Time	
Reconcile statements	Friday	13.00	1 hour
Departmental summary	Thursday	13.00	1 hour
Process invoices	Friday	11.00	1 hour
Post cheques	Every day	12.00	1 hour
Contact suppliers	Monday	11.00	1 hour
Petty cash reconciliation	Wednesday	10.00	1 hour
Contact customers	Tuesday	12.00	2 hours
Deposit bankings	Every day	14.00	1 hour

Monthly work schedules – management accounts				
	Monday	**Tuesday**	**Wednesday**	**Thursday**	**Friday**
Week 1	Overhead cost report (1 hours)		Overhead cost report (2 hours)	Budget report (2 hours)	Manufacturing cost review (1 hour)
Week 2	Materials cost report (1 hour)	Materials cost report (1 hour)	Labour cost report (3 hours)		
Week 3			Materials cost report (1 hour)		Manufacturing cost review (1 hour)
Week 4	Data collection (2 hours)			Cost coding (1 hour)	Variance analysis (1 hour)

You are planning your work at the start of the day on Monday of week 2. You have been asked to complete a non-routine cash book task by 10am, which is already included in your to-do list.

(a) **Complete your to-do list for today, Monday of week 2. Refer to the management and financial accounts schedules and place the tasks to be completed into the to-do list below.** **(4 marks)**

Note: You may put each task into the to-do list more than once if the task takes more than one hour to complete.

Tasks:

Budget report	Deposit bankings	Post cheques
Contact customers	Labour cost report	Process invoices
Contact suppliers	Manufacturing cost review	Product cost analysis
Cost coding	Materials cost report	Reconcile statements
Data collection	Overhead cost report	Variance analysis
Departmental summary	Petty cash reconciliation	

Monday, week 2 to-do list	Time
Cash book	09.00 – 10.00
	10.00 – 11.00
	11.00 – 12.00
Lunch hour	12.00 – 13.00
	13.00 – 14.00
	14.00 – 15.00
	15.00 – 16.00

You are often asked to complete non-routine tasks. However, on one day in each four week cycle you are too busy with routine tasks to accept non-routine work.

(b) **Identify on which day in which week you will be the busiest with routine tasks from the management and financial accounts schedules.**

Place the day of the week and the week number into the table below. **(2 marks)**

Days and weeks:

Monday, Tuesday, Wednesday, Thursday, Friday

Week 1, Week 2, Week 3, Week 4

Day of the week	Week number

The non-routine cash book task in today's to-do list is finalising the cash book below for a colleague who is away on study leave.

Cash book

Details	Cash (£)	Bank (£)	VAT (£)	Trade receivables (£)	Cash sales (£)
Balance b/f	15				
M Alonso		2,400		2,400	
J James	1,020		170		850
I Guana		960		960	
Cash		985			

Details	Cash (£)	Bank (£)	VAT (£)	Trade payables (£)	Cash purchases (£)
Balance b/f		4,550			
P Read Ltd		1,500		1,500	
A Gator		390	65		325
D Phin		210	35		175
Bank	985				

(c) **What will be the cash and bank balances brought forward the start of the following day?** **(4 marks)**

Tick whether each amount will be debit or credit.

Balances	Amount (£)	Debit	Credit
Cash balance b/f			
Bank balance b/f			

(d) **What will be the totals of the cash and bank columns when the balances have been inserted?** **(2 marks)**

	Amount (£)
Cash total	
Bank total	

Task 2   (12 marks)

MM has recently recruited Julie, who will join MM from another employer. Julie has some relevant accounting experience from her previous job, but will not be familiar with MM. Initially, Julie will have responsibility for recording petty cash transactions and will also be responsible for ensuring that there will be adequate stationery supplies available to colleagues in the accounts department. Julie will also deal with other ad hoc duties as she becomes familiar with the work of her colleagues in the accounts department.

As Julie is due to start work next week, you have been asked to provide some notes to help her settle into her role. You have decided to begin the notes with the main roles of the finance function.

(a) **From the list below, identify the FOUR main roles of the finance function at MM by placing them into your notes.** **(4 marks)**

List of roles:

Ensuring the security of the manufacturing processes
Ensuring the confidentiality of accounting information
Managing staff in other internal departments
Ensuring the reliability of financial data
Producing monthly bank reconciliations
Producing statutory financial statements
Providing accounting information to other internal departments
Providing systems support to other departments

Notes for Julie **Main roles of the finance function:**

It is now Julie's first week at MM and you are helping with her induction into the organisation. You have been asked to highlight important policies and procedures on MM's intranet that Julie should familiarise herself with.

(b) From the list below, identify FOUR policies or procedures Julie should familiarise herself with by placing them into your notes.

(4 marks)

List of policies and procedures:

Annual leave entitlement policy
Research and development policy
Sales team selling targets
Sickness and absence reporting
Vehicle maintenance checking procedures
Warehouse despatch procedures
Accounts department study leave policy
Stationery ordering procedures for the accounts department

Notes for Julie

Policies and procedures you need to be familiar with:

Julie has been working with you for a few weeks now and you are aware of some concerns in relation to her performance. During meetings, Julie appears uninterested and does not participate. There have also been instances of Julie misunderstanding instructions and not meeting deadlines. You decide to help Julie to develop the skills which are important in her role.

(c) **Identify FOUR ways Julie could develop the necessary skills to help her in her role** **(4 marks)**

Ways for Julie to develop her skills	
Prepare for meetings by thinking of relevant issues in advance to raise and discuss.	
Work on your own and don't ask for help or guidance.	
Identify the speaker at meetings so that you can develop a network of colleagues and work contacts.	
Take your mobile phone into meetings and set it to silent mode to text friends who are difficult to contact as they have limited free time.	
Wait until the person speaking has finished before asking questions.	
Take notes at meetings so that you can remember what was discussed and any decisions made.	
Interrupt the speaker during meetings to ask questions.	

Task 3 (12 marks)

MM has supplied goods to Premier Products Ltd. You have been asked to complete the invoice by calculating the invoice amounts.

(a) **Refer to the price list and complete the FOUR boxes in the invoice below.** **(4 marks)**

Price List:

Product code	Price each (£)
ADA14	5.50
BDA14	6.00
BDA16	3.50
CDE24	2.40
DOX18	9.00
DOX28	9.50

Invoice:

	MM Manufacturing	
	5 Liverpool Way	
	Brayton, BA42 5YZ	
	VAT Registration No. 983 3624 07	
	Invoice No. 2178	

To:
Premier Products Ltd
121 Old Road
Grungetown, GR78 9DR

Invoice date: 12 June 20X6
Delivery date: 12 June 20X6
Customer account code: PP007

Quantity of units	Product code	Price each (£)	Net amount (£)	VAT amount (£)	Total amount (£)
65	CDE24				

Terms of payment: Net monthly account

Your next task is to enter the invoice into the appropriate daybook.

(b) **Record the invoice in the correct daybook by:**

- **selecting the correct daybook title, and**

- **making the necessary entries.** **(6 marks)**

∇ Drop down lists for task 1.3 (b):

Cash book	Premier Products Ltd
Discounts allowed daybook	MM Manufacturing
Discounts received daybook	
Petty cash book	
Purchases daybook	
Purchases returns daybook	
Sales daybook	
Sales returns daybook	

Date 20X6	Details	Account code	Invoice number	Total (£)	VAT (£)	Net (£)
▽						
12 June	▽		2178			

MM Manufacturing is considering offering its customers a 5.0% prompt payment discount for payment within ten days of date of invoice.

(c) **Calculate the amount that Premier Products Ltd would deduct if a 5.0% prompt discount was offered on the invoice in (a) and the invoice paid within ten days.** **(1 mark)**

£ [   ]

(d) **What is the latest date by which MM should receive the payment from Premier Products Ltd if the prompt payment discount was taken?** **(1 mark)**

▽ Drop down list for task 1.3 (d):

12 June 20X6
17 June 20X6
21 June 20X6
22 June 20X6
12 July 20X6

▽

Task 4 **(16 marks)**

It is now early September and you are in the process of preparing MMs' purchases ledger control account as at 31 August, as shown below.

Purchases ledger control

Details	Amount (£)		Detail	Amount (£)
Bank	44,214		Balance b/f	78,954

You now have the totals of the purchases and purchases returns daybooks and must record the appropriate amounts in the purchases ledger control account.

Purchases daybook extract

Date 20X6	Details	Total (£)	VAT (£)	Net (£)
31 Aug	Totals	31,572	5,262	26,310

Discounts received daybook extract

Date 20X6	Details	Total (£)	VAT (£)	Net (£)
31 Aug	Totals	1,350	225	1,125

Purchases returns daybook extract

Date 20X6	Details	Total (£)	VAT (£)	Net (£)
31 Aug	Totals	600	100	500

(a) **What will be the entries in the purchases ledger control account?** **(4 marks)**

Tick whether each amount will be debit or credit.

Balances	Amount (£)	Debit	Credit
Entry from the purchases daybook			
Entry from the discounts received daybook			
Entry from the purchases returns daybook			

(b) **What will be the balance carried down on the purchases ledger control account?** (2 marks)

Amount (£)	Debit	Credit

Your next task is to reconcile the sales ledger with the sales ledger control account as at 31 August. These are the balances in the sales ledger on 31 August.

Credit customers	Balances	
	Amount (£)	Debit/Credit
Baikal	15,987	Debit
Eerie	14,628	Debit
Louise & Partners	358	Credit
Michigan plc	17,242	Debit
Superior Ltd	11,746	Debit
Windermere	23,255	Debit

You have inserted the balance of the sales ledger control account in the reconciliation statement below.

(c) **Complete the reconciliation statement by:**

- **inserting the total of the balances in the purchases ledger, and**

- **calculating any difference.** (2 marks)

Reconciliation statement	Amount (£)
Sales ledger control account balance	82,130
Total of the sales ledger balances	
Difference	

Your manager wants to know what may have caused the difference shown in the reconciliation statement.

(d) **Which TWO of the reasons below could NOT explain the difference you calculated in (c) above?** (2 marks)

Reasons	
A credit note was entered twice in the sales ledger control account.	
An invoice was entered twice in a customer ledger account in the sales ledger.	
A receipt was entered twice in a customer ledger account in the sales ledger.	
A discount allowed was entered twice in the sales ledger control account.	
An invoice was entered twice in the sales ledger control account.	
A discount allowed was not entered in a customer ledger account in the sales ledger.	

The list of balances in the sales ledger in (c) above shows the account of Louise & Partners has a credit balance which arose as a result of the customer making two payments to MM.

Your colleague has prepared a draft letter to be sent to Mr Browne at Louise & Partners enclosing a cheque to clear the balance.

(e) **Review the draft letter and highlight SIX errors. Errors may be wrongly spelt, incorrectly used or technically incorrect.**

(6 marks)

Dear Mr Brown, Our purchase ledger shows an erroneous overpayment recently made by MM Manufacturing has resulted in an amount of £538 owing to you. Please find enclosed a check for the amount due. If you require any further information relating to this payment, please contact me and I can provide supporting documentation and information. Yours faithfully,

Task 5 (12 marks)

MM has recently committed itself to improving its Corporate Social Responsibility (CSR) activities. You are part of a team that has been asked to prepare a staff summary of the benefits of positive Corporate Social Responsibility, and identify CSR initiatives that staff could become involved with.

(a) **Complete the two sections of the staff summary, by choosing THREE benefits to MM of having a positive attitude to CSR and THREE CSR initiatives to raise local community awareness that employees could become involved with.** (6 marks)

Possible benefits of CSR to MM (choose THREE):

Producing more products will mean using more resources even if good CSR practices are introduced.
CSR will help to improve the reputation of the organisation.
CSR will help to attract and retain staff.
There will be some costs incurred in order to introduce CSR initiatives into the organisation.
CSR will help to reduce costs associated with wastage and inefficiency.
Professional consultants will need to be hired to provide staff with appropriate training and awareness of CSR.

Possible CSR initiatives to raise local community awareness (choose THREE):

MM could donate surplus or waste resources, such as paper and cardboard, to local a local nursery for use by children in play activities.
MM could change its manufacturing and production processes.
MM could permit members of staff to have leave of absence from work to act as a volunteer in a local charity.
Offering staff training and supporting those wishing to gain further qualifications.
MM could sponsor members of staff who undertake fund-raising activities for a local charity.
MM could try to ensure that all staff minimise costs and expenses to the organisation.

MM Manufacturing
Staff Summary
Corporate Social Responsibility
Benefits of CSR to MM Manufacturing.
CSR initiatives to raise community awareness.

MM recently introduced a new initiative to improve the local environment, by agreeing to clear an area of parkland and to plant trees, shrubs and flowers so that it will be used by the local community. MM therefore organised a fund-raising event, with all funds raised used for the park clearance and development activity. The CSR team is responsible for reporting on the costs of the event.

The budget costs were:

Hire of venue £750

Food and drink £10.50 per person

1,250 people attended the event. The actual costs are shown in the table below and you have been asked to compare these with the budgeted costs.

(b) Complete the table below by:

   - inserting the total budgeted amount for each cost

   - inserting the variance for each cost, and

   - selecting whether each variance is adverse or favourable.

(6 marks)

∇ Drop down list for task 1.5 (b):

Adverse
Favourable

Parkland clearance cost performance report				
Cost	Budget (£)	Actual (£)	Variance (£)	Adverse/ Favourable
Venue hire		850		∇
Food & drink		12,900		∇

Task 6

(24 marks)

A departmental manager at MM is interested in how costs behave at different levels of output. He has requested that you prepare a cost analysis for product ZXY at different levels of output. You are told that fixed costs are £15,000 and variable costs are £8 per unit.

(a) **Complete the table below to show fixed, variable and total and unit costs for each of the three levels of output for product ZXY.**

(12 marks)

Level of output	Fixed costs (£)	Variable costs (£)	Total costs (£)	Unit cost (£)
4,000 units				
10,000 units				
15,000 units				

(b)   In the box below, write a short report for the departmental manager comprising:

- a brief introduction outlining the areas you will be covering in the report

- an explanation of what a variable cost is, giving an example

- an explanation of what a fixed cost is, giving an example

- a description of what happens to the unit cost as output falls, for example from 15, 000 units to 10,000 units, and the reason for this.   **(12 marks)**

Your report must be clear and structured appropriately.

Task 7   **(12 marks)**

You are preparing for the August 20X6 accounting month-end at MM.

Your first task is to transfer data from the sales daybook to the ledgers. An extract from the sales daybook is shown below.

Date 20X6	Details	Invoice number	Total (£)	VAT (£)	Net (£)
31 Aug	Crosby Ltd	MM3258	660	110	550

(a)   Show whether the entries in the general ledger will be debit or credit entries.   **(3 marks)**

Account name	Debit	Credit
Sales		
VAT		
Sales ledger control		

(b)   What will be the entry in the sales ledger?   **(3 marks)**

▽ Drop down list for task 1.7 (b):

Crosby Ltd
Purchases
Purchases ledger control
Purchases returns
Sales
Sales ledger control
Sales returns
VAT
<empty>

Account name	Amount (£)	Debit	Credit
▽			

You have found an error in the accounting records. A cheque receipt of £2,468 from a credit customer had been recorded as £4,268.

You have partially prepared journal entries to correct the error in the general ledger.

(c)   Complete the journals below by:

- **removing the incorrect entries, and**

- **recording the correct entries.**   **(4 marks)**

Do not enter a zero in unused debit or credit column cells.

Journal to remove the incorrect entries

Account name	Debit (£)	Credit (£)
Sales ledger control		
Bank		

Journal to record the correct entries

Account name	Debit (£)	Credit (£)
Bank		
Sales ledger control		

You have also identified that discounts allowed during August 20X6 were omitted from the general ledger. You have prepared the journal entries below to correct the omission.

Journal

Account name	Debit (£)	Credit (£)
Discounts allowed	360	
Sales ledger control		360

(d) **Record the journal in the general ledger by dragging the appropriate entry into each account below.** **(2 marks)**

Discounts allowed

Details	Amount (£)	Details	Amount (£)
Balance b/f	723		

Sales ledger control

Details	Amount (£)	Details	Amount (£)
Balance b/f	84,364		

Entries:

Discounts allowed	360

Sales ledger control	360

2 Mock Assessment Answers

Task 1

(a) Completion of to-do list

Monday, week 2 to-do list	Time
Cash book	09.00 – 10.00
Contact suppliers	10.00 – 11.00
Post cheques	11.00 – 12.00
Lunch hour	12.00 – 13.00
Deposit bankings	13.00 – 14.00
Materials cost report	14.00 – 15.00
Unallocated/available time	15.00 – 16.00

Tutorial note: the materials cost report could be done between 15.00–16.00 if required, with the unallocated time between 14.00–15.00 to deal with any other issues that may arise.

(b) The busiest time within the 4-week period

Day of the week	Week number
Wednesday	Week 2

On this day, the following activities using all six hours of the working day must be completed:

- Reconcile petty cash – 1 hour by 10.00
- Post cheques – 1 hour by 12.00
- Deposit bankings – 1 hour by 14.00
- Labour cost report – 3 hours by the end of the day

(c) Cash and bank balances brought forward

Balances	Amount (£)	Debit	Credit
Cash balance b/f	50	✓	
Bank balance b/f	2,305		✓

(d) Totals of cash and bank columns

Totals	Amount (£)
Cash total	1,035
Bank total	6,650

Task 2

(a)

> **Notes for Julie**
>
> **Main roles of the finance function:**
>
> Ensuring the confidentiality of accounting information
>
> Ensuring the reliability of financial data
>
> Producing statutory financial statements
>
> Providing accounting information to other internal departments

(b)

> **Notes for Julie**
>
> **Policies and Procedures you need to be familiar with:**
>
> Annual leave entitlement policy
>
> Sickness and absence reporting
>
> Accounts department study leave policy
>
> Stationery ordering procedures for the accounts department

(c)

Ways for Julie to develop her skills	
Prepare for meetings by thinking of relevant issues in advance to raise and discuss.	✓
Work on your own and don't ask for help or guidance.	
Identify the speaker at meetings so that you can develop a network of colleagues and work contacts.	✓
Take your mobile phone into meetings and set it to silent mode to text friends who are difficult to contact as they have limited free time.	
Wait until the person speaking has finished before asking questions.	✓
Take notes at meetings so that you can remember what was discussed and any decisions made.	✓
Interrupt the speaker to ask questions during meetings.	

Task 3

(a)

MM Manufacturing

5 Liverpool Way

Brayton, BA42 5YZ

VAT Registration No. 983 3624 07

Invoice No. 2178

To: Invoice date: 12 June 20X6

Premier Products Ltd   Delivery date: 12 June 20X6

121 Old Road   Customer account code: PP007

Grungetown, GR78 9DR

Quantity of units	Product code	Price each (£)	Net amount (£)	VAT amount (£)	Total amount (£)
65	CDE24	2.40	156.00	31.20	187.20
Terms of payment: Net monthly account					

(b)

Sales daybook ▽						
Date 20X6	Details	Account code	Invoice number	Total (£)	VAT (£)	Net (£)
12 June	Premier Products Ltd ▽	PP007	2178	187.20	31.20	156.00

(c)

£	9.36

(d)

22 June 20X6   ▽

Task 4

(a)

Balances	Amount (£)	Debit	Credit
Entry from the purchases daybook	31,572		✓
Entry from the discounts received daybook	1,350	✓	
Entry from the purchases returns daybook	600	✓	

(b)

Amount (£)	Debit	Credit
64,362	✓	

(c)

Reconciliation statement	Amount (£)
Sales ledger control account balance	82,130
Total of the sales ledger balances	82,500
Difference	370

(d)

Reasons	
A credit note was entered twice in the sales ledger control account.	
An invoice was entered twice in a customer ledger account in the sales ledger.	
A receipt was entered twice in a customer ledger account in the sales ledger.	✓
A discount allowed was entered twice in the sales ledger control account.	
An invoice was entered twice in the sales ledger control account.	✓
A discount allowed was not entered in a customer ledger account in the sales ledger.	

(e)

The amended letter should be as follows (errors amended in bold type)

Dear Mr **Browne**,

Our **sales** ledger shows an erroneous overpayment recently made **to** MM Manufacturing has resulted in an amount of **£358** owing to you. Please find enclosed a **cheque** for the amount due. If you require any further information relating to this payment, please contact me and I can provide supporting documentation and information.

Yours **sincerely**,

Task 5

(a)

MM Manufacturing Staff Summary Corporate Social Responsibility
Benefits of CSR to MM CSR will help to improve the reputation of the organisation CSR will help to attract and retain staff CSR will help to reduce costs associated with wastage and inefficiency
CSR initiatives to raise community awareness MM could donate surplus or waste resources, such as paper and cardboard, to local a local nursery for use by children in play activities. MM could permit members of staff to have leave of absence from work to act as a volunteer in a local charity. MM could sponsor members of staff who undertake fund-raising activities for a local charity.

Tutorial note: Although some of the possible items listed may bring CSR benefits, the report requires you to identify those initiatives which are particularly relevant to the local community.

(b)

Parkland clearance cost performance report				
Cost	**Budget (£)**	**Actual (£)**	**Variance (£)**	**Adverse/ favourable**
Venue hire	750	850	100	Adverse ∇
Food & drink	13,125	12,900	225	Favourable ∇

Task 6

(a)

Product ZXY – output and costs

Level of output	Fixed costs (£)	Variable costs (£)	Total costs (£)	Unit cost (£)
4,000 units	15,000	32,000	47,000	11.75
10,000 units	15,000	80,000	95,000	9.50
15,000 units	15,000	120,000	135,000	9.00

(b)

Introduction

This report:

- explains and gives examples of variable and fixed costs
- describes the effect of a fall in output on unit costs.

Variable costs

A variable cost is one which changes in relation to the level of output. An example of a variable production cost would be the direct labour costs used to manufacture a product. Note that this should not include wages and salaries costs of office staff, for example.

Fixed costs

A fixed cost is one that remains the same irrespective of the level of output. An example of a fixed cost for a factory would be the cost of insuring the premises.

Description of what happens to the total cost per unit as output increases

The total cost per unit increases as output falls. This is because fixed costs do not change with output so are shared between a reduced number of units when output falls. Even though the fixed cost per unit increases when output falls, the variable cost per unit will remain unchanged at £8 per unit.

Task 7

(a)

General ledger entries

Account name	Debit	Credit
Sales		✓
VAT		✓
Sales ledger control	✓	

(b)

Sales ledger entries

Account name	Amount (£)	Debit	Credit
Crosby Ltd ▽	660	✓	

(c)

Journal to remove the incorrect entries

Account name	Debit (£)	Credit (£)
Sales ledger control	4,268	
Bank		4,268

Journal to record the correct entries

Account name	Debit (£)	Credit (£)
Bank	2,468	
Sales ledger control		2,468

(d)

Discounts allowed

Details	Amount (£)	Details	Amount (£)
Balance b/f	723		
Sales ledger control	360		

Sales ledger control

Details	Amount (£)	Details	Amount (£)
Balance b/f	84,364	Discounts allowed	360

Appendix 1: Bookkeeping Transactions

Introduction

This chapter recaps the key aspects of the underlying Bookkeeping Transactions Unit.

UNIT LEARNING OBJECTIVES STILL RELEVANT FOR THE SYNOPTIC ASSESSMENT
LO2   Process customer transactions
LO3   Process supplier transactions
LO4   Process receipts and payments
LO5   Process transactions through the ledgers to the trial balance

LO2 Process customer transactions

Calculate invoice and credit note amounts

- Understand the difference between total, net and VAT amounts and how to calculate them.

- Bulk discounts and trade discounts should be deducted before amounts are included in an invoice or credit note.

- Prompt payment discount allowed to customers (i.e. settlement or cash discount) is accounted for only when a customer takes advantage of the discount terms.

Enter sales invoices and credit notes into books of prime entry

- The sales day book is a list of credit sales invoices issued in date order, which records the transaction date, invoice reference number, customer name and account reference, along with the total, VAT and net amounts.

- The sales returns day book is a list of sales credit notes issued in date order which records the transaction date, credit note reference number, customer name and account reference, along with the total, VAT and net amounts.

- The discounts allowed day book is a list of prompt payment discounts allowed to credit customers which records the transaction date, customer name and account reference, along with the total, VAT and net amounts.

- Ensure that you understand, and can calculate total, VAT and net amounts based upon the following relationship:

	%	£
Net amount	100	500
Add: VAT amount e.g. 20%	20	100
	———	———
Total amount	120	600
	———	———

- Ensure that you understand, and can calculate total, VAT and net amounts, given any two of the three values in the relationship:

  e.g. net amount = total amount/120

  e.g. VAT amount = total amount/120 × 20

  e.g. total amount = net amount × 120/100

- Make entries in the sales day book as follows, with equivalent information recorded in the sales returns day book and discounts allowed day books as required:

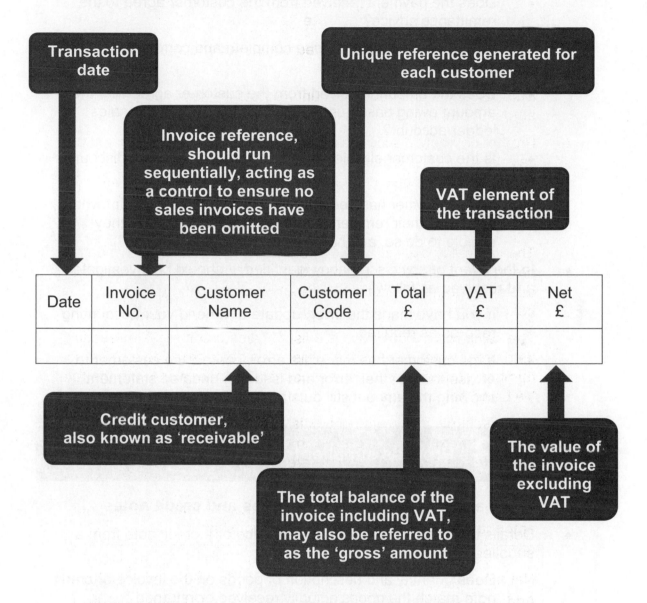

- Total the columns in the sales day book, sales returns day book and discounts allowed day book respectively and cross cast the totals to ensure that they are arithmetically accurate.

Check the accuracy of receipts from customers

- Details to check upon receiving a remittance advice include:

  - Does the payment received from the customer agree to the remittance advice?

  - Are all details on the cheque complete and correct so that it can be banked?

  - Does the amount received from the customer agree with the amount owing based upon their individual customer sales ledger account?

  - Is the customer eligible to take any prompt payment discount offered?

  - If the customer has deducted prompt payment discount when preparing their remittance and making payment, are they eligible to do so, and has it been calculated correctly?

- In the event of any discrepancy identified, it should be investigated and resolved as follows:

  - If you have made the error, update or amend your accounting records as required

  - If the customer has made the error, contact the customer to advise them of their error and issue an updated statement showing the amount still outstanding.

LO3 Process supplier transactions

Check the accuracy of supplier invoices and credit notes

- Details to check upon receiving an invoice or a credit note from a supplier include:

  - Does quantity and description of goods on the invoice or credit note match the goods actually received or returned?

  - Does the price charged by the supplier agree with what was previously agreed with the supplier?

  - Check that any bulk or trade discount agreed with the supplier has been deducted before calculation of the amounts stated on the invoice or credit note.

  - Check the calculations of net, VAT and total amounts on the invoice or credit note to ensure that it is arithmetically correct.

  - Check the date and terms of payment, including possible prompt payment discount, are correct.

- In the event of any discrepancy identified, it should be investigated and resolved as follows:

  - If you have made the error, update or amend your accounting records as required

  - If the supplier has made the error, contact them to advise them of their error and confirm how the discrepancy will be rectified e.g. a credit note will be issued or a further delivery of goods will be made by the supplier.

Enter supplier invoices and credit notes into the books of prime entry

- The purchase day book is a list of credit purchase invoices issued in date order, which records the transaction date, invoice reference number, supplier name and account reference, along with the total, VAT and net amounts.

- The purchase returns day book is a list of purchase credit notes issued in date order which records the transaction date, credit note reference number, supplier name and account reference, along with the total, VAT and net amounts.

- The discounts received day book is a list of prompt payment discounts received from credit suppliers which records the transaction date, supplier name and account reference, along with the total, VAT and net amounts.

- Ensure that you understand, and can calculate total, VAT and net amounts refer back to the previous section if necessary) based upon the following relationship:

- The discounts received day book is a list of prompt payment discounts received from credit suppliers which records the transaction date, customer name and account reference, along with the total, VAT and net amounts.

- Make entries in the purchases day book as follows, with similar information recorded in the purchases returns day book and discounts received day books as required:

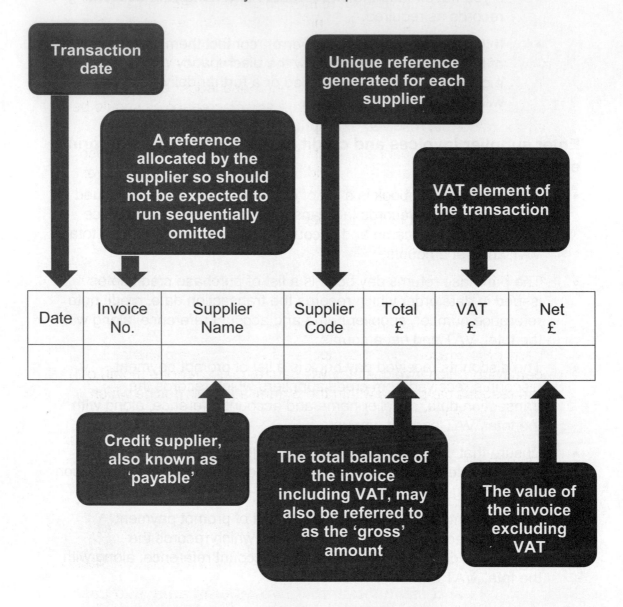

Date	Invoice No.	Supplier Name	Supplier Code	Total £	VAT £	Net £

Transaction date

A reference allocated by the supplier so should not be expected to run sequentially omitted

Unique reference generated for each supplier

VAT element of the transaction

Credit supplier, also known as 'payable'

The total balance of the invoice including VAT, may also be referred to as the 'gross' amount

The value of the invoice excluding VAT

- Note that the purchases day book will often include analysis columns to analyse the net amount of each invoice into appropriate cost classifications and facilitate coding as preparation for posting of totals to the ledgers.

- Total the columns in the purchase day book, purchase returns day book and discounts received day book respectively and cross cast the totals to ensure that they are arithmetically accurate.

Prepare payments to suppliers

- Suppliers of goods and services on credit will usually send a monthly statement of account to each of their customers, detailing any balance outstanding at the beginning of the statement period, along with invoices and credit notes issued during the month, together with cash received and discount they have allowed to their customer.

- This should be checked against the purchase ledger account for the supplier to ensure that it is accurate – any discrepancies should be investigated and resolved appropriately.

- Examples of discrepancies which may arise between the supplier statement balance and the individual purchase ledger account for that supplier include:

    - cash in transit to the supplier, not on the statement

    - goods in transit from the supplier not yet received

    - discount or credit notes not yet accounted for by one party or the other

    - omitted or duplicated transactions.

- Many organisations use the supplier statement as a basis for identifying which invoices they will pay (e.g. all over one month old) or a responsible person within the organisation will decide which invoices should be paid.

- Before raising the payment, care should be taken to identify whether any prompt payment discount can be claimed and for that to be calculated correctly.

LO4 Process receipts and payments

Enter receipts and payments into a two-column analysed cash book

- A proforma two column cash receipts book is shown below:

CASH RECEIPTS BOOK						
Date	Narrative	Reference	Cash £	Bank £	VAT £	Receivables £	Cash sales £
Totals						

- This will be updated using information from the following sources:

  - listings of cheques received, or the bank paying-in slips

  - remittance advices received from customers

  - bank statements to confirm direct credits received from customers.

- A proforma two-column cash payments book is shown below:

CASH PAYMENTS BOOK

Date	Narrative	Reference	Cash £	Bank £	VAT £	Payables £	Cash purchases £	Admin £
Totals								

- This will be updated using information from the following sources:

  - listings of cheques raised to pay suppliers, or the cheque book stubs

  - bank statements to confirm direct debits and standing order payments and any bank charges or interest paid.

Enter receipts and payments into an analysed petty cash book

- A specimen analysed petty cash book is as follows:

	Receipts			Payments							
Date	Narrative	Total £	Date	Narrative	Voucher no	Total £	Postage £	Cleaning £	Tea & Coffee £	Sundry £	VAT £
1 Nov	Bal b/f	35.50									
1 Nov	Cheque 394	114.50	1 Nov	Market	58	23.50			23.50		
			2 Nov	Post Office Ltd	59	29.50	29.50				
			2 Nov	Cleaning materials	60	15.07		12.56			2.51
			3 Nov	Postage	61	16.19	16.19				
			3 Nov	Market	62	10.57		8.81			1.76
			4 Nov	Newspapers	63	18.90				18.90	
			5 Nov	Market	64	12.10				10.09	2.01

- Receipts will consist mainly of replenishment of the petty cash float from the main bank account, normally using the imprest system:

- Payments will normally comprise relatively small amounts for sundry items e.g. cleaning materials, stationery and postage.

Total and balance the cash book and petty cash book

- As with any other accounting record, the cash book and petty cash book totals and analysis columns should be totalled as a basis for determining the period end balance and in preparation for posting accounting entries into the ledger accounts.

LO5 Process transactions through the ledgers to the trial balance

Transfer data from the books of prime entry to the ledgers

Book of prime entry	Debit – £	Credit – £
SDB – credit sales	Sales ledger control account (gross)	VAT
		Sales revenue (net)
SRDB – sales returns	Sales returns	Sales ledger control account (gross)
	VAT	
Discount allowed day book	Discount allowed (net)	Sales ledger control account (gross)
	VAT	
PDB – credit purchases	VAT	
	Expenses – analysed (net)	Purchase ledger control account (gross)
PRDB – purchase returns	Purchase ledger control account (gross)	Purchase returns (net)
		VAT
Discount received daybook	Purchase ledger control account (gross)	Discount received (net)
		VAT

Cash book payments	Expense	Cash payments
	Non-current asset	
	Petty cash	
	Purchase ledger control account	
	Wages and salaries	
Cash book receipts	Cash book (total)	Sales ledger control account
		Cash sales
Petty cash book payments	Cleaning	Petty cash payments (total)
	Postage	
	Sundry expenses	
Petty cash book receipts	Petty cash receipts (total)	Cash book

Total and balance ledger accounts

STEP 1
Total both the debit and credit side of the ledger account.

STEP 2
Insert the higher of the two totals on both sides of the ledger account.

STEP 3
On the side with the smaller total insert the figure needed to make this column add up to the total - 'balance carried down'.

STEP 4
On the opposite side of the ledger account, below the total insert the same figure - 'balance brought down'.

Extract an initial trial balance

- This is produced immediately after all double entries have been made as a quick check to confirm that there are an equal total of debit and credit entries in the accounting ledgers.

- It is not a guarantee that the accounting ledgers are free from error.

- Prompt payment discount allowed to customers (i.e. settlement or cash discount) is accounted for only when a customer takes advantage of the discount terms.

- A specimen trial balance is presented below:

	Debit £	Credit £
Sales		5,000
Opening inventory	100	
Purchases	3,000	
Rent	200	
Car	3,000	
Receivables	100	
Payables		1,400
	6,400	6,400

KAPLAN PUBLISHING

Appendix 2: Bookkeeping Controls

Introduction

This chapter recaps the key aspects of the underlying Bookkeeping Controls Unit.

UNIT LEARNING OBJECTIVES STILL RELEVANT FOR THE SYNOPTIC ASSESSMENT	
LO3	Use control accounts
LO4	Use the journal
LO5	Reconcile a bank statement with the cash book

LO3 Use control accounts

Produce control accounts

Sales ledger control account				
	£			£
Balance b/d	X	Returns per SRDB		X
Sales per SDB	X	Cash from receivables		X
		Discounts allowed		X
		Irrecoverable debts written off		X
		Contra entry		X
		Balance c/d		X
	–––			–––
	X			X
	–––			–––
Balance b/d	X			

Purchases ledger control account			
	£		£
Payments to payables	X	Balance b/d	X
Discount received	X	Purchases per PDB	X
Purchase returns per PRDB	X		
Contra entry	X		
Balance c/d	X		
	–––		–––
	X		X
	–––		–––
		Balance b/d	X

VAT control account			
	£		£
VAT on credit purchases	X	Balance b/d	X
VAT on cash purchases	X	VAT on credit sales	X
VAT on sales returns	X	VAT on cash sales	X
VAT on irrecoverable debts	X	VAT on purchase returns	X
VAT on discounts allowed	X	VAT on discounts received	X
Balance c/d	X		
	–––		–––
	X		X
	–––		–––
		Balance b/d	X

FOUNDATION CERTIFICATE SYNOPTIC ASSESSMENT

Reconcile control accounts

- Reasons for discrepancies between the control account total and the total of sales ledger or purchase ledger balances include the following:

    - errors casting the daybook totals posted into the control accounts

    - transactions omitted from the day books (and therefore, the control account also) but included in the ledger account balances, or vice versa

    - casting errors to determine an individual ledger account balance

    - omission or duplication of individual ledger account balances

    - debit ledger account balances classified as credit balances, or vice versa

- Note that some errors may affect the control account balance, whilst other errors may affect the total of the ledger account balances

- For reference, a specimen reconciliation of a sales ledger control account: with the total of sales ledger balances is below

Sales ledger control account

	£		£
Balance b/d	18,971.12	Discount allowed omitted	10.00
Undercast of SDB	1,500.00	Irrecoverable debt omitted	20.00
		Adjusted balance c/d	20,441.12
	20,471.12		20,471.12
Balance b/d	20,441.12		

	£
Original total of list of sales ledger account balances	21,761.12
Duplicated ledger account balance	(800.00)
Adjust for credit balance initially included as a debit balance (i.e. 2 × £260.00)	(520.00)
	20,441.12

LO4   Use the journal

Produce journal entries to record accounting transactions

- A journal is a record of accounting entries which have not been in any other book of prime entry

- Examples of journals used to record accounting transactions include the following:

  - accounting for irrecoverable debts

  - accounting for contras between the purchase ledger control account and the sales ledger control account

  - to record the opening entries for a new business

  - to record accounting entries relating to VAT and payroll

- A proforma journal record is as follows:

Date	Ledger account name	Ledger account ref	Debit – £	Credit – £
31/12/X4	Wages expense	WE1	13,500.00	
	Wages control	WC1		13,500.00
Being recording of total wage expense for the month				
Date			£	£
31/12/X4	Wages control	WC1	10,000.00	
	Bank	CB1		10,000.00
Being net wages paid to employees				
Date			£	£
31/12/X4	Wages control	WC1	500.00	
	HRMC	HR1		500.00
Being tax-related deductions which are payable to HM Revenue & Customs				

Produce journal entries to correct errors not disclosed by the trial balance

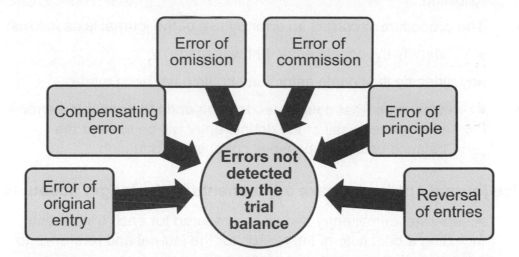

- Errors not disclosed by the trial balance mean that either no double entry has been posted, or that an equal value of debits and credits has been posted, but there is a problem with either the monetary amount and/or the ledger accounts used were wrong

- The procedure to correct an error by use of the journal is as follows:

  - identify the double entry that was made

  - identify the double entry that should have been made

  - determine what double needs to be done to correct the error

Produce journal entries to correct errors disclosed by the trial balance

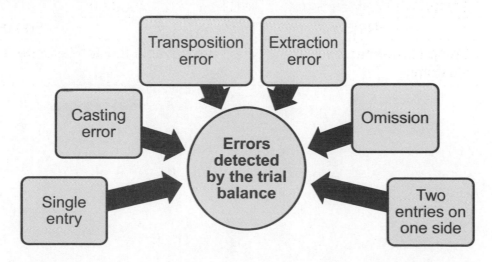

- Errors disclosed by the trial balance mean that an unequal value of debits and credits has been posted into the ledgers, such as the following:

- The procedure to correct an error by use of the journal is as follows:

  - identify the double entry that was made

  - identify the double entry that should have been made

  - determine what double needs to be done to correct the error – note that one half of the double entry will be to clear the balance on the suspense account in this situation

Use journal entries to make adjustments in the ledger accounts

- A separate journal entry should be prepared for each transaction, including a brief note of the reason for the journal and reference to any supporting documents as follows

Date	Ledger account name	Ledger account ref	£	£
31/12/X4	PLCA	PLA1	350.00	
	SLCA	SLA1		350.00
Being recording of contra between PLCA and SLCA				

Redraft the trial balance following adjustments

- Any journal adjustments, whether to make accounting entries, or to correct errors whether or not they were disclosed by the initial trial balance, it is important to extract an updated trial balance to confirm that the value of debits and credits is in agreement

LO5 Reconcile a bank statement with the cash book

Locate differences between items on the bank statement and entries in the cash book

- The procedure for a bank reconciliation is as follows:

  - agree items on the bank statement are also included in the cash book – tick off matching items

  - update the cash book for items on the bank statement but not in the cash book

  - update the cash book balance

  - prepare the reconciliation statement, beginning with the bank statement balance and adjusting this for outstanding lodgements and unpresented cheques

Use the bank statement to update the cash book

- Examples of items on the bank statement not initially recorded in the cash book include:

  - direct credits or BACS receipts

  - bank charges and interest

  - standing orders and direct debit payments

Produce a bank reconciliation statement

- Begin with the bank statement balance and adjust for items in the cash book, but not on the bank statement at the date of the reconciliation, such as unpresented cheques and uncleared lodgements

BANK RECONCILIATION STATEMENT AS AT 30 JUNE 20X1

	£	£
Balance per bank statement		(1,160.25) O/D
Outstanding lodgement:		
cleared 2 July		6,910.25
		—————
		5,750.00
Unpresented cheques:		
121 – cleared 5 July	538.00	
122 – cleared 3 July	212.00	
	—————	(750.00)
		—————
Balance per cash book		5,000.00
		—————

Appendix 3: Elements of Costing

Introduction

This chapter recaps the key aspects of the underlying Elements of Costing Unit.

UNIT LEARNING OBJECTIVES STILL RELEVANT FOR THE SYNOPTIC ASSESSMENT
LO2   Use cost recording techniques
LO3   Provide information on actual budgeted costs and income

LO2 Use cost recording techniques

Calculate cost of inventory issues and inventory valuations

- FIFO (first in, first out) – this assumes that the issues into production will be made from the oldest inventory available, leaving the most recent purchases in inventory

- LIFO (last in, first out) – this assumes that the issues into production will be made from the newest inventory available, leaving the oldest purchases in inventory

- AVCO (average cost or weighted average) – this assumes that the issues into production will be made at an average cost, derived from taking the total cost of inventory and dividing it by the total number of units in inventory

Calculate labour payments

- Time-related pay – staff are paid for the hours they spend at work, regardless of the amount of production or output that they achieve.

- Overtime – overtime refers to the total additional pay that staff earn for working overtime.

  - the overtime premium refers to the additional pay (above standard) that staff earn in their overtime hours.

- Piecework -output related pay, or piecework, is where a fixed amount is paid per unit of output produced – irrespective of the time taken.

  - staff may (or may not) be guaranteed a minimum amount, regardless of the number of units they make.

- Bonuses – staff may be paid additional amounts by management due to good performance which can be measured e.g. quantity produced.

  - bonuses can be paid to time-rate or piecework employees.

Calculate overhead absorption rates

- A system needs to be developed for either finding average overheads per unit or absorbing them into units. This is particularly important when a company makes more than one product.

    - unit basis – using this approach, each unit gets the same level of overhead.

    - labour rate basis – using this approach, overheads are absorbed at a rate per direct labour hour. This means that for every hour someone works on the unit an hour's worth of overhead is given to the unit as well.

    - machine hour basis - using this approach, overheads are absorbed at a rate per direct machine hour. This means that for every hour of machine time worked on the unit an hour's worth of overhead is given to the unit as well.

- Total cost per unit can therefore be determined as follows:

	Unit cost £
Direct labour cost - 2.5 hours@ £8.00	20
Direct material cost – 1 kg @ £3.00	3
Direct expenses – royalty payment to licence holder	1
Prime cost or direct cost	24
Production overheads (calculated and absorbed on an agreed basis)	8
Total cost per unit	32

Use cost behaviour to calculate unit and total costs

- Cost behaviour needs to be understood so that total cost and cost per unit can be estimated for different levels of activity:

- The 'high-low' method is a way of splitting total cost between fixed and variable elements so that it can be used for budgeting and costing:

    - the total fixed cost element will not change for different levels of activity

    - the total variable cost element will change for different levels of activity

Calculate the direct cost of a product

- Refer to the earlier cost per unit compilation – it includes direct materials, direct labour and direct expenses:

- The direct cost of a manufacturing process can be compiles as follows:

	£
Opening Inventory of raw materials	7,000
Purchases of raw materials	50,000
Closing Inventory of raw materials	(10,000)
DIRECT MATERIALS USED	**47,000**
Direct labour	97,000
DIRECT COST	**144,000**
Manufacturing overheads	53,000
MANUFACTURING COST	**197,000**
Opening Inventory of work in progress	8,000
Closing Inventory of work in progress	(10,000)
COST OF GOODS MANUFACTURED	**195,000**
Opening Inventory of finished goods	30,000
Closing Inventory of finished goods	(25,000)
COST OF GOODS SOLD	**200,000**

LO3 Provide information on actual and budgeted costs and income

Compare actual and budgeted costs and income

- Comparison of actual and budgeted costs and revenues will highlight variances between the two figures:

  - a favourable variance will improve profit - .i.e. actual cost is less than budgeted cost

  - an adverse variance will reduce profit i.e. actual sales income is less than budgeted sales income

Apply exception reporting to identify significant variances

- After variances have been calculated, they should be evaluated to determine which are the most significant, and only the most significant variances should be investigated:

  - significance may be determined by either a monetary amount e.g. investigate all variances in excess of £2,000, or as a percentage of the budgeted amount e.g. only investigate variances in excess of 5% of the budgeted figure

  - variances, and the outcome of any investigation work, should be reported to a responsible person to take action

Specimen variance report for May

A variance in excess of 10% of budget is deemed to be significant and should be reported to management.

The variances have been calculated and, based upon the criteria, have been identified as being either significant or not significant.

Element	Budget £	Actual £	Variance £	S or NS
Sales	126,500	145,700	19,200	S
Direct materials	22,000	22,200	200	NS
Direct labour	76,000	75,000	1,000	NS
Production overheads	64,000	34,000	30,000	S
Admin overhead	2,400	5,400	3,000	S

INDEX

KAPLAN PUBLISHING